MASTERING STM32 CUBEMX

Unlock the Power of STM32 with CubeIDE for Embedded System Development

By

Peng Huang

TABLE OF CONTENTS

DOWNLOAD CUBEMX 5 AND CUBEIDE...4

INSTALLING CUBEMX 5 AND CUBEIDE..5

INSTALLING CUBEMX 5 PACKAGES 8

OVERVIEW OF STM32CUBEMX 5..11

OVERVIEW OF THE CLOCK CONFIGURATION TAB 21

CODING AN INPUT OUTPUT DRIVER......................................24

CODING AN INPUT INTERRUPT DRIVER.................................43

CODING AN INPUT INTERRUPT DRIVER (MULTIPLE INPUTS)................53

CODING GPIO DRIVERS FROM SCRATCH USING DATASHEET
INFORMATION (PART I) 59

CODING GPIO DRIVERS FROM SCRATCH USING DATASHEET
INFORMATION (PART II) 80

CODING ARM ASSEMBLY APPLICATIONS IN CUBEIDE 87

CODING GPIO DRIVERS FROM SCRATCH IN ASSEMBLY LANGUAGE
(PART I) 95

CODING GPIO DRIVERS FROM SCRATCH IN ASSEMBLY LANGUAGE
(PART II) 105

CONVERTING KEIL MDK ARM ASSEMBLY SYNTAX TO GCC ASSEMBLY
SYNTAX..112

CODING A HARDWARE TIMER TO GENERATE PRECISE DELAYS 120

CODING A HARDWARE TIMER DRIVER FOR OUTPUT COMPARE
FUNCTIONALITY 134

CODING A HARDWARE TIMER DRIVER FOR COUNTING EVENTS 141

CODING A HARDWARE TIMER DRIVER FOR GENERATING PWM SIGNALS
....147

CODING A HARDWARE TIMER DRIVER FOR GENERATING PRECISE
INTERRUPTS 151

CODING AN ADC DRIVER FOR SINGLE CONVERSION MODE................157

CODING AN ADC DRIVER FOR CONTINUOUS MODE CONVERSION.....163

CODING AN ADC DRIVER FOR INTERRUPT CONVERSION MODE........170

CODING AN ADC DRIVER FOR SINGLE-CHANNEL DMA MODE 175

CODING AN ADC DRIVER FOR MULTI-CHANNEL DMA SCAN MODE...180

CODING SPI DRIVERS FOR POLLING TRANSFER MODE 190

CODING SPI DRIVERS FOR INTERRUPT TRANSFER MODE....................195

CODING SPI DRIVERS FOR DMA TRANSFER MODE 200

CODING UART DRIVERS FOR POLLING TRANSFER MODE 203

CODING UART DRIVERS FOR INTERRUPT TRANSFER MODE...............213

CODING UART DRIVERS FOR DMA TRANSFER MODE 223

CODING MULTIPLE UART MODULES 227

UNDERSTANDING THE USB CAPABILITIES OF DIFFERENT DEV BOARDS
....238

CODING USB DRIVERS FOR HUMAN INTERFACE DEVICE (HID) -
KEYBOARD FUNCTIONALITY...239

CODING USB DRIVERS FOR VIRTUAL COM PORT FUNCTIONALITY (TX
ONLY) 248

CODING USB DRIVERS FOR VIRTUAL COM PORT FUNCTIONALITY (RX
AND TX) 252

CODING   ACCESSING HARDWARE DRIVERS FROM MULTIPLE THREADS
....261

CODING   ACCESSING HARDWARE DRIVERS FROM MULTIPLE THREADS
USING A MUTEX..271

CODING CREATING THREADS MANUALLY 274

CODING   SENDING NOTIFICATIONS BETWEEN THREADS 279

DOWNLOAD CUBEMX 5 AND CUBEIDE

We are going to see how to download Cube M X five and the new cube IDC released by STMicroelectronics. So I'm a Google over here. I'm simply going to search and download the SDM 32 Cube remix. Okay, let's see so we can come to the S-T dot com. That's the official Web site of STK Micro-electronics. Click over here, open in a tab over here. And here it is. As crude as. And I'll click get software. The latest version is five point five, as we can see over here, over here. If you want to select a previous version, you can select that as well. I'll just click get software over here. And it gives this license agreement. I've read this before, so I'll simply go ahead and accept. Once that is done, you've got to input your e-mail address and your name over here. And once I looked in, I'm brought back here.

STM32CubeMX is a graphical tool that allows a very easy configuration of STM32 microcontrollers and microprocessors, as well as the generation of the corresponding initialization C code for the Arm® Cortex®-M core or a partial Linux® Device Tree for Arm® Cortex®-A core), through a step-by-step process.

The first step consists in selecting the STMicroelectronics STM32 microcontroller or microprocessor that matches the required set of peripherals

For microprocessors, the second step allows to configure the GPIOs and the clock setup for the whole system, and to interactively assign peripherals either to the Arm® Cortex®-M or to the Cortex®-A world. Specific utilities, such as DDR configuration and tuning, make it easy to get started with STM32 microprocessors. For Cortex®-M core, the configuration includes additional steps that are exactly similar to those described for microcontrollers

For microcontrollers and microprocessor Arm® Cortex®-M, the second step consists in configuring each required embedded software thanks to a pinout-conflict solver, a clock-tree setting helper, a power-consumption calculator, and an utility that configures the peripherals (such as GPIO or USART) and the middleware stacks (such as USB or TCP/IP). Eventually the user launches the generation that matches the selected configuration choices. This step provides the initialization C code for the Arm® Cortex®-M, ready to be used within several development environments, or a partial Linux® device tree for the Arm® Cortex®-A.

STM32CubeMX is delivered within STM32Cube.

Click, download. So the first time I said get software, you can either click, download or wait for the download to begin automatically as it has begun over here. So I am downloading it now. Right. The download is complete. I'm going to download the SDM 30 to Cube. This is a new IDC released by S.T. Microelectronics say SDM 32 or SDM Cube? IDC said it's called. Put load here. And then, all right, click over here. So this idea is free of charge. And there are no, quote, limits, unlike Karl, your vision, where the trial version gives you 32 kilobytes of code limit. This one here, you can have however large your code is and it's all for free. So I'm brought over here. I can download the version that corresponds to my operating system. I'm currently running Windows. As you can see. So I'm going to click this over here for the Windows install. I get software and this license and agreement is brought up again. I'm going to accept. And we were brought here again. I'll log in. And it's going to start automatically. My computer's a bit slow today, okay? It started downloading, let's call it both. Six hundred and sixty five megabytes. So this would take a while. So in the next lesson, we shall see how to install both the SDM 32 Cuba mix and the SDM 32 cube IDC.

INSTALLING CUBEMX 5 AND CUBEIDE

We are going to install our esteemed Thatta to Cuba. So this is the complete download package. I'm going to write. Click over here to extract it or extract here. And its Finnish extract in order will click over here. There's a content interest in a may have downloaded the. I may have done that, the Mac OS version, so I'm sure you downloaded a Windows version, so I'm going to download a Windows version. No, see, OK. No. The download package comes with the Windows version. The Mac version. And the Linux version.

The reason why I think it's just a Mac version is because it is the only folder I see over here. I'm going to sort of create a new photo here, hear a call in my downloads for the DLC Cube Imex. And I'm going to extract into the fold rather than have it mixed up with everything else over here. Just fix this clean up. Yeah, okay. Just bear with me. So this is the Cuba mix. Come over here now. Oh, extract it here. so we have the Windows version here. The mock version and a Linux double click in the Windows version here to install it. So, yes, over here. OK. It says the application requires a Java runtime environment. This. So if you don't have a Java runtime environment, you would have to install that. So that's a different computer than the one I use every day. So I don't have Java here. So I would have to install this Java runtime environment. GRV. Okay. So it's bringing me to the Java Web site to download a GRV. Okay, download. It's open in Internet Explorer, so just bear with me. Click here to download, click it to save.

Click here to run it. Install. It's installed in. Okay. Right. See what happens next. So I'm gonna go back to our maker's row. Try to install it again. Double click, this is team 32. Cuba makes five. Java hasn't completed installation yet. She wants to leave the Java show. Let's see. Gerri is still running. The current installation is just taking a bit longer than I expected. So let's wait for it. It says you have successfully installed Java. Okay. Should be fine, though, if we're still unable to get access to it. We may have to restart the computer. Okay. I mean, stalling. Keep that makes. Now click. Yes, right here. OK. For LA it started and a click next over here. I've read this before so I just click to accept it next and then step this. So you can kinda take a look at the um the privacy policy as well as the terms of use before you accept it like this. Over here. A click over here. And this installation foda or keep it the same click next target. Right. Uh, it says the target directory will be created with a click. Okay. And a click next to over here. And this is installed and now it's gonna take a while. It's still stolen. Okay, so I'm going to click next. And then I'm going to click done over here. The installation is complete. Right. So next, I'm going to install the keep IP. That's my downloads folder. I'm going to create a folder to extract it into a Korda's Cube IDC Raw. I'm simply going to crack the Kubi into this folder and then extract it over here. It's a structure in. Still extracting. Don't extract him. I'm going to install it by double clicking on this over here. Quick, yes, over here. Click next over here. I agree, but keep the, um, the destination forward at the same click next. Click it or kick it. Oh. Keep everything here. The same next time. And it started. It's still stolen. This would take a while, so I just post. Okay. The installation is complete. Click next over here, create a desktop shortcut. Click finish.

INSTALLING CUBEMX 5 PACKAGES

We shall see how to install some third packages into our estimate, 32 Chebet mix. I'm going to open the Cuban mics we installed earlier. Simply come over here a steam 32 and it's a piesse. You click here. And it says, cha cha cha cha re 32 bits detected Java G 64 bit as strongly advised with order to some features might not be available. So please install 64 bit. So, Eddie, Jay, everyone thought it was 32 bit. The one that the link led us to. So we've got to install 64 bit. If you experience this sort of issue, then it's simple. You simply need to install 64. It is good that we are doing all of these things together so that you don't end up having roadblocks. So you just come to Google, search Java or download GRV 64 bit in Google and or just. Right. Click on the first link to see what shows up. Let's see.

Okay, it brings me here. If it brings you to the documentation tab, just click on the download stuff. Then let's see. Download to pro me here. Okay, so this download tab, when you come here, the first time, it would look like this to you, just scroll down to the bit where you see GRV over here. Click Jeary Download. And it brings us over here. Oh.

Click here to accept the license agreement. You can read up on this over here. So click here. Once it's accepted, come over here to download the O, download the dot e e version, Windows X 64 over here. That's actually so click. This one here. It requires signing a contract. We may have to create an account for a coup or a coup. Interesting. OK. So you've got to create an account and then proceed to download Chiari. So I just locked in and to Jerry. I started downloading as soon as I locked it. So it turns out now even Oracle requires you to sign up before you can download things like the runtime environments. It's a bit ridiculous. That's anyway. Here we go. Okay. Okay. The installation is complete, double click here to install it. Click Yes, over here. This is from the Cuba mixed message, which is, of course, Cuba mix when it opens. Course, we are installing that geography now. It's hidden behind here. We're just close. Cuba makes it from here. These terms. Okay, quick next. It's going to go through the same process again. Right. So now the download is complete, check out Cubitt mix again. Now that the download is complete. Come over here. And then I'm going to start SDM 32. Cuba makes. Okay, now we're over. No, we've been able to open successfully without that warning. I'm gonna come over here to help. Help. Top over here and I'll click manage and better software packages.

And over here, we were given a list of packages. We've got iStore packages for the day microcontrollers that we're going to be generating code for. So if you are going to be using your cube that makes for F zero, f1, f2, F3, F4, F. You've got to install packages for each and every one of them. You're going to be using EF four in this course. So I'll come down here and I'm going to download the package for the esteemed 32 EF four series. Well, right here, they've got different versions of the package. I'm going to select the latest version over here by clicking here and I'll click install now. And this is going to take a while to download and then extract it. So we've got a wait. So to install other packages, I can come to the, um, tub to install The Simpsons package over here on the SDM 32 MCU packages. I installed the one for F for O come to arm and then I'm going to select the latest Simms's package available and I'll click install now and it's going to go through the same process.

OVERVIEW OF STM32CUBEMX 5

We shall give a quick overview of SDM 32 Cubitt Mix. Okay, so my Cuba makes us open over here to create on your projects. I can just click. I can open an existing project. If I had existing projects, that would be listed here. But I do not have a need. So there's nothing here I can start to from access MSU Selecta, Access Booth Selecta or Access Cross Selecta. Right. One other key point is the the tops we've got over here. We've got a file type for new project to load project and a list of recent projects. If we have a need, we've got a Windows type. And this allows us to set the, um, the font size, et cetera. And then we've got this one, this very important one to help one. When you click on Help Top, you can check for updates. You can manage embedded software packages. Let's say you want to install A, B, I, e for Bluetooth low energy. You run a store, a Bluetooth, low energy package or some other package. You've got to come to manage embedded software packages to do that. And you can set your user preferences by clicking over here as well. Over here, you can give consent for data to be sent to SD microelectronics to sort of monitor the usage of Cuba. Makes, you know what to improve the product. I said is written over here. If you don't want to do that, you can simply on check this. Right. And, um, you can check for updates as well by clicking this. So I'm gonna start a new project by coming over here, access to board select click here. It's open. It's the first time, so it's taken a while. It's still got certain things to download, and on Zipp, it's quickly doing that. And it's opened. So here we are. We've got our various development boards over here. We've got the discovery ports. Different types. Cross. Amanda Port Selector.

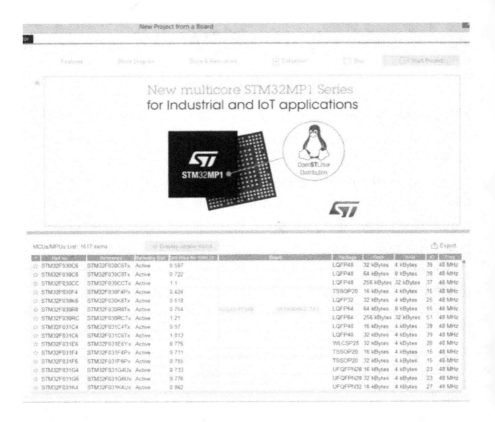

If I want to select just the MCU Chip, I can click over here and simply search for that chip. I'll see SDM 32 for one and then it will list. And when you check here, it keeps the parameter, keeps the price range as well. Over here, the price starts from two point two eight four two three point four five. I can reduce the price range. If I can afford all of this to reduce the options. These are the options that I have if I want the price to be within this range. Right. Because the key that makes it set up from, you know, prototype into development such that you have a clear picture of what you are dealing with over here as well. It gives the peripherals available on a particular port. We can filter by peripherals as well. So what should I say? I want to. I want a HDD and other peripherals. I can just a neighbor determine which hits enter and Cuba makes you suggest other mce use that I can use. So let's see. You can select this one by Crosswell. I type this a cortex for. That is why I just call text and voice highlighted. I can delete this such that led to Cuba mext make that choice for me. I'm going to select Coatex M 33 over here and it gives me the options. These are the options and these are the peripherals available as well. Right. So this for the MCU selector, let's see, Herbal criticism seven. I've included Criticism seven and it's increased my list and we can check for the line. So by here, what do we want? F one series, F zero series, et cetera. And then. Okay. That's what I meant by the lines. F one, f zero, etc.. And then the prize, the package as well. You can select the package if you are into designing your own BCBS. You can filter by packages as well. Right. So I'll just close this and then I'll come back to the board selector and then I'm going to just select the new clue F for one, one for E.T.. There is the new clue, F for one one over here. Just double click this. And when you highlight it, it tells you the specifications of the board. If it's obsolete, it would tell you it's obsolete. But this is active. Therefore, it is written at a market price. The retail price is over here. This is thirteen dollars and the futures of the board are listed over here or are listed over here, I should say. And if you want access to the data sheet as well as other documentation, you can click these tops over here to take a look at them. Okay. So once I've highlighted, I can double click it or just click start project over here like this.

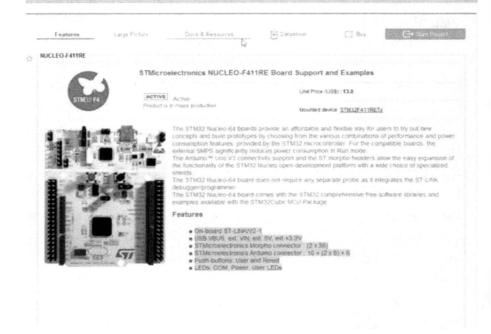

And when you select a board, it would ask you, what do you want to initialize? Or peripherals with default mode. I'll click. Yes. And it's setting up the project. Okay, so that's what it looks like. So there's one nuclear I see you right here. These are the default setups and we've got the push-Button enabled for us. We've got the LDA also set as an output pin. And then we've got the you got to be a two and P three. And then we've got other things with regards to the zero wire interface and the clock setters. Okay, so this is known as the pin out of you. We've got a pin out and configuration tab over here. We click to set a pin. Let's see. I want to set it in as an output pin. I will simply click this and select GPL output and it becomes an output pin. Let's say I want to rename this. All right. Click this and see. And to use a label, I can simply call this my output. And then it becomes an output to be a simple cluster if I want to set it to a different type of pin. I simply click and select the type that I want. This is known as the. This is known as the pin out penult and configuration view. Right. And I can drag a click and hold two drugs to move it around. It's allowable to do that. I can zoom in. I can zoom out. I can rotate if I want. Right. Okay. So there's the penult view and we have these. So, you know, in microcontroller setup when we select a pin. We've got to do further configurations. And what I mean by this is to set up something like a U at a U. Art is an alternate function on the MCU, meaning we take a GPL, your pin, and then we set it as an alternate function as you got before we are able to use it. So, for instance, if I want to say this, as you said, it's done over here after I have selected it as U. S. I've got to come over here and configure its alternate function. So under system core over here, we are given you know, we are given options to figure out what GPL you and these often we wouldn't talk much about. We just explained them when we required them racc. Over here are the bits that won't be forgotten. These lines are a clock high speed extend or we're not using this or we are saying bypass. Or we can simply say disable, acyclic, disable. You realize that this changes to yellow, but I can say bypass, which is its default mode, is back to green and low speed extends or here. We are using a crystal for it. So if I disable that, you see that it's been to get disabled from here. So as I click disable, it becomes yellow. Right.

Yellow means you've set the GPL. You've got to go and do its actual alternate function configuration. So whenever you see a pin as yellow, it means its setup is incomplete. So I'll see you ceramic and then it's back to green. Right. And then stop over here. The single wire. I can disable it. I'll show you. That is on the other side. I just disabled it when I saw it. Use zero wire. It turned back to green. Right. And this you can disable the pin by selecting reset. Okay. Right. And we've got Topps here for auto configuration. If we want another configuration for our HDD, we simply click on a lock and then we select our ADC. This MCU has a single ADC module. But this single module has about sixteen channels. So if we want an ATC, this is where the configuration will be done. But we're not using an ADC now. So ATC is under analogue. We've got timers. And this tab allows us to figure out various general purpose timers as well as a real time clock. We've got connectivity as well. This deals with things like the AI to see the SBI and the U. S. As we can see, the "you too" is set up over here. That is why it is green and that is why we've got it correct or taken over here. So to see the configuration or to change the configuration or simply click here and you can see it says Mode is Synchronoss and then hardware flow control disabled. Okay. When I disable this when I come over here mode and disable it. When I come over here and change it or disable it, you see that these payments will be affected because these parents are the ones connected to the U. But let's say I go single wire, you see. Now we've disabled. Exline shows that the IRS is back to yellow, meaning its configuration is incomplete. Single wire or half duplex means just one direction communication. Go back to Synchronoss and then this is here. And the configuration of the actual ADC or the actual you. I should say, it is down here. Things like the box rate we can change over here. The word length we can change and select the pirate to the data direction, et cetera. If we are using DME, we can click over here and add a GPL. You, as we know, are P2, P3. When we selected these opinions, they were added here automatically.

And whether we want to set ADC interrupt, we come to infix settings and fix stands for Nesse. That fact or interrupt controller.

So yeah. So connectivity provides us access to war connectivity modules and these are the I2 see S.P.I and the U. OK. The next one is multimedia. We have two s over here which we can use for sound and other things. We've got computing and we've got this module known as the CRC Mean and Cyclic Redundancy Check. We can use that as well. You want to add a middle word such as a file system. We've got futz efforts that we can include here. We can also include a real time operating system like free our toes. And we can include the embed tearless if we want, as well as USP devices. Right. So we talk about them deeper when we are using them. The next step up here is known as the core configuration. So we can simply click here. And this gives us a few of our clocks. We can, um, we can increase the clock frequency. It says over here that Max is hundred megahertz. So we've got to keep it. They might and we can know the process for our various peripherals. For instance, over here, it tells us that the plug for what time is the time is connected to the MPB one. The APB one bus clock currently is set at two four, making a hit the clock to be called cortex system time unassisted. Time is clock is eighty four, etc.. So over here we have exactly the values that our farish peripherals would have for their clocks. So let's say I want to increase the clock to one hundred. I simply need to type one hundred hits here. And it's going to configure everything appropriately. And it sort of arranged everything.

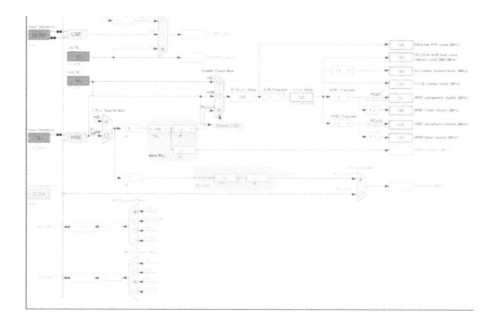

And over here too, we can see they are using the high speed internal edge as I hear those for high speed internal. Remember, in our setup we said bypass high speed extend or HFC. That is why this is selected at high speed in turn on this being used. And we are also using a low speed external. Right. Often used in low speed extend or let's see. Uh. So we said no split x10, no use this ceramic, um, ceramic resonator. And I think there is a ceramic resonator or slate. Oh, no. PCV on a microcontroller. What I should say. OK. So that's a quick overview of the clock top. And then, um, the next step I see is there's this TEUs here which you use for checking the, um, the power consumption and other things with regards to your board. You find our top priority in the process is to collect the project money. And over here you can give your project a name because I'll call this simple and then you can decide on the toolchain you want to use. So I can say I want to generate the code for SDM 32 Kupe idee, um, MBK or the other IDC if I prefer. So this allows me to generate code for various ideas. And you can come over here. This is another topic called code generator. OK. It says the project's location cannot be empty. So we've got to give a location for a project. Let's see. A crater food called Cuba makes. Okay, so. Right. So let's say we want to generate projekt for SDM 30 to keep idee like this. And then there's the code generator here. And over here, you can take such that your files are separated into various plots, H and that C files. I often do this or you simply take it like this. And then once you've selected the idea you wish to use, you can simply click generate. And it would generate it for you. We'll see how that works when we start dealing with actual projects. And there isn't much any more. We can also generate a report. Over here, we can generate a report for our setup. Simply come to file, generate a report right here and there. Would you like to create the project for us? Click here. Because the project hasn't been created yet. a report has been generated. So I'm going to open the folder and the report comes in to form. What is the TSD file? As well as a PDAF encapsulating all these selections you made. So I'm open to PDAF so that we can take a look at it. So there's the PDAF project to name and the MCU you chose as well as the date. All of it exists. And, um, this is the pin out. And your clock conflagration is also included here. As well as the other setups that you have, the RACC set up values, we find him here. This is art. Everything is included here. So this report. Right. So that's a quick overview of the estimated two keys.

OVERVIEW OF THE CLOCK CONFIGURATION TAB

We shall give an overview of the clock configuration tab. It's over here. We use this type of right here to figure out a system clock. So based on what board you selected during the board selection, if you selected the nuclear board or the disco board, the default setting will be different. Right over here, the default is nine to six megahertz. This is the nuclear broad, it's nine to six mega heads. And the maximum can be one hundred megahertz. If you have the disco body could. The default is 16 megahertz. If you have a different version of the F4 microcontroller, you could have a different value here. But in any case, it always indicates the, um, the maximum down here. So unless I want to say this to the maximum, I can simply type one hundred and hit enter over here like this and is going to search for the solution because he has to update all the various parts in order to be able to work with this frequency. So it's been able to find a configuration out, providing me with its Yoki of 100. And by doing that, it's adjusted the frequencies here as well. Right.

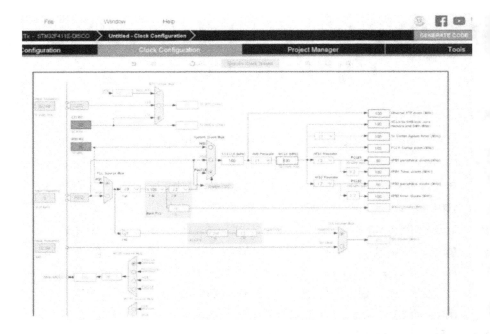

So any one of that and you can see it, there are parts that are great out, this party is great out. And if you want to know what the great out part belongs to, you, just put your point out there. You will receive the info. This is for the eye, too, as a cloak. And it's not, it's not set. So if we go to our pin out and enable the eye to us, then we expect this part to be enabled. Let's check out and see. I'll come back to pin out and then I'll come to multimedia. So I'll see eye to eye with us. And then I'll just select a word. Healthmaster duplex. Right. Once that is done, I'll go to Kolok Conflagration. And because I changed something now, the clock on immigration has a conflict. So it asks, do you want to run an automatic clock issues solver? I can click, yes. And then you will solve the issues for me. So, yes, I cannot find a solution. so the reason I cannot find a solution is I would have to. Just some of the settings here, which can be done from the. These cities as well. Right. So, what I wanted to show you is that this pilot was disabled. Knowing that we've been unable to pay for that requires this plot. We can see that this part of the clock is enabled by the robot here. This multiplex belongs to the RTC, the real time clock. So it is because we're not using the real time clock in our project, we see that it is disabled as well. Right over here. This one belongs to this one says MCE oh to source UKCS. If we want to get more information about it, we can just drop all modes. And when I put my mouse here, it keeps me informed as to how to enable this. It says MCO output is not available to enable it. One of the following RACC modes or IP moves need to be set. Right? So because we know using this part, that is why it is great out as well as this part. We can also adjust the clock off the various passes. So if we want to adjust the clock for the APB to time up, it may be two bros four times, meaning all the time is connected to EPB two. If you want to adjust the crop for them, you can simply type here. So let's say I type 50 megahertz. Because I want to set a plan B, two is two. This is gonna find a solution that works and by itself it would adjust for me. I can do it for all of these over here. And one other thing whereby here we have high speed internal or neighborhood. That is why we have this year because of a high speed extension or is disabled. We don't have the option to select this. So let's see how to enable high speed extension or I'll come back to a PIN configuration over here. Come to System four and then RACC and then high speed, high speed quelque HFC. I'll see. Ceramic crystal or resonator? And this one here. The nuclear board hasn't got. The nuclear board hasn't got a ceramic crystal. So this won't be required for a new clue. But if you have that described as a ceramic resonator on the body, the reason why Cube allows us to make this option is that the idea is you buy this microcontroller and order a project. And if I and it's your project, you add your own ceramic resonator. It's not going to be a dev board. This is for you. You know, production. Great solutions. So anyway, I've enabled this. Let's go to the clock and see. So Nundah is often a neighborhood. I can choose HSC as my clock source. Now I have the option to select both of them. Right. So there's a very quick overview of the clock configuration. There isn't much here. We just use it to adjust our clock as well as the peripheral clocks. That's all you need to know with us. Well, if we have any more information regarding the configuration of the clock for a particular peripheral, we'll talk more when we get it.

CODING AN INPUT OUTPUT DRIVER

We are going to see how to generate GPA your code using the SDM 32 for using the SDM 32 Kubi mix. And then we go to Cube Idee and then write the code for it. So I've opened my cubitt makes five over here. But before we do the let's download the manual for the SDM. Thirty two hall library halls stand for hardware abstraction layer hall shall come over here and. Over here and Google, you can just search SDM 32 Hall Drive driver Mindo, and then you select this first link. Right. Click and then open in a new tab. This first link that says SDM 32, that dot com. You saw. I know. And then this. And this. The name description of SDM 32 F for Hall and L. L drivers when you're right click it would open this PDA for you. So we're going to. We're going to save this. This is going to be your reference for the functions that you can use to enable the various drivers. So I'm gonna save this and then I'm I'm just gonna keep the name. So I'll save it as it is. Right. It's saving. OK.

29 HAL GPIO Generic Driver

29.1 GPIO Firmware driver registers structures

29.1.1 GPIO_InitTypeDef

Data Fields

- uint32_t Pin
- uint32_t Mode
- uint32_t Pull
- uint32_t Speed
- uint32_t Alternate

Field Documentation

- uint32_t GPIO_InitTypeDef::Pin
  Specifies the GPIO pins to be configured. This parameter can be any value of GPIO_pins_define
- uint32_t GPIO_InitTypeDef::Mode
  Specifies the operating mode for the selected pins. This parameter can be a value of GPIO_mode_define
- uint32_t GPIO_InitTypeDef::Pull
  Specifies the Pull-up or Pull-Down activation for the selected pins. This parameter can be a value of GPIO_pull_define
- uint32_t GPIO_InitTypeDef::Speed
  Specifies the speed for the selected pins. This parameter can be a value of GPIO_speed_define
- uint32_t GPIO_InitTypeDef::Alternate
  Peripheral to be connected to the selected pins. This parameter can be a value of GPIO_Alternate_function_selection

29.2 GPIO Firmware driver API description

29.2.1 GPIO Peripheral features

Subject to the specific hardware characteristics of each I/O port listed in the datasheet, each port bit of the General Purpose IO (GPIO) Ports, can be individually configured by software in several modes:

- Input mode
- Analog mode
- Output mode
- Alternate function mode
- External interrupt/event lines

During and just after reset, the alternate functions and external interrupt lines are not active and the I/O ports are configured in input floating mode.

All GPIO pins have weak internal pull-up and pull-down resistors, which can be activated or not.

So this is good. One other thing. So in this course, we will be using the, um, the SDM 32 F for one one new clue. And Disko bought, um, the reason we use in the nuclear disco is because they have, oh, say, 90 percent of the upper for us are the same. Apart from some 10 percent difference. Well this, uh, this means that the new clue has a U. You can use the U out of the nuclear. Without adding an then or you know, f TDA to us. B connector. Whereas for the disco you have to extend all F TDA to us. B connector. And the disco has a USB port that can allow us to program USP. Oh TEGA USP devices. Whereas the new clue hasn't got that. However, the microcontrollers are the same. They all have SDM 32 F for one Feherty. So the same quote should work on both ports. Just that we may have to. Well you don't have to pay for connection. You may have to connect your own exten or device. For instance, um, the ality on the new on the nuclear is connected to p a five. I think by default the LCD on the disk will be connected to other pins. So you may have to set up those pings, but it's the same microcontroller. Oh, you can just connect an entity to the p a five of your disco board. If we are using the new clue in that particular lesson the effect should be the same because the microcontroller chip is the same. Okay, so I'm going to come over here. Uh, we'll stick here and then I'll go back to Google and I'm gonna search the, um, I think the user guide for the board so that we can, uh, see the, um, the penult, how our peer fros, how well, uh, our input output devices are connected, I should say. So I'll say SDM thirty two for one new clue. User guide. Then I hit Enter. So there's this first link that says Estimated two new clues. Sixty four Board User Guide. All right, click from over here. I don't know what this one says. This is not a PDAF, this is a PDAF. So we can take a look at the PDAF. OK. So does the user guide for the nuclear. I'm gonna save this as well. Whenever you are going to start a project, especially when it's a new board, you've got to get your documentation ready. So I'm starting this process with you. I'm going to do the same for Disko. So I'll change the word. A new clue here to disco. And then we have Discovery Kids, MCU, and it's a PDA. So, right, click open in a tub and it's open and over here. And there's the one for the disco.

Right. All right. Click Save. Then I'll save this, so I've got three documents, of course, one for each port. And it may happen that you have different SDM, 32 boats. You may, in fact, have the, um, the F3 or the F4 version, although things will be very, very easy if we have the same boats so that you don't need to spend time converting things to your particular port. Okay. So that being said, let's start off by creating the, um, input output. Mm hmm. Project. So I'm going to come over here. New project. It's open and it's brought me to the MCU selector.

You can come to this top four board selector so we can actually use the board selector. I'm going to use the new clue here. But you will be able to do this with a Disqus. Well. So I'm going to say SDM 32 over here. F4. And then over here. Funny enough. Yes. Sean showing just the, um. The discovery kids. They're not showing the other ones for Hubble. One one. Okay. So no problem over here. When you search the air, search is not working perfectly. They're not sure when the boards whose, um, reference modules, we just download it so we can come back to MCU MP, you selecter this Pittaway come to this top and now we can search or see SDM 32 F for one one. And over here it tells me, you see there is no clue here. And then there is this school here. So double click this. And this is it. And it says this is active. You can still buy pot for this particular port. Nothing is deprecated here. And it gives the, um. It gives an overview of the components and the specifications of the board. Once we are once we verify that. Okay. This the board we want, then we can click start projects. But interestingly enough, it gives the market price here as well. So if you're buying it from somewhere and the price is twice this price, you should know the person is. Yeah. The person is over charging. Okay, so click here to start a project, initialize all peripherals with default mode. You can click. Yes. Over here. Right. It's open in. Okay, it's open now. So this is, oh, estimated it to four one one. Like I said, this microcontroller is the exact same microcontroller on the disco board. However, the schoolhouse connected more LCD and it's connected a push button at a different place. And it's making use of the U.S. Pippin's for USB device configuration, et cetera. So anything you write here should be the same for this school. A new clue. If you don't have that particular, um, I or device connected, you may have to connect your own. That is the only difference. Okay, so this is our LCD. It is connected to, um, five us. We can see over here. We can zoom in here. We can zoom in and you can click to drug. You can click to zoom in, then click to drugs. So it is the entity and we have our outlines. And just through these same lines that we program the board. Okay. So I'm going to clip it out. What I'm going to do is come over here. Obviously, this has been out and then we see a clip out. Yes, sir, everything is cleared. Okay, so we've cleared it. So if you have a board from scratch like this and let's see the board, we didn't know where the, um, the LDA and the and the pushbutton were connected. We called a user guide, which we downloaded. It's over here. So let's start with a nuclear first and then we take a look at a disco. This is the disco kit. There's a new clue. A double click, this to open. And it's opened. And what I want to see is the schematic diagram of this port, and in case you want to create your own SDM 32 microcontroller. This is a very useful document. It gives you reference on how to design a circuit. Okay, so I'm gonna scroll down. It's down here. Okay. Right.

Figure 29. ST-LINK/V2-1

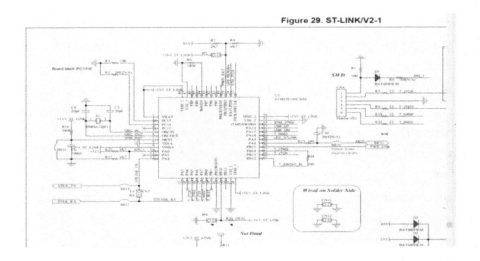

So we're almost there. Cuckoo slow over here. Okay. There's one here that talks about the S-T link debugger. So we need the other document, the actual microcontroller. Right. So this is the microcontroller. And it gives the penis. So to find the push button on the microcontroller, we can see it from here. This is the schematic symbol for the push button if we trace its connection. We realize that is connected to P.c 13. So we can enable the P.C 13 PIN as an input pin and we can just use this as a switch. Wow, experiment. And what you see over here is what is known as a sort of bridge. If we want to disconnect P.S. 13 from this physical blue push button on our nuclear board, we can cut off this bridge over here and you can find this sort of bridge under the board or on the board. And it's labeled P. 17, S.P. one seven. Right. And the LDP, a five. Over here. This is Pier five. How about the if not indicated is the LCD. And I suppose because this schematic applies to all SDM 32 F4 boards. Right. So always is a four one one V.T.. There is F a four zero X X X as well. So that is why it looks a bit generic. Okay. So this is the schematic. It it's shown us where the push buttons and, um, the Kingdom X told us where the ality was.

Figure 28. STM32 MCU

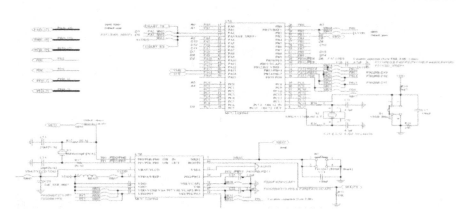

So yeah. But in case you end up with a um in the um in your normal life or in your everyday work, should you find a document that is not showing everything. You probably go back to the Internet and find another document that tells you exactly where the ality is. If we wanted to do that, we would do that. But I already know where reality is. So we can proceed with that. Okay. So this is that it was for the new clue. Let's take a look at the disco board. This team 32 Discovery. Oh, double click to this. And then what we want to see is the. Is this schematic diagram as well? go slow. so this one is actually more straightforward. Know, what I mean by that is they've indicated the simple power flows or the simple IO devices here is telling this 2012. This is page number 33. Over here, it's indicating that maybe twelve is the P. Twelve is the green ality on the discovery port. Peaty 13 is the orange LCD PD. 14 is the red LCD. Fifteen is the plurality. So if we want to set these Eltis to blink, meaning said it must. These are the GPL of your penis. We need to interact with each other. And the push button on the discovery board that is connected to me is zero. So if one set a discovery board, if we want to set the, um, the push button as an input pin, then we have to use pin number P zero. Okay. Right. So we can go back to our Cuba mix and set our stuff. So let's do some housekeeping stuff. First, let's set what debug debugging to clock. I'll come over here. System clock and then I'll click the system over here. Debug the bughouse is zero wire over here and do not keep this the same RACC over here or just come over here. Uh, high speed clock. I'll say bypass clock and then low speed clock. I'll see crystal and ceramic resonators. Right. And then once that is done, I can close this and then. Because I said I'm going to flush this onto the new clipboard. I'm gonna be using the nuclear pinout. So it's a p a five. I'm gonna say this as GPL your output. And then we can rename over here by right click and then enter the user name to rename again. Right click enter user name. So I'll simply give it a name. Ellerby. And now the name must change. And we saw that the push button is connected to P.S. 13. So let's find the easy 13. Easy. Thirty twelve is over here. This is P.S. 13. So this is your GPA, your input. And then right click and then I'll give it a name, DTN for Button. Right. So once we're done, we can actually go ahead and generally talk code. Right. So this is the clock configuration. We can leave this the way it is. And then we can come over here. And then. We can, um, we can give our project a location and then a storage forwarder, a place to store the, um, the project.

I'm gonna give this a name. I call this input output like this. And then I'm gonna browse to change the location. Let's see. We've got a story to this forwarder. A quick Pocan over here. So the project name is Input Output, and I'll keep everything the same. Over here, the toolchain we use is the SDM 32 cube idee e. If you're using a different chain, you can select the appropriate one from this list. So like this. And before we do that, we can generate the report. If we want, we can come. Let's see. We can click over here, Gendre, to report, and then would you like to create a project? First, I can say yes to create a project and then the report has been generated. We can click over here to open the folder. So these are projects for them. Where we saved our project. The report comes in this text file as well as in P.D.A format. And this has all the selections we made, including the date, the board type. I know everything else. Okay. Um, I'll keep this open or minimize this. Right. So. Okay, one other thing. We can come to advance curtains over here. Let's see. Is there something to change? We can leave these the same as the over code generator. We can see an April fool's asset and this allows us to be able to check to offset our function to see what our functions have, the right parameters or arguments to pass to them if they're wrong. Argument is passed, and is going to invoke something known as the asset function. And this one he has set or free pins as analog. And what this does is it helps save power. And, um, I think in the four boards, the pins, the four status, the floating state. And if you leave all of your pins floating, it takes more power. So if a plane is not currently in use. You have to set it to analog if you want to optimize for power consumption. We're not using that. So I'll leave it. I'll come back to Project Hub to select my two chains. Everything is looking good. I click over here to generate. Write it down, generation. We can say open food up to go to the foda, so there's the food. That's where we started. We can double click to open our project. Oh, I'm opening to Cuba. Max, I should have opened the idea. Um, yeah. Right. So. So the icon that shows I.D., we can double click on it. So double click this. It's got no name. I think there's a bug in the cube I.D.. Okay, so if you open this, you would select your default workspace. You can keep it the same. And then, um, you can just click to launch. Okay. Right. So it's done open and can click here to expand, and it's even showing our PDAF over here. We come to the source. We have our Mendo to see files over here. Okay. That's what we have. So this is what is generated by the cube. It makes its generator, the clock configuration. And then this initializes the GPL. You according to what we chose. As you can see over here, we have Ali Dippin cause we selected the LDP to be an output pin. So we said it too early D. And then the mood is output mode. Push-Pull And then there's no pool over here with any set of speed cetera. And we have that button that also sets us on inputs. Been over here. So for those of you taking this course, I assume you're familiar with how to initialize. To set up the drive over a particular pair you are just here to see how it is done in the Cuba mix.

```
 * @brief GPIO Initialization Function
 * @param None
 * @retval None
 */
static void MX_GPIO_Init(void)
{
    GPIO_InitTypeDef GPIO_InitStruct = {0};

    /* GPIO Ports Clock Enable */
    __HAL_RCC_GPIOC_CLK_ENABLE();
    __HAL_RCC_GPIOH_CLK_ENABLE();
    __HAL_RCC_GPIOA_CLK_ENABLE();

    /*Configure GPIO pin Output Level */
    HAL_GPIO_WritePin(LED_GPIO_Port, LED_Pin, GPIO_PIN_RESET);

    /*Configure GPIO pin : BTN_Pin */
    GPIO_InitStruct.Pin = BTN_Pin;
    GPIO_InitStruct.Mode = GPIO_MODE_INPUT;
    GPIO_InitStruct.Pull = GPIO_NOPULL;
    HAL_GPIO_Init(BTN_GPIO_Port, &GPIO_InitStruct);

    /*Configure GPIO pin : LED_Pin */
    GPIO_InitStruct.Pin = LED_Pin;
    GPIO_InitStruct.Mode = GPIO_MODE_OUTPUT_PP;
    GPIO_InitStruct.Pull = GPIO_NOPULL;
    GPIO_InitStruct.Speed = GPIO_SPEED_FREQ_LOW;
    HAL_GPIO_Init(LED_GPIO_Port, &GPIO_InitStruct);

}

/* USER CODE BEGIN 4 */
```

So I'm not going to spend time explaining each member of the initialization structure. What does it mean to be in pain mode, et cetera? I'll just give a surface overview of these. I have a list of courses showing how to write your own drivers from scratch in assembly language in A better to C and in C++. No libraries used just from scratch. So, yeah. The purpose of this course is to show people who have taken those courses or who are familiar with these, um, these techniques how to accomplish the same thing using the Cuba max generation. So that is why we are here. Okay,

35

so Cuba generally functions for us. So all we have to do is write the code to test it out. So when we come over here, we have these comments that guide us, um, that guide us for, you know, put in our code in particular areas. For instance, it says this is where you put your use. It includes from this side to decide. Does Y say you saw code begin included. So if I want to do it. And then I have my own dot h file. I put it over here. That is what Cuba once was. So it's got these blocks here for guidance. Often I just clean them. But you might find them useful. So I'm gonna leave them there. And when we come to our main function is to start off by initializing in the hardware abstraction layer. This is the hall. And this is what allows us to use the whole library. So this is initialized. And then once that is done, it causes the system clock config function that we saw over here. It is code. So once this is done, then it would initialize our GPL u. And it 's. This is the execution of GPL. You it. Basically it's set in our button, pinned to input and then our early dippin to output. Right. So once this is done, we can go ahead and read the button and then talk about it with reality. So if we want to know which functions are available to us, then we can go to the whole library reference module, which we downloaded earlier. Right. So let's see. OK. So this is the PDAF we downloaded earlier. Gonna open it and I'm just going to press control and then F and then I'm gonna search GPI over here. So I would jump straight to the aspect of GPL. You can tell this is a reference document. It's not meant to be read. It's meant for references. And one can tell this from the number of pages, a score of one thousand eight hundred pages. So you just have to come here and then get, you know, your reference. So out of such GPA, you. And then it will bring me to, um. What does it say over here? Says the whole system. For handling GPS use. Okay. Oh. Search to move to the next one. Okay. So this is what we want. We want the section that talks about GPA, you. Oh GPA you generic driver click over here would open. And this one here talks about how the GPA you in its function is written by them, how the GPA, your peers define the mode, etc. and then the GPA, you FAMM where API is over here. It talks about how to use this driver. We can read a bit. It says enable the GPA you HP clock use in the following. Right. Using HARL racc GPA U. X clock and enable. And if we check the QB mix, Cuba already does that for us. Cuba makes us enable a clock. Okay, so basically this document deals with people, not people who want to write what Cuba makes from scratch and then more. So it says first enable this. And then you've got to configure that pain mode, whether it's, you know, pull up, pull it, etc.. Cuba makes us do all of this for us. And then GPL u haul G. How gpl you innit. This one here. Initializes the GPL function. And then you can initialize it as well. So this whole GPL you in it is what Cuba makes refers to us and makes GPL you in it. You see over here the function is how GPL you in it. But when we go to our project over here, we don't find that. We find M x gpl u. S. This is just to show that. Okay. This was written by Cuba. Schmick's. Right. So yeah. That's what it means. But what is left out of this is how to read a pin and write the pin because we didn't tell the we did until Cuba Amex or we cannot tell. Cuba makes 10 to pin on for five seconds and then turn it off and then torgau this. The logic is not part of the Cuba X generation. So that is what we need to add over here. It says I do operation functions.

3. In case of external interrupt/event mode selection, configure NVIC IRQ priority mapped to the EXTI line using HAL_NVIC_SetPriority() and enable it using HAL_NVIC_EnableIRQ().
4. To get the level of a pin configured in input mode use HAL_GPIO_ReadPin().
5. To set/reset the level of a pin configured in output mode use HAL_GPIO_WritePin()/HAL_GPIO_TogglePin().
6. To lock pin configuration until next reset use HAL_GPIO_LockPin().
7. During and just after reset, the alternate functions are not active and the GPIO pins are configured in input floating mode (except JTAG pins).
8. The LSE oscillator pins OSC32_IN and OSC32_OUT can be used as general purpose (PC14 and PC15, respectively) when the LSE oscillator is off. The LSE has priority over the GPIO function.
9. The HSE oscillator pins OSC_IN/OSC_OUT can be used as general purpose PH0 and PH1, respectively, when the HSE oscillator is off. The HSE has priority over the GPIO function.

29.2.3 Initialization and de-initialization functions

This section provides functions allowing to initialize and de-initialize the GPIOs to be ready for use.

This section contains the following APIs:

- *HAL_GPIO_Init()*
- *HAL_GPIO_DeInit()*

29.2.4 IO operation functions

This section contains the following APIs:

- *HAL_GPIO_ReadPin()*
- *HAL_GPIO_WritePin()*

And it says how the GPL you read it and then how GPL, your right opinion. And from these names one can tell. We use them for reading and right into the pins and we have how GPL you told your pin. So we can look at Repin. So the function name is how GPL you read pain. It takes the GPL. You put this is this type of the office of the GPL you put. You have GPL, you sub X over here. This X stands for the port. It could be GPL, you A, B, C, D, et cetera. So the first argument is the GPL you put in, the second argument is that GPL, you pin and then it returns, GPL you state. So if you call this function, how would you pay for your read pain? We have to pass the port and then the pin and then we are going to get a state. That's the return value of this. And as you can see over here says the X stands for a two K. Like I mentioned, the GPI U. Port. And the next function here says, how are you? Right. And this one here doesn't return anything. It's a void. Function returns void. It takes two arguments. Yeah. It takes the um that I shouldn't say it's a void

38

function. I should just see its return void caused by saying that one might assume it doesn't take arguments or talks. Well, um, how gpl. You're right. I mean, it takes the GPL U. Port. And then it takes the GPL your pin and then it takes the state. You want to write to the pin. So how GPL your rights in the port that you pay your pin and then what you want to write. High state or no states to the point. That's what this does. And then another interest in function, which is going to be your assignment, is going to be, um. This one here, how GPL you toggle pin. This one takes the port and then the pin. You want to talk, you remember toggle this just to flip something. Meaning if it's on its own, turn it off. If it's off, turn it on. So that's why you just need to. The Dippin, you don't have to pass the state to talk, no function would get this state by itself and then flip it. So you just need to pass the port and then the pain of the port. And we have other functions which you can take a look at. Out of interest. So now. Right. We know what we want to do. We would simply want to read the pen, the push button, and then we write the state of the push button to reality. Meaning if we'd read and the push button is on, we want to turn the light on if it's off or turn off. So let's run the experiment. I'm going to minimize this. Okay. So we have this G.P.A. who has been initialized and what a great way to create a global variable here. Call this you see you in eight on a score T or call this BOTTEN status or something. Yeah, okay. So then once this is done, I'm going to come in. Just minimize this. Once this is done, I'm going to come into our main function here. I'm going to come into our infinite loop while one over here just gonna clean these. Goodness no. I'm gonna clean these comments. I think it's gonna be easier for you. Yeah. The reason I was hesitating is, yeah, some students complain. I like cleaning comments. Yeah. Cause there's an older version of this course known as, um, Cuba makes four. It's a free version. And, um, it was the same process I open and then I clean comments trying to make the, um, the IDB look much more clean and focused. Turns out not everyone was happy with that. Okay, so now we can get this is our entire main function. You see, it's better like this. It's clearer for the mind. Okay. So while one over here, what we want to do is call our whole GPL your read function. So I'm gonna see how cheaply I can underscore, read and then pin like this and then I'll pass gpl u. Over here. What. Um a pass. What entity is connected to P. A five hour pushbutton is connected to P.S. 13. So what I can do actually is pass the um I could pass the name of the push-Button port. I'm sure Cuba gave it a symbolic name. You see, it's got a name here. GPL U. Port B10 GPL your port. So it renamed the Port Port C to BTR and GPL your port. Course we said PTM should be a button pen so I can use this and we can find all of such names in the main dot h file. So just right. Click over here and then um we can go. We can open the H file over here. We should be able to do this. We can just say Togo source and header by right clicking in. I should be here somewhere. OK. Torgau source slash header. Okay, so this is the head of this Mendo H. As you can see, BGN pain is just G.P.A.. You pin 13 BGN GPA, your port is just Port C, Ellie Dippin GPA, you pin five LDC GPA, your port is Port B because we know ECPA five for the L.A. D. Right. So um, actually I'll copy this BITA and Port Y controversy here. So we know we read our whole GPA, you read it takes the port and then it takes the um Dippin which is a BGN pin. And then it would return to Penn State. I'm going to store it in our forever that we created here. So I'll see what BGN status calls this. OK. So after this line executes, we would have the state of the push button stored in this very well. So then we can come over here and call the GPL your rights pin. So we'll see how GPL, you know, scores. Right. And this one takes the port as far as I can mount and the port we know is the lady port, which is called Lady G.P.A. Port controversy to copy pasted over here. The second argument is the, um, the pin, which is ality pin. Let's get a name, a lady pin controversy to copy and paste over here. And then the state. We want to write it up. That's the third argument when a write to button state control seems to copy and control V to paste and close over here. Right. So this is it. We can build and see how it works. So we can click here to build. Let's build in. And it's built successfully. We can click here to run or just click over here. Depak. I clicked on this blog here. Right. So so like this esteemed 32 Coatex M c, c plus. Plus. And it's going to open a debugger. First, we've got to edit the launch configuration properties. So name input output debug.

```
22  #include "main.h"
23
24
25  void SystemClock_Config(void);
26  static void MX_GPIO_Init(void);
27
28
29  uint8_t buttonStatus;
30
31  int main(void)
32  {
33
34      HAL_Init();
35
36
37      SystemClock_Config();
38
39
40      MX_GPIO_Init();
41
42      while (1)
43      {
44          buttonStatus =   HAL_GPIO_ReadPin(BTN_GPIO_Port,BTN_Pin);
45          HAL_GPIO_WritePin(LED_GPIO_Port,LED_Pin,)
46
47      }
48
49
50  }
51
52
53  void SystemClock_Config(void)
```

You can keep everything here the same and say, OK. Okay, so there's the debug the debug perspective or the debug view. So if we want to run our code, we simply click the play button. If we want to stop. We click here. If we want to step over. Meaning two step. Line by line. We use these ones. Step into. Step into a function. Step over to step over function. Right. If we want to enable in a few ways such as the disassembly view, the debug view, such as the disassembly view, the watch window. For those of you who are familiar with Carl Empty. Okay. And then i.e. are embedded workbench. There is this window known as the watch window over here. It is called the expressions view. So we can come to window over here and sure view and we have all the views we have over here. We have the memory for you. If one enable that, we do just click to open it. So a lively expression is here. This one here. You can use it to watch your global variables. So this is this expression over here. Right. So we can copy this. I'll copy this. And then I'll click add expression and then I'll pasted over here. Right. So let's run a while code and see what we have. Open this. This the value it guarantees here as you click the play button over here. And the push button is one. When I press it is zero. Because the button. I suspect it is octave high. It is octave low. I should say mean in its default state is high. When you press it, go slow. Right. So basically, if you flush this onto your board, the LCD should be on because that button is on the button as octave low. When you press, then the button go slow. You can see the watch window. You can see over here, button status has changed. Two value zero. When I release it, it will go to one. I've just released it. I'm going to press again. When I press, the elite goes off as well. And then this becomes zero. When I release, it becomes one. Right. So this is the, um. This is it. This is how simple it is to create inputs, outputs with the, um, the Cuba mix.

CODING AN INPUT INTERRUPT DRIVER

We are going to see how to create interrupts for our cheap inputs. We are going to see how to enable, extend or interrupt Cuba makes and then program it in Cuba to eat. But before we do this, we have to see how the external interrupts are connected and the microcontroller. So we already know that a push button is connected to PC 13. So we keep that in mind. We need another document here. We have a number of documents thus far. We have the descriptions and the user guide of the Hardware Obstruction Leya Library, which is the hall. We also have the user guide for the new clue into this report. What we need now is a reference module for the microcontroller itself. Thus far, we don't have the reference manual for the microcontroller. We have one for the library, the whole library, and then for the Nuclear Discovery Board. You might think the documents for the Nuclear Discovery Board are supported. MICROCONTROLLER No, it just talks about these boards, how they are connected schematically. Do you have a push button, et cetera? We need a document that tells us about it registers in the chip itself. So we're going to go to our best friend, Kyouko to, you know, ask for some help like we did earlier. So I'll come over here or estimate 32 F one one. And then the word, oh, search here is reference module over here. And this first link here, it's a PDF. So we can click this. I'm opening in this new tub.

it's over here and there's the reference point. I'm going to save that as well. Click over here and advance on this 32 bit. we can keep it. I'll change the name. I don't want to get confused. ASTM 32 F for one one ref my know that's what I'm going to call this. we can open this. No, don't lose for that. Now I think I should close the browser. Can I open this? So we want to find out where our interrupt lines up. So I just come here like I do. These are reference modules you don't need to read. I read that. You just need to know where to find what you're looking for. So I'll press control and then I'll search for an interrupt. Right. And then over here it says

44

interrupts. Let's see what this first one here could do for us. This one. Let's see. I just start from the top search interrupt and then. Oh, it interrupts again. Let's see how many interruptions we have, OK. Interrupt. And which one we're looking for, one that is called the interrupt controller I. So extend or interrupt the configuration register. Um, we can use a different word, we can use SDI for external interrupt, and I know this stuff because of experience, right? So I know what to search for actually. we have it over here. External interrupts Event Controller Page 201 or double click this over here. And it talks about the external interrupt. It talks about the address.

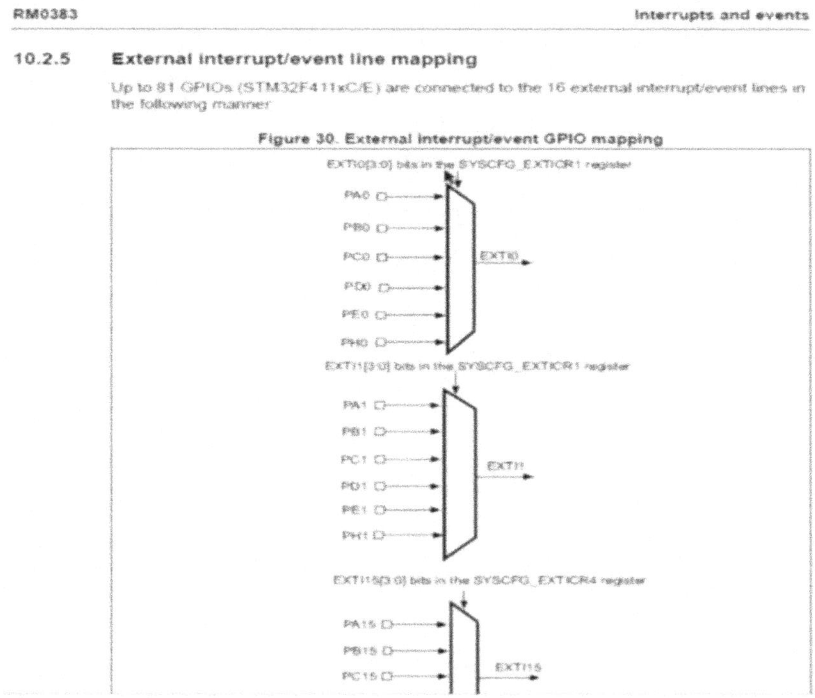
RM0383 Interrupts and events

10.2.5 External interrupt/event line mapping

Up to 81 GPIOs (STM32F411xC/E) are connected to the 16 external interrupt/event lines in the following manner

Figure 30. External interrupt/event GPIO mapping

And then it brings us to this table, this very important table. Right. I'm going to zoom in. So this one tells us external interrupts slash event G.P.A. Krupin. So over here, it's telling us that all things zero are connected to external interrupts you over here. It's written text zero. So on the peninsula of every port, whether it's A, B, C, D, E or H, you use external interrupts zero and then open one external interrupt one all the way to fifteen. So from this we can tell that our button should be connected to external interrupts. Uh, thirteen since it is connected to PC thirteen. So this is what we came for. Right. I'm going to minimize this now. We can go to our estimated 32 QNX to set this up. I'm going to select my board, it's the new clipboard. And I'm going to open up and come over here. Claire Penult, I started from scratch because it would take some time for you to get used to it. That's why I didn't start in the middle. So let's initialize the normal stuff. The Cool Stuff System Call says over here, a single wire passes over here. I'm just going to say bypass for the high speed clock, low speed accident or C, use this ceramic resonator. And then what we're going to do is our PC 13 or is it. PG 13 is over here. I'm going to right click this time rather than choose input. I'm going to choose keepa. You extend or interrupt because I want to use interrupt and then we know our lead is five. So I'll come over here then.

This is the output and we can rename this. Right click and use a label to call this lady. And then over here, right click until you see the label BTN like this. OK. Next we need to go to the configuration top to select our interrupter line. So there's an extra step involved in this one. That is why it's essential that we do it. Um, so I'll come over here too. Systems view over here and then the Enviga over here. This should open a system for you and Vic. Right. So what we want is external interrupt line 13, but we see that the cube mix allows us to select this for interrupts ranging from 10 to 15. So our 13 falls within this range. So we take this. So there's no dedicated Etext I line 13.

There is a dedicated line for interruptions of 10 to 15. So we take this, once that is done under Enviga, we can go to our project and then give it a name. We can call this input interrupt. And then we can select our two Jane Q idee and then we can generate the project. Oh, click open project to open it so the project is done opening this old project from our workspace. So I'll close this and then. This is all new input interrupt, so come over here, open source, and then I'll just do a bit of cleanup. I'll clean up by reducing the number of comments. So this is what it looks like after taking up the comment. Right. This is our main function. So, um, we saw the init function, the key player in its function already. So what we are going to do this time is let the interrupt turn on the LCD. To do this, we have to take a look at the function that allows us to deal with interruptions. We can find this in our While Drive manual, the document we downloaded earlier. Right. So if we don't want to always go back to the, um, the dereference manual, one way of doing this, one way of knowing all the functions available to a particular Peverel is to open the implementation file of the peripheral so you can come to drive us over here, drive us. And then this one, SDM three to four hold drivers and then we are dealing with GPU. So you select the whole underscore GPL, you don't see fault double click to open it and you can either go through the entire driver file or you can come over here and take a look at the outline, the outline here, its list, the number of defines and the number of functions defined in this file over here. These are the defined statement, GPL, your mode, etc. These are the functions we have. GPL you in it, D in it, repin right beento Gilpin in and then we have exten or interrupt your Q handler over here and then we have the extend or interrupt callback. So we know these two functions. Deal with the interruption so we can take a look at the Iraqi handler. You can just double click this and then it will bring it over here for you. And then he says this function handles extended or interrupt requests. Krupin specifies the pins connected to it, extend or interrupt line, and then it returns none. So we can just pass the pin here for the external interrupt and then this will deal with it. Another way is to use this one here. The extend or interrupt callback. It says open specifies the pin connected. We can use this callback function. The callback function basically allows us to add our execution in this function. If you want to perform a computation, if you have got an algorithm that needs to compute when to interrupt, as you put it in this function such that whenever the interrupt occurs, this function is executed. And the reason we see this week keyword here is that it means this function can appear twice.

```
494    */
495  void HAL_GPIO_EXTI_IRQHandler(uint16_t GPIO_Pin)
496  {
497      /* EXTI line interrupt detected */
498      if(__HAL_GPIO_EXTI_GET_IT(GPIO_Pin) != RESET)
499      {
500          __HAL_GPIO_EXTI_CLEAR_IT(GPIO_Pin);
501          HAL_GPIO_EXTI_Callback(GPIO_Pin);
502      }
503  }
504
505  /**
506    * @brief  EXTI line detection callbacks.
507    * @param  GPIO_Pin Specifies the pins connected EXTI line
508    * @retval None
509    */
510  __weak void HAL_GPIO_EXTI_Callback(uint16_t GPIO_Pin)
511  {
512      /* Prevent unused argument(s) compilation warning */
513      UNUSED(GPIO_Pin);
514      /* NOTE: This function Should not be modified, when the callback is needed
515               the HAL_GPIO_EXTI_Callback could be implemented in the user file
516      */
517  }
518
519  /**
520    * @}
521    */
522
523
524  /**
525    * @}
```

You know, we cannot pick up appear multiple times in a while, you know, our project, whenever we see week, whenever there is a situation where we have this function defined twice with one starting with wheat and the other one not having a week and just having this part of it, the one starting with week is not going to be comp. It's not going to be run, I should say. So this allows us to be able to copy this function, paste it in our mandatory file and then delete the weak keyword there and then write our own version of it while keeping this where it is without cleaning it. Because what happens is often when you have two identical functions in your project, the compiler is going to complain and tell you you've got multiple definitions of the function. But if you put a week before the ones you don't need so that you just delete the week keyword when you need a particular version, then you can get away with it.

So I'm going to copy this over here. Control. Easy to copy. I'll come to amend or C fall. I can put it anywhere I want. I can put it above you or let me put it right beneath the main function. I'll come over here and we can read what it says. This function should not be modified when the callback is needed. The whole GPL you extend or Kobuk could be implemented in the use of all this or use of it. So we want this to execute. So we delete the week here and then we can just take the note. We've read it. So what we want to do is when they interrupt. Here's when to interrupt. Which is connected to our input case. What we want to do, we want to do something when I do something over here. Right. And remember the interruption when we press our button basically that is why we connect it to the push-Button extend or interrupt. So what we want to do is talk about the ability. So we'll do so together.

```
37
38      MX_GPIO_Init();
39
40
41      while (1)
42      {
43
44      }
45  }
46
47    void HAL_GPIO_EXTI_Callback(uint16_t GPIO_Pin)
48    {
49        /* Prevent unused argument(s) compilation warning */
50        UNUSED(GPIO_Pin);
51
52        //Do something....
53        HAL_GPIO_TogglePin(LED_GPIO_Port, LED_Pin);
54
55    }
56
57  void SystemClock_Config(void)
58  {
59      RCC_OscInitTypeDef RCC_OscInitStruct = {0};
60      RCC_ClkInitTypeDef RCC_ClkInitStruct = {0};
61
62      /** Configure the main internal regulator output voltage
63      */
64      __HAL_RCC_PWR_CLK_ENABLE();
65      __HAL_PWR_VOLTAGESCALING_CONFIG(PWR_REGULATOR_VOLTAGE_SCALE1);
66      /** Initializes the CPU, AHB and APB busses clocks
67      */
```

CDT Build Console [InputInterrupt]
23:56:55 Build Failed. 3 errors, 0 warnings. (took 2s.395ms)

We use the whole Jhpiego underscore toggle pin and then the first argument is going to be the part which is really the GPL, your port. And then the second argument is going to be the which is early dippin like this. Right. So what is going to happen is we talk about this whenever we interrupt. so there's nothing else we need to do. We don't need to write anything in the main function. This is the beauty of this. So you can think of this as a background threat, something in the background that is just triggered whenever there's an interrupt. And this type, this interrupt is triggered by pressing the push button in our case and this particular example. So this is it, right? So I'm going to click over here to build. We've got three errors, it could be from our implementation of the early DGP report, so I probably messed up the name of the lady who was caught in the early DGP report. This is correct. Let's copy the exact same word. the port shouldn't be capital letters, just start with a capital letter about the Pinelli dependence should be fined hubo how the hell you togo? Let's confirm how G.P.A. Togo paid back in the GPL. You don't see far. I'm going to check the outline and see what the function is like, how the GPL you told Gilpin's is cheap. Right. OK. Looks good, I'll come over here. Click here to build. I should close this, it's built successfully and then we can run this click over here, so like this is 32. We're going to keep everything the same, say, OK. So this expression, live expression is from our previous project. I can just close this, drop this away a bit and then we can click here to run the code, currently the lead is off when I press, as you can see, when my hand is pressing the LCD on, this means the interrupters or Keryn. When I leave my hand, it goes off when I press the interrupt. yes. And what we find in the interrupt service routine is executed. So this is it. This or there is for this project. If you have any questions at all, just let me know. And if you find it in the course, use it to take some time off to leave a review and I'll see you in the next lesson. Have a nice day. Bye bye. So as you can see, when I press the toggle, look at what is in the interrupt service routine. So sometimes when I press it sort of stays on because of something known as the bounce. Then when you are working in embedded systems and you are dealing with push buttons, you've got to account for depos, because when you press a button rather than the press or caring, once it occurs multiple times, so often you've got to put a time there. Some people often implement deboned use in time. So the really the Dippin for a number of milliseconds and then read it again to make sure there's the actual state. So the reason why you might see some jitter is because we've not, you know, put a system in place to prevent the bounce. So there is multiple reading of the same press cos I think I'm pressing just once, but because it's so fast, the one time press becomes ten times press. If we were to count and if we were to view the number of times the button is pressed, you realize that what I would consider a one time press could be 10 or 20 times in the reading of the PIN. In a way, if you don't understand all of this, you need not worry about that.

CODING AN INPUT INTERRUPT DRIVER (MULTIPLE INPUTS)

We're going to see how to work with multiple extensions or interrupts. So I'm going to create a new project from. All right. Yeah. Click over here. You project. Also liked my board. This team has four. One, one. Or just like the nuclear board here. And I'm going to disable Claire, or the pin out was a clip in out over here and I'm going to start off. I know we have just a single button on the nuclear board, but we would find a way to run this experiment.

I'm going to set a wire. P.S. 13 over here, which is where our push button is connected to extend or interrupt GPL, you extend or interrupt 13. And then I'm going to set P five to our ality, which is simply GPL, your output like this. We can use Spears zero as our next button, although there is no second button on the board. We can nominate peers over here. So I'm going to go to pin p0 and say as GPL, you extend or interrupt you like this. Okay.

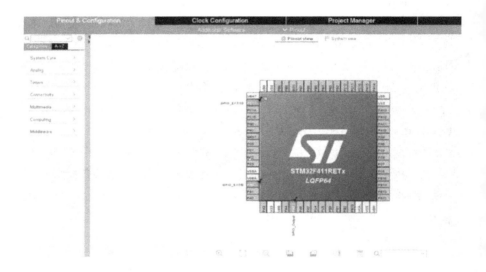

So we can make our experiment a bit more interesting by 10 in the early days using P.S. 13, which is where our push button is connected and turn it off using PSU so we can go to our system's view and then click on our GPL. You are over here to set up the pins. I'll click over here to open it. So I'll start off by clicking on, um. We have our peers who are here. We know it selected its default mode as extend or interrupt mode with Brize in edge trigger. That is fine. A whopping five is said to, um, output, Push-Pull. That is fine as well. These are peers. Right. So the spears, you extend or interrupt, rise and, uh, rise, rising edge trigger. P.S. 13, we want to change that to fall in an external interrupt mode with falling edge trigger detection. Right. OK. Once this is done, we've got to go to the NVC tub.

And they will all interrupt and enable us. Now we can go ahead and generate our project, come to generate code over here. I'll call this or call this multiple. External. Interrupts and then also likes my tune change over here is the esteemed 32 Cube. And then we can click over here to generate. This is our project. I'll clean up a bit. So this all may not seem far. And if we come down here, we will see all of the code calibrated in the GPL. You in it. We have to interrupt.

And to see further interrupt information, we can come to the SDM 32 F4 on the score. I did not see this fall over here and now we'll see our two interlocked, uh oh, two interrupt handlers. So we have 10 or 15 to 10. I am an RCU handler. And this is what would handle the interrupt request for P.S. 13. And then we have to extend or interrupt zero hour cue handlers. And this, of course, is DPL you pin zero. so now we have to implement a while Kobuk for interruption. So we have to go to our GPL you module. So I came to drive us over here. How drivers sors and then G.P.A. you don't see. And we can simply start off by searching the week keyword on that score on a score week. And we have this callback function here. Oh, GPL, you, XDR. Kobuk. So we can just copy this, reimplement this. No, I mean, let's see the file. So I copy this and then I'll come up here. I can close this. I'll come up here and put this here like this. And then I would delete the weak keyword. Yeah. OK. So you may be wondering, we've got one callback function, but we've got to interrupt. How do we work with this? And there is a single parameter over here which is GPL you pin. OK. We can do this by using an if statement. We can simply check what a pain is to interrupt coming from and then we execute. Well, we want to execute. So over here I can simply see if this parameter here, GPL yappin. If this equals G play, you pin zero, which is the same as our peers zero. If this, of course, GPA points zero, then we want to do something here. And we said I would do something to turn on the ality, but do something. And over here, we can see if the GPA you pin a course GPA, you pin 13. Want to do something again? So over here, you can do whatever you want, but I'm just going to turn it on here. Turn off the ality here and turn it on in the next interrupt. So I'll see how GPI you. And then two, turn on. We use the right pin. Right. Been like this. And then this takes the port, which is GPL. You see, that's where it is connected. The PIN number is keeping you on the scorpion on this score five. And then we want to write zero to it. Want to turn it off. So we use reset. So we say G.P.A. you on the Scorpion and the score reset like this. And over here, if the interrupt is coming from P.S. 13, we want to turn on the depen.

```c
16
17     *********************************************************************
18     */
19  /* USER CODE END Header */
20
21  /* Includes ------------------------------------------------------------*/
22  #include "main.h"
23
24
25  void SystemClock_Config(void);
26  static void MX_GPIO_Init(void);
27
28
29  void HAL_GPIO_EXTI_Callback(uint16_t GPIO_Pin)
30  {
31
32      if(GPIO_Pin ==  GPIO_PIN_0){
33          //Do something...
34              HAL_GPIO_WritePin(GPIOA,GPIO_PIN_5,GPIO_PIN_RESET);
35
36      }
37      if(GPIO_Pin == GPIO_Pin_13){
38          //Do something.. I
39          HAL_|
40      }
41  }
```

Problems   Tasks   Console   Properties

No consoles to display at this time.

So we say G.P.A., you hold GPI, you on the score, right. PIN like this and then we pass the same thing. GPL U. A. And then the penis G.P.A.. You pin five. Cause that is where it is connected to a five. You pin on the score five. And we want to make a cheapie. You. No scorpion on this corset sets means. Right. One to it, okay. We have this over here. So from this arrangement, I hope you can tell that we cannot have, uh, two PIN numbers in a multiple interrupt arrangement. And what I mean by two PIN numbers is that if you have the same PIN number but different ports, you can all use multiple interrupts. You have to have different pin numbers, if any can be the same ports, but different PIN numbers. The reason why that is, is that what is taken here is the PIN number. So pin zero here means it could be pin zero four. Put a pin zero for ports B, C, D, E, F, et cetera. So you cannot have pin zero for port A as one extent or interrupt and pin zero for port to be as an ETA as another extend or interrupt cause there would be no way to differentiate the two of them. Right. So we can go ahead and build a project or click over here. I have one error here because of this. This pin here should be all cup two letters. So I appealed again. It appealed successfully. I'll get onto the board by clicking on this. Selectors say, okay. I say, OK. Here we are here. We can click here to run. Right. So you can try this on your board so you can simply connect on the external button to the P zero. This is the, uh, that nuclear user guide we downloaded. This is the position of P is you. It's over here. You can just use this P note. Oh. This one here. This is how I bought a four one one r e p. Is you. Is this pin over here? Right. So based on the setup, if you have more interruptions, you can just use the if statement to deal with them one by one like that.

CODING GPIO DRIVERS FROM SCRATCH USING DATASHEET INFORMATION (PART I)

This lesson is about using the cube I.D. to create perimeter code. And what I mean by bare metal code is right and the driver's without use in Cuba makes all the whole library, meaning access in the registers directly after this lesson. Go ahead and see how to write a driver's assembly using cube I.D. as well without using the cube and making it in the whole library. And this lesson is going to be in this cube, imex cube, imex cube I.D. cause as well as another course that I have on bare metal programming in that other cause.

The development environment we use is the Carl MBK. So I'm going to include this lesson in that other course as well. The reason I'm saying this is that the language I'm going to use in this lesson would be assuming you've never written bare metal code. So I'm just going to assume you have no idea. And I'm going to take you step by step. If this lesson appears in the bare metal cores, student watch and of course, already know some of the steps. So it would sound a bit repetitive to them. That is why I'm given this warning, because we are going to do it from scratch. It's going to be from the student of the SDM, Teddy to Cuba mix perspective. The estimate to Cuba students perspective, because this is not focused on bare metal. So I'm going to explain some of the things as I do it. But if you find this lesson in the bare metal, cause this would be like we spoke about this before. Just bear with me. And it's better to have it repeated than skipping stuff. So let's get started. So to, um, to be able to access the arm, to be able to access, to be able to access the registers, we need to know the register addresses and the offset how they are arranged and what's the debits in the wrappers are in the registers represent the registers that uh, 32 bit in size every register. That is why the arm is a third.

It's one of the reasons why ARM is a 32 bit microprocessor. So we have to know what bits number one is used for. It's number two. It's number three, et cetera. To find this information out. We need to download another document. This time, we're going to download the reference module for the microcontroller chip. We've already downloaded the data sheet for the, um, the chip, which gave us a quick overview. We had about one hundred and forty eight pages. The data sheet gave us the block diagram, um, showing us how the various peripherals are connected to the different pass matrix or matrices that the board has. And this allows us to know what Plock each pair can have in the data sheet. The reference manual, on the other hand, gives us a detailed explanation of each and every register India in the microcontroller chip. So we'll need these documents. And he has over, I think, over 800 or 1000 pages. So it's a reference document. It's not meant to be taken all at once, you know. Anyway, um, so I'm gonna go to the Web browser and, um, and download it. So you can just go to Google and type SDM three to four one one reference manual. I have four boards. That is why this is the word you may have phones, you, etc.. OK. This first link says PDAF. So let's right click this and open this. OK. So here we go. As I said, this has eight hundred and forty four pages. We are simply going to download this. And I can rename this call. Oh, call this the reference, my door. I mean, they all have these long names. Ref Miyo. OK. So once we've downloaded this, we'll go ahead and create a new project and then list out some of the, um, the, um, the activities or some of the steps we need to take to get this project running. Okay. So I'm simply going to minimize this. And this is our Kubi. I'm gonna create a new project, file the new look at it for you over here and I'll select SDM 32 to project. This one here, not this one. This one is the M3 to project. It says Initialise and SDM 32 targets Selecter. So does the target selector.

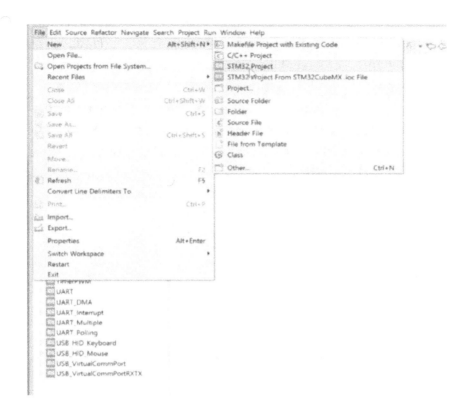

Please bear with a resolution for some strange reason. It's open with, um, with these, um, smaller fonts. But this is the same page that we use and, um, in what Cuba makes to select our board. So we just come here and select our board, SDM 32 for one one. So we searched over here. And then over here, we can choose the board we have. So I just select one or select my nuclear board by what matters. Yes, the microcontroller. No, whether it's nuclear or disco is the name of the microcontroller which we searched SDM three to four one one. And I'm, like I said, to bear with a small font here. For some strange reason, Cuba opened this way. And then you are familiar with this page. All right. It is the same page from the Cuba mix that we selected on our board. So we shouldn't be an issue. So once I've found my board, I'll click on next. And then once I've selected the board, I'm going to give the project a name. I'll give this a name. Let's see. I'll call this GPI. You. QPR, you bare metal. so next. And this I kept the same, it's a You Project Cube. Get the prototype estimated to Cube. OK. Target. I'll leave this the same next time. And then this is the board. The reference board we selected is the find firmware package. You can keep this the way it is. And then a click finish.

This kind of project is associated with SDM 32 Kubin mixed perspective. Do you want to open this perspective? If we want to open this perspective, we can say yes, but we don't need that. So I'll say it. No. Because we're going to keep Bermejo. We don't need Cuba, Max. We don't need the whole library. We are going to go to the datasheet and reference my no. Find the registers and manipulate them ourselves. OK. So there's the page that shows up. This page has been opened to allow us to easily, you know, configure our pins. So if you were to be creating a project using cube I.D., you can still use this method and then use the whole library by just starting from cube I.D.. This opens. You select your pins and then you move on. What this means is you don't always have to start from the cube and mix and come to the cube to eat. You can access the cube mix from here. But we don't need all of that.

We said we are doing Bamma talks who are close to this and then I'll come to see. There is just what we have here. It brought the whole library. We don't need a whole library. You brought this. It couldn't help it. So that's what SD is doing here. So the system generated the whole library regardless because it assumes 99 percent of the time. If you get on a project, you need the hardware abstraction layer, which is the whole library. So we have the whole library here. But we don't need that. What are we going to be using as just a single header file? Which we find in the CMC is okay. So I'm going to quote the source folder. This is our project. This was located right. Click at New and in our other folder called The Source Our Like This. And this is just to show that, you know, we have a source folder in all of the project, the project structure. You often have your source inside your source, inside your source for. You have your main Ötzi Fall and the other files you need. So I have this source photo here. And then I'm going to come over here inside this source folder. I'll close this. This is still our project, GPL. You underscore Babymetal inside a source. All right, click add. New item or or new. Why am I seeing a new item? Okay. New. And then select followed by here. Then this fall is going to be the main dot c. And then finish. Okay. So now we have our main view here. And I'm going to include our SDM 32 head of file. The head of file that gives the register addresses and locations we see include. Besty M 32, f four. We're using the F for board x x dot h x. X means Of four essentially. And I'm simply going to say int main. Over here. And this is void. I want to just write this and test and see that we build successfully before we go on. Okay. And we can put our infinite loop in here. Open and close. Right. So once this is done, we can click here to build. Let's see what we have learned in all of the whole library drivers. We can delete them, but we don't need to delete them. This was just a demo. But if you don't want to, if you don't want this whole library stuff to take space on your firmware, we don't need any of that here. They can be deleted. We're not using them. You see, we know we aren't as tempted to underscore each. We don't have it in our projects or we can delete everything related to it. OK. So we have no errors. No warning. Right. So the setup looks good. So in this example, what we're going to do is basically to go to the LCD on our nuclear board and this can be in a SDM 32 F4 board at all. The only difference is that you would have to connect the LTT differently on your particular body if you are the disco board on disco. The LCD is connected elsewhere. But if you want to follow along without changing anything, you may need to connect on X10 or ality to a port so that you can use the same pin. The reason I'm saying this is that the nuclear board elite is connected to P five. So we're going to be enabling P five as an output pin, using bare metal, using the bare metal method. If you may call it that. So, you know, in modern day microcontrollers, before you use any part of the microcontroller in a module or in your peripheral, you have to enable clock access to that part. And the reason why we do this is because of something known as the clock gating mechanism. Microcontrollers from the past long ago, about maybe two decades ago, didn't have this clock Gayton mechanism. And what I meant is if you turn on the microcontroller or all the parts sort of consume some power. Right. Cos they all have clock access open to them. So due to the rise of, you know, low power development, finding ways to optimize, you know, power usage, et cetera. And we became one of the solutions. So what this means is by default, the microcontroller has the clock cutoff from the different parts. If you want to use a particle apart, you enable clock access to just that part two. If I want to use the HTC One, I enable clock access to the ADC one without an enabling clock for the other parts, such as you, art and other peripherals. So this is what the clock cages about.

```
#include "stm32f4xx.h"

int main(void)
{
    while(1){

    }
}
```

And the bus, the bus of the arm of the microcontroller tells us how the clock lines are connected. So to start off, let's take a look at the, um, the bus connection of the peripherals. We said we're going to be dealing with GPI, you port. So we want to know where the port is connected. If we can find a bus of Port A. Then we know how to enable clock to port A SO to find the bus, we need to go to the SDM three to four one one datasheet document. This is different from the reference document. The datasheet document is the document with the M with a block diagram. We need to take a look at the block diagram. I think I have the data sheet here. So if you don't

68

have that, you can just go on line, search SDM 32 F for one one datasheet. And this is the um, is a called data sheet. Liz, let's see what is written up here. so this is it. This is classified as the datasheet when India and the arrangement and the other one is classified as the. The reference to my notes written here. Datasheet. Over here. So we need to take a look at the block diagram. So I'm going to scroll down here. We just posted this one over here. I'm going to zoom in. OK. Well, assuming a bit. so this diagram here shows us the, um, the buses connecting the various parts of the microcontroller. So there are two buses. Generally, we have the HP, the APB bus and the HP bus. HP allows us to allow faster access. Basically, you can access a particular part of the microcontroller with fewer clock cycles when using the HP as compared to the APD. APB is the legacy buses from the past and the HP is the more recent one. But they keep both to allow portability. So over here you see HP over here.

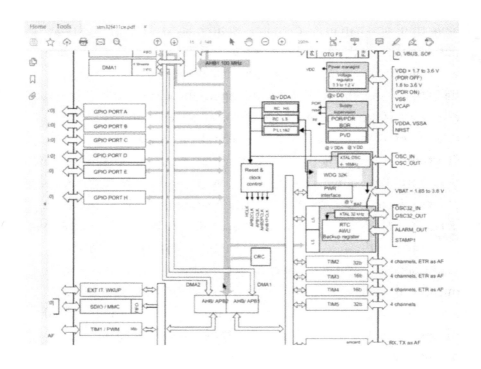

And then we have APB and HP are further divided into HP, one APB one, et cetera. So to know how a particular component is connected, you just have to trace the arrows, the arrows connecting it. And then from the arrow, you know which bus. So this is GPL, your port. If you look at UK ports, we see this arrow connection to G.P.A.. You put a and then connect into this other bus here. When we look at the name of the bus, the bus is called a HP one bus. So we know to access GPL, you put it to enable it. We need to enable it using the HP one meaning there is something in the HP module without allowing us to enable G.P.A.. You put a is the same for ports B, C, D and E, you can trace them. But if we were to use a different peripheral such as t I am M2 meaning time two, we know that we can trace and locate it bus from here. It's connected to the APB, one bus, the APB, one bus gives us access to time or two. So after knowing this we know GPL, you say it is HP one. So we can just keep a comment up here, a HP one like this. OK. And we said we're dealing with P five. P A five. That's it. Well, it is connected. Right. So to enable the HP one, we need to go to the data sheet and see what HP looks like. So we need to go to data sheets and search HP one and Naples, register the register for enabling HP one. I mean, reference manual. This is the data sheet. So we need to open the reference manual next. Does the one that gives us the register information. So come over here. That will click this to open. And there's the reference manual. This one is bigger. So there's a trick for dealing with this. You simply search for what you are looking for. You all do control. If you open the search box here and then I'm going to search for the HP one. And then I hit enter. And then it's probably here and then. Oh, hit enter again. I'm looking for an HP one enabler register. So this one here says RACC, a HP one pair, four o'clock enabler register. This is the one we're dealing with. So click this. And when I come here it tells me over here. It shows the 32 bit register. And we say 32 bits because we count from zero. So if you count from zero through thirty one, you end up with 32. Right. So over here it says pit zero is GPA you enable between GPL, you B enable B to GPL, you see a network cetera. So let's go to pit zero. Over here, the bits I explained or that decoded if you want to see it. So if I scroll down here to go to the part where it tells me BOPE, it's zero like it said in the diagram, but zero is GPL you enable. And it says, I Allport a clock and enable set and cleared by software. And over here it gives a simple Truth table, if you want to call it that. It says if it is set to zero then I put a clock is disabled. If it is set to one then I o clock. When they said to one, then I put a clock. It is enabled. So to enable clock four point eight we have to set this over here to one. So yeah, that is point number one. So we know what to do here. So we can, um, we can take note of the we can, um, say set the register called RACC, HP one enable register set bitz zero. Oh see I said it's zero or Qasi HP one, two, one does what we want to do to enable clock access. Right. Next, So once we do this auction clock access is going to be available to keep you put in. Now we can choose whichever pin we want on the port to use for our purpose. But we said we use MPLX five. This brings another explanation which regards the way microcontrollers work. So any microcontroller at all. Um, when dealing with GPI, you GPI U stands for general purpose input output. When dealing with GPA, there are at least two registers that any microcontroller would have, what, eight, eight bits. Sixteen bits. Thirty two bits. There are at least two registers when it comes to dealing with GPL. You and these two registers are the um the direction register and the data register. These are at least two, but you would never in modern day microcontrollers, you would find more than two, but all of them contain this, at least to the direction register used to set the GPL. You remember, GPL stands for general purpose, input output. We use that direction to set the direction, whether we want it to be input or output. We use that direction to do that. Direction register. To do that. And they, um, the data register, based on whether you choose to set it as input or output, would either contain the data or would give the data that is to be able to put it out. Right. So at least they have these two registers. So these are the generic names of the registers. Um, data register and direction register. So I mentioned. OK. So given this fundamental, um, given this, um, fundamental knowledge, microcontroller manufacturers, um, build upon this to add more options to it. So I mentioned in GPL you can have it either as input or output because of the complexity of modern day microcontrollers. Our GPI, you pin p five is not simply a GPO. We can configure p a five also into an s p i o n s p i. O stands for special purpose input output. So because we have this other option in this so-called Direxion Register, our options are no longer to choose input or output. There's another option known as alternate function option. So we can also set it to an alternate function. And by setting it to an alternate function, we can say we want to use P a five as a U at our x p, meaning you are to receive Peine or you are to explain or as a plutonium generator in all. I said that. So these are peripherals such as you at ADC, DHC, the special purpose peripherals, the base pair for the general purpose is the simple G.P.A. you about all of these peripherals. They deal with Paines as well. So you have to configure the pin to be a special purpose being to use it. So with this, then we access the same, the same direction register. Right. So direction register. Right. However, when you go to the data sheet and the reference my notes or from silicon manufacturers, you wouldn't find the, um, the word direction register. They've given us this functionality or registered different names. If you go to the, um, the data sheet of the Texas instrument. Um, Tim Forese, one, two, three. This is still called the Director Register. But, you know, SDM 32. This is called the Mode Register, so it makes sense. You are setting the mood. So yeah, in other manufactures, I'm sure an B would have a different name for this same register, but fundamentally they do the same thing. So this brings us to finding our register. And then, um, and then dealing with it. So we're going to go back to a work reference my no and find a note register. And see how the more register or the direction. Remember when I say mode and direction, I'm using it interchangeably because I gave you the prologue. I gave it an introduction using the word director register. So you can think of them as the same. So we go to the, um, the reference manual, find this direction register or more register and see what we have to do to this register to set out what, a five as an output pin because P five can be output, it can be input and it can be a special purpose as well.

```
#include "stm32f4xx.h"

//PA5

//AHB1

//set bit0 in RCC_AHB1ENR  to 1


int main(void)
{
    while(1){

    }
}
```

CDT Build Console [Gpio_BareMetal]
16:13:11 Build Finished. 0 errors, 0 warnings. (took 14s.631ms)

We have to say we want this pain to be output for this project and we have to find that. Okay. So let's go to the, um, the reference model. I think I still have it open over here, so I'll come back to the top on scroll back to the top control F to search F here and then I'm going to search mode. Ah. And then now hit enter and then it's probably here under GPL your register. He says g.p or Port Moad registered. The R stands for register. That is why it's written mode.

Ah. So we can click here to read about it. Okay. It says GPL you Portmore Register and GPL your GPA you on this uh subscript X mode register. And it says X stands for a, e and H e all the way to H I should see. And this means GPA. You put a person C D all the way to H over here like we said or register 32 bits if they are not thirty two. Although the other two bits, not all of them have all. It's been used, for instance, this one down here. We don't use the upper upper arm. Fifteen bits. Sixteen bits. They're reserved. OK. So this one would register. And it's broken down into mode zero. Through mode. Fifteen. Right. More to zero. Take the first two bits. Zero and bit one more. Fifteen takes the last two bits to thirty and a bit. Thirty one. So let's read about what mod zero is. One word. One is what mode two is, et cetera. Over here it says. Mode. Mode. Subscript y. And over here it gives bits zero through one meaning they take one bit. Um. Yeah. And it says Port X configuration Y equals zero through fifteen. Meaning Y. Here. Represent more to zero mode one mode to all the way toward fifteen. Right. So he says these bits are written by software to configure the eye or direction mode. You see the eye using the Y direction here. Yeah. So you said the eye or direction mode. It says when we set the two bit two zero zero, we've set it as input. When we set it to one zero, we've set it as general-purpose output mode. When we set it to zero, we've set it to alternate function mode. And when we said it to one one, we said it to unlock mode. So we have four different modes or directions here. Right. So what, um, what we have here. It's not clearly stated here. But not one here. These two bits are useful. Configuring all this is mode zero. I should see more zero here. These two bits, which are bits and bytes, one more zero is useful, configuring all pins, zeros of every port. So if I'm dealing with P is zero. I have to use more than zero. If I'm dealing with please you. I have to use more to zero. If I'm dealing with p.c zero point zero p e p h zero or more two in the same way mod five over here. Whereas Mode five, mode five over here is for or pin pin fives. So this is the one we're looking for. We have to set mode five two two one zero. So what does this mean? It means we have a 32 bit, 32 bit binary number and that that's pit number ten. We have to set it to one. We have to make sure bits number 10 is set to one. Number eleven is set to zero, all the other bits. We don't care about them. They deal with other pains. But specifically, four bits. Number ten and eleven. We have to make sure. We have to make sure they are set to. Yes, sir. To bits. One and zero, as we have over here, if you don't understand, is to live in. Live it in the questions area. So mode five is for P five. So what is Mod five? Would five deal with pit number ten and eleven. So we set pits number ten to one. And then bitz number eleven to zero. By doing this we'll set it to general purpose output mode and output mode is what would output our L.E. delight.

8.4.1 GPIO port mode register (GPIOx_MODER) (x = A..E and H)

Address offset: 0x00

Reset values:
- 0xA800 0000 for port A
- 0x0000 0280 for port B
- 0x0000 0000 for other ports

31	30	29	28	27	26	25	24	23	22	21	20	19	18	17	16
MODER15[1:0]		MODER14[1:0]		MODER13[1:0]		MODER12[1:0]		MODER11[1:0]		MODER10[1:0]		MODER9[1:0]		MODER8[1:0]	
rw	rw	rw	rw	rw	rw	rw	rw	rw	rw	rw	rw	rw	rw	rw	rw
15	14	13	12	11	10	9	8	7	6	5	4	3	2	1	0
MODER7[1:0]		MODER6[1:0]		MODER5[1:0]		MODER4[1:0]		MODER3[1:0]		MODER2[1:0]		MODER1[1:0]		MODER0[1:0]	
rw	rw	rw	rw	rw	rw	rw	rw	rw	rw	rw	rw	rw	rw	rw	rw

Bits 2y:2y+1 **MODERy[1:0]:** Port x configuration bits (y = 0..15)

These bits [...] the I/O direction mode
00: Input
01: General purpose output mode
10: Alternate function mode
11: Analog mode

8.4.2 GPIO port output type register (GPIOx_OTYPER) (x = A..E and H)

Address offset: 0x04

Reset value: 0x0000 0000

31	30	29	28	27	26	25	24	23	22	21	20	19	18	17	16
Reserved															
15	14	13	12	11	10	9	8	7	6	5	4	3	2	1	0
OT15	OT14	OT13	OT12	OT11	OT10	OT9	OT8	OT7	OT6	OT5	OT4	OT3	OT2	OT1	OT0
rw	rw	rw	rw	rw	rw	rw	rw	rw	rw	rw	rw	rw	rw	rw	rw

Bits 31:16 Reserved, must be kept at reset value

Bits 15:0 **OTy:** Port x configuration bits (y = 0..15)
These bits are written by software to configure the output type of the I/O port
0: Output push-pull (reset state)

So let's take some notes. I'll come over here. Set. Set. Bit ten to one. And bit eleven to zero in GPL. You are a mode register. And this will give us output mode. OK. So after this we would have this set us output mode. Now how do we write to the GPL Open? Remember we said there are at least two registers you have to deal with. There is the direction register and the data register. Well, yeah. The data register allows us to get the data. I get it or give it based on whether we've configured it for input or output. So when we turn on the ality, when we want to turn it off to how we do the on and off to do this, we would have to access the data register. And just like the direction register, silicon manufacturers give this register different names also. So in some data sheets or reference modules, you find it's called the data register. In others you'd find no data register, but a name is still descriptive of its function. So over here, it is called the Output Data Register. Over here, they've broken the data register into inputs, data register and output data register such that when you are dealing with GPA, you set it as an input. You use the input data register. And when you are dealing with it as an output, you use the output data register. So let's find the output data register and see what it presents to us. When I come up here and then I'll do a control f and then our search o t r does what it is called or hit enter and it brings me over here. GPL, you put an output data register. Click this over here. And this explains what we've got. You can close this. So it says what it says. It says GPA. You put the data register. No problem. And over here we have only r y meaning Y is from zero through fifteen. The top is reserved. So we have output data. Register. What is your one, two, three. And these correspond to the PIN numbers. So if we are dealing with PIN five, then this is where our output is going to be. We are going to write our output here. We're going to write one, two bits, number five over here. And by writing one, two bits, number five, ten P a five is going to be set high. It's going to be set on its own. It's going to be set to one, whichever you prefer.

```c
1  #include "stm32f4xx.h"
2
3  //PA5
4
5  //AHB1
6
7  //set bit0 in RCC_AHB1ENR  to 1
8  // set bit10 to 1 and bit11 to 0 in GPIOA_MODER
9  //write 1 to GPIOA_ODR bit 5 to se|
10
11 int main(void)
12 {
13     while(1){
14
15     }
16 }
17
```

So we take note. Right. I'll see. Right. One, right, one, two GP, are you a GP, are you a. Oh, dear. Bit five. To set P a five on and write zero. I'm just putting this here for your revision, right? Zero to set it off. Right. So we have everything we need. And then, um, we can, um, we can, um, conclude here and continue the next lesson we've recorded over, I think, 30 minutes. So he's getting a bit long. You can, um, stretch your fingers. I had my university professor once tell me, you know, when you move your fingers, when you move your joints, when you move them, especially the little joints rapidly, it keeps you awake. So every now and then in class, he makes us stand up and then, you know, flex our fingers and then take off our shoes and flex our toes. You can imagine. Apparently it keeps people awake.

CODING GPIO DRIVERS FROM SCRATCH USING DATASHEET INFORMATION (PART II)

I'm going to minimize this this all documentation. We are done with the documentation. We can go to the fun stuff now. Okay. So we have all we need. We said we would have to access the RCC, um, HP one enabled register and then set it zero to one. So what we're going to do is create a symbolic name to hold these, um, these bits setters. To do that. I'm gonna use a defined statement. I'm gonna say define a Y here. I should assume in a bit. Doesn't seem to zoom in. Also define a Y here. And then, um, I'm going to say over here. I'm going to say one shift. Zero. This means that I'll give this a symbolic name. You've got to put a name here. This we say it upl you e e n. OK. So what this means is the GPL, you e underscore e n is the same as having one in the position zero of a 32 bit number. This here means this. This bit here. Right. This bit here. Okay. It means I have said two bits. This is how you write binary notation. Zero B. And then we have one, two, three, four. One, two, three, four. One, two, three, four. You two have eight of them. Wanted to yeah. One, two, three, four. Just bear with me. I think I want to break everything down into less. I don't want to keep anything. OK. So we have, you know, four multiplied by eight. That is 32. So 40. So this is the register. This is our register. Right. So if I do shift, if I do it, I if I execute this, it means I want to shift this value to this position. So this here. Gets Bond shifted to position one. And if you recall, we said sets, but gets one shift at two positions, zero shift disvalue one into this position, zero. OK. If you recall what we said, we said it said Bitz zero in RACC, HP one enabler registered to one. So that is what we're doing with this here. And we've renamed this

this two GPL you a underscore E. So simply by writing this, we get this, we get this action here. Okay. I think you understand. If you don't, you can leave it in the Q&A area. OK. The next one says set bitz 10 to one and bits eleven to zero in GPL you in GPL you a mode register. So I'll leave this one for you to do it on your own. Based on what we've done here, you can give it in a name you want. I just happened to give this the symbolic name GPL. You B underscore E and you can give this action a different name. OK. Once you've tried it on your own. Let's try this together. So we do define. And then I'm going to give this the name node register. Underscore five on a score out. And this basically means I'm trying to set pin five two outputs. That is the description I have in mind. So we said, what set? Bit number 10 to one. So we want to set one over here to position ten. Like this. Right. And then bit number eleven to zero. So by default, there's zero. So we need not do this part just like over here. There was zero and we just needed to change. But zero two one. So over here I can. A copy of this put us here for you. So this is. We have four over here. We have two right here. We have turnover here. OK. So this is what we get from this. And we can count. This is zero. One, two, three, four, five, six, seven, eight, nine, 10. So this is pit number 10. So, like I said, it's eleven. We don't have to touch that. And we said, Right. One, two, GPL, your order pin. And they know the rest. OK. This is part of the logic of the code. Um, should we do this? let's just make it, let's make it very readable by adding this. I'm gonna add a defined statement here. I'll call this oh D-R five. Well, are five said, because our penis. Woody is five. And thus we said we write in one two position five to one over here to position five like this. You know what that would look like? And then we would have another one to set it to zero to turn it off. So I call this new one defined Odia five underscore reset. And this one here I'm going to see. Right. Zero to position five. And the reason we just access the bit we want rather than OK. Another way we could do this if we want to write zero to a register is simply say register equals zero. But what's going to happen is it's going to set all three to a bit to zero. Such that if another part of your program is using different bits in the same register, it is going to disable it as well. But the method that we use and we only set in the bits and resetting the bits we need, you see, we just touch in the parts that we need without sort of changing anything in the other bits, because oftentimes in a single register you have different parts of your program using it very often. In fact, I think in most programs you would have, you know, just think of a program where you have different parts using the same port. You have one part of your program using GPL. Another part is still being used. You play it for different things. You have to use this form of programming. We call it friendly programming. so this is what we're going to create a defined at, uh, a symbolic name before four in five us. Well, by using a defined statement. So is there going to be shift one, two, five. So this is Ellie Dippin. We call this Ellie Dippin. And then this is basically shift one two, position five. so we have all of them. Oh, Rita will stuff, yeah. Oh. Oh, keep these comments there. So let's start. We said we do this. So to access this, to access this register. We say RACC. It is arranged for this fall. The, um, the registers are arranged in a structured format. And the, um, the register offset. This is sort of a range specifically to, um, too much d d too much d the position of the members in the structure such that if the registers if the register has an offset of zero, it's the first member of the structure. And if it has an offset of less C for it? S the next member, it's properly arranged like that. And this allows us to be able to use structures to access different memory locations that are arranged properly. And I have another course showing how to create this structure and build this from scratch. We can take a look at the embedded systems, object to a rented program in C and C++. We create this file, which creates an example of this file. Go to the datasheet. We get all the information, arrange it using structures and add new types. And then we created and then we will write a library in C++ as well as C language and test it out. So to access this, we go to the RCC module and the member we're looking for is the HP one. You can see that as soon as I brought the Arrow operator, it's giving me all the members of this structure. So the member we're looking for is the HP one enabled. So click this and I'm going to put this vertical line here and then I'll see it is equal to this value that we created. Put it over here like this. OK. The reason I'm putting this vertical line is so that we only change despite bit zero, without this vertical line, without its vertical line. The new content of it will be one and it will read this. There will be this. But as we saw, each one is used by ports. Put A, B, C, D, all ports almost use HP one. So if we were using a different port and we simply write this, which is equal to this, if we write this without this vertical line, then let's zoom a bit. One, two, three, four, five. Do or be set to zero means the other ports will be disabled. But by putting this on all operators we say keep everything the same. Just sets are zero to one. This is friendly programming. OK. Right. So once that is done we um we go to the merge register and then we set a mode. So we say GPL you say. It's also a structure. And as soon as I do the arm, the operator, we receive, the members of this structure and the member we're looking for is the Mode Register. And then the mode register, we apply the same friendly programming and then we see mode five outputs. We set in two outputs like this. Right. And then once this is done, we can go ahead and down 10 on the ALYDA and turn it off. Remember, as we said, you need just two. You need just two registers in more than the microcontroller together with plug gate in. You need to enable clock access to the port. You need to set a direction or that mode. And then you need data, the data register to set the data. So we are going to access that data register and then we'll be done. So we can say GPL you it is our well, one lo GPL, you say, or D.R, which is the output data register. And what we want to do is if we want to simply toggled reality, we can use an Audur five set to turn it on or audio or five. We said to turn it off. Oh, we can simply use one. And use the Togo operator such that it's always Togo's goes. This is the Torgau operator. We can say Togo Togo this on. So on becomes five. One becomes five. It starts on. And then it goes off. And then it starts on. It goes back on. This is going to be toggling it on and off. Yeah. And I know we can put a bit of a delay here. What I mean by pseudo delays, we are simply going to put a for loop to make it, you know, to make us see that blink cause is going to run this and then totally take off and then run spin for a while. Um, I'll say it. I call zero I is less than. Oh, yes. Less than we can see.

```c
#include "stm32f4xx.h"


//set bit0 in RCC_AHB1ENR  to 1
#define GPIOA_EN (1<<0)   // 0b 0000 0000 0000 0000 0000 0000 0000 0001

// set bit10 to 1 and bit11 to 0 in GPIOA_MODER
#define MODER_5_OUT (1<<10) // 0b 0000 0000 0000 0000 0000 0100 0000 0000

//write 1 to GPIOA_ODR bit 5 to set PA5 on an write zero to set it off.
#define ODR_5_SET   (1<<5)
#define ODR_5_RESET (0<<5)

#define LED_PIN (1<<5)

int main(void)
{

    RCC->AHB1ENR |= GPIOA_EN;

    GPIOA->MODER |= MODER_5_OUT;

    while(1){

        for(int i=0;i<)
            GPIOA->ODR ^= ODR_5_SET;
```

CDT Build Console [Gpio_BareMetal]

Nine hundred thousand. And then I plus plus. Like this. So this is basically to waste time. Count zero to nine hundred thousand. And then when you get here, you are five. Whatever it is, set it to its opposite state. So if you are five, if at this time it is one. Set it to zero. The next time you come. If it is zero, set it to one. Okay. Let's build and see what we have. Click over here to build. It's Putin. OK. We've got no arrow, no warning. OK. This is an excellent program. Okay, we can, um, we can run our click over here. Dybbuk. Know it's Lodin. And then I'll say, okay, over here. Right. It says download is verified successfully, meaning we can either access the debugger and see the LCD move or we can run it to the debugger. If you want to run into debuggers, often we use the debugger to analyze the internals of the microcontroller, such as the global variables, the memory, the registers, etc. But if you have some output such as naledi, if you simply want to see it, you can just click exit. And what we do for click and debugging is to actually flash onto the board. Right. So we don't need to be here to see it, but we can click here to run as well. Kooiker resume. And then let's see, my LCD is not blinking. Let's see. Oh, stop. Click to stop. Let's see what we have. OK. So when I clicked to stop this other man that he opened, man, and when we created our project, um, SDM Daddy to Cuba, I may not see it created as Mendo see. And then we created our may not see. And they are found in the same location. You see, this may not be seen. This is our mind to see the wonder we've been using. This is the other main not seen. OK. So I see. So this is found in quar source may not see and ours is found in source, may not see. So what happens is when you create a project with Cube Ida E, it keeps the source file over here in your source like this. Whereas when you create from Let's Cuba the source file is not in core. It does. The core doesn't exist. That is why we created a source, because we thought it didn't exist. So what we're going to do is we're going to copy this and not see which is a Mendota C that we've been working on to control A to select or control C to copy. And then you come to call over here. This whole project core source may not see this other one. Then. Select or delete? Control V to page to control. S to save. And then we can delete the source folder that we created. Cause when we create from scratch. In Cube idee e. It creates a source folder for us stored in this other forward unknown as core. So this folder here which we created. I'm going to come here and delete our mind, not see first. Delete this. I see. delete. It's my friend. And then the folder. Right. Click delete this. Yes. The lead. This. OK. So let's pull it again.

```
4
5  //set bit0 in RCC_AHB1ENR  to 1
6  #define GPIOA_EN (1<<0)   // 0b 0000 0000 0000 0000 0000 0000 0000 0001
7
8  // set bit10 to 1 and bit11 to 0 in GPIOA_MODER
9  #define MODER_5_OUT (1<<10) // 0b 0000 0000 0000 0000 0000 0100 0000 0000
10
11 //write 1 to GPIOA_ODR bit 5 to set PA5 on an write zero to set it off.
12 #define ODR_5_SET  (1<<5)
13 #define ODR_5_RESET (0<<5)
14
15 #define LED_PIN (1<<5)
16
17 int main(void)
18 {
19
20     RCC->AHB1ENR |= GPIOA_EN;
21
22     GPIOA->MODER |= MODER_5_OUT;
23
24     while(1){
25
26         for(int i=0;i<900000;i++){}
27         GPIOA->ODR ^= ODR_5_SET;
28     }
29 }
30
```

Um. Yeah. I'll click over here to build. Putin. It appealed successfully. Let's go to debug or click over here. OK. It says. Download verified successfully. Click here to run and you can see my LCD is blinking just like we predicted. So you can experiment with this further. You can delete this if you delete this once, Plinky is just gonna stay on because it's going to toggle so rapidly your human. I want to be able to capture it. And like I said, that debugger, we use it to flush the code. Most of the time. So even if you exit the debugger, you see that your code is still flushed into memory and it's blinking just like it ought to blink. So that's all the rage. If you have any questions at all, just leave it in the questions and answers area. And if you'll find the course useful. Kindly take some time off to leave a lovely review even if you're not finding it useful. I'll be glad to know what you think about this mode of teaching or simulator.

CODING ARM ASSEMBLY APPLICATIONS IN CUBEIDE

We are going to demonstrate how to write assembly code using the Kubi d e. I'm going to create a new project from over here, a new SDM 32 project. My boat selector is going to load up. So here we go. So I should point out. If you load it. The project selected a target selector and it doesn't show this Piano over here. Simply click a console and start the project creation project and start a project creation process again. Um, because sometimes when you try to create a project and it tries to load the, um, the target selector, it doesn't load everything. It doesn't load the part that allows you to search for your board. If you experience the click console, there is a console down here. There is a console here. If you experience that, just click the console over here and start again. Yeah, I think Cube I.D. two has a number of bugs that, you know, updated versions. Would, um, would you sort of get rid of it? Um, yeah. Look at what I'm having here. So the pano disappeared. Just what I was talking about. So in this case, what I would do is simply console and then just start again, click console over here and then start again. New look at this. Oh, goodness. SDM 32 Kube SDM 32 Project Knocking Project. So it's going to load up the targets elected again, and this time I hope you load it up properly. So I'm gonna search for my boat again. Do pardon the arm. The resolution here. It's from the cube I.D.. It's not from my side. ASTM 32 by boat is estimated to have four one one. Just search for a boat here. And this is the same screen we find on Cuba mix. So there's nothing strange.

Just search your boat, your microcontroller if you are using a different microcontroller and then go ahead and select it. So once your board is selected, you just click next. And then you give your project a name. I'll call this simple assembly. I'll keep everything the same. Or click next and click finish over here. And it's going to create a project. It says this. This kind of project is associated with Cuba. Max, do you want to open this perspective? No. I'll say no. I think it would open regardless. Right. So the setup is complete and we have this here. I'm going to close this. We don't need to write assembly code. And then, um, this is our project. We come to call our source file here in the source folder. And then, um, our. We don't need all of this. We don't even need to see. I'm simply going to delete the main dot. See. Right. Click, click, delete. Over here. Like this. And then. Okay. We don't need the rest, but we can keep them there. I'm going to create a main dot file. Right, click. New file. I'll give this a name meaning, but miss. Right. And this is all me. Yes. So we write the assembly code here. OK. So to write assembly code, we start with the directives. The directives are not they are not instructions. Then they tell the compiler how to compile the code. So in assembly language, you could have two different compilers of the same instruction set to different. They would have this India directives. Well, that's what that means, is that the code we're going to write here should run exactly the same way on the, um, um, compiler or the AB assembler, I should say, our symbol. No compiler, cause the assembly code is assembled. It's not compound. So the ARM assembly will run this, just that the directives would have to change. So over here we're using the GCSE assembler and we start off by using the section direction to say this is a code section. We just see a DOT section. And then we see the text to say this, who holds a code and then we can use the C.P.U to indicate to ACP. We are using the cortex and forward to another directive that is the C.P.U we are using. And then we can use the DOT global and global without a dot GPL. And then we say mean to make this the subroutine made this label made to make it accessible from a file outside of this one. So I say mean and then I'll come over here and then I'll create to mean so many labels or create to me like this. And then we start off by moving, we're gonna say move into register our five zero x zero x um you're X six four. And I think this is the number hundred. This is just for testing to show that we can write assembly code here. Now we're going to say move into the register. AR4 is gonna move less, add a number the number zero. How about that? And then once that is done, we're going to create another label here. We called Loop so that we can jump to this label. And over here we are going to see how well we say @ @, the content of our five at one at the number one to the content of Register R5 and then start a resort in R5 would do that by writing this. We take this operand we added to this and then this the destination. So the content of this register, add this to it, then store it here. Right. And then we see that Hobaugh adds the content of our four. I'd like to. I'm writing it in this way to let you understand. So first we take the content of our four, we add one and then we start a resort back into our four. Right. So we call in this loop. And then, um, let's see, what else can we add to this experiment? Think we can simply test this out? Because this is a simple assembly just to test that we can create and run assembly code. So we're going to end, but we're going to branch to this label here. This label is not accessible yet. So we're going to make sure when we execute this instruction, we execute this next one. And then we would execute a third one that would bring us to this label. So we use the A B instruction, which means branch. And then we passed the name of the label like this. And we use the end directive here to indicate this is the end of our assembly assembly program. So control is to save. And then, um, yeah, we can build and see what we have. Click over here to build. It's built in. It's Putin. We have three errors. Let's see. I'm going to open this up. What does it say? Immediate expression is required. Okay. Yeah. I forgot to put this here, okay. If you're using a number, you have to put a harsh sign like this. So that is one of our eras of click to build and see what this is, what created the other arrows build. Okay.

It's looking good so far and it's built successfully. No warning. Okay. So now let's go to our debug fuel to check our registers. What indeed we get these values stored in the registers. Click over here. Debug SDM 32 to. Oh. Okay. I'll click okay over here. It's open in. And it's finished. Open it. So we have different views here. We have the live expression, if we have a breakpoint. We have juice. We have registers. If you don't have any of these views here, you can come to window, show view and then talk about any of them on. So if you didn't have the Register's view, you can simply click to have it. So click on Registers View and oh, expand this. And this will give us a view of our general purpose. Reddish This. So this is our Schiro. This is the value of our zero now. This is our one. Our two are three or four or five. And then the other registers are down the course we have, we have, we are floating point registers. That's why we see the D. But we look not just the R registers. The general purpose registers to use this to execute our instructions line by line. Best means step into this means step over. This means step return. We're going to use this step into. And whenever you see this arrow pointing to a line, it means this is the next instruction to execute. This is what is going to be executed next. So I'm going to click on to step into and it's executed this. What did this do? Did this moved a zero x six four to register our five? Let's see. What are our five. Has this. US can see our five was the number one hundred. One hundred in hexadecimal form is zero x six for the next says. The next instruction says move to number zero to register our four. So let's run this and see what a r four. B zero. Well, our voice currently zero. So there'll be no difference. But let's run it regardless of click over here. Step in two. OK. So nothing has changed. We know that the next instruction says branch to the label loop. So if we execute this, we want to jump to this place, branch to this place or click to execute this. OK. And now we are here. So the next instruction says go to the content of the register. And add one to its content and store the results back into our five. So currently our register AR five has the number one hundred. After this, an instruction we expected to have the number one hundred and one because we are performing one hundred plus one.

So click over here. Step into. And I can see are five. One to one, right? So next it says go to register for take it content, add one to it to our four plus one, and then store the resorts back into our four. Click here to step in to. And we just executed. And then I can see her for one. And that's the end of our program. OK. So this shows that we can run our assembly code, which cube idea? And that is how we create an assembly project. You simply create your project. You delete the M the main dot s file demand or C falling creates a main dot s file. And it's important that we call this. Where is it? It's important. We call this main dot. We call this label made because in the in the system. Uh, reset handler. It looks like this. This subroutine called me as its starting point. So if we give it a different name, it wouldn't work. So let's say I give it a different name. Five, for instance. Let's see, the starting label is called MI five, and I'm making this accessible. If you use the global, it means you want to make it global so the other files can access it. So let's say this is it and I click here to build. OK. What does it say? We have two arrows. What does it say over here? Return exit studies. So basically what is happening is a what quote has no starting point. So that is why we are using the word mean. If we had a main doxie fall, then we can give our label here in your name because the starting point of the program will be in demand. Ötzi. But because we do not have me not see, we use this control. S or build and then the arrows should disappear. No. As you can see, no longer have any arrows. Right. So that's all there is. If you find in the course useful for just, you know, leave it in the in the review area. OK. I just can't help it. Before you go, I would want to show you why Maine is the is the word that we need to use to make it work. Okay. So we need to go to our system d'hote. S fault and take a look at the routine known as the reset handler. And this is the first portion that is executed whenever your boat starts up. Okay. After the boot sequence, of course, um, we come to over, uh, this forward here setup. And then there was this file on, uh, dot. S file. It's called this long name start up on the score, SDM 32 f F4 and then dot s or double click to openness. And what we're looking for is the reset handler. So this is the reset handler. Right. This is how it starts. It's. This to S.P.. Espey means stop points, so you'd need not know that. But the important thing is, after it's executed, it punches to this other label known as loop copy data in it. So let's go to Leupp, copy data in it and see. This is loop copy data in it. So this is still part of the reset. I'm glad that the reset unlock comes here and then they execute these lies one by one. And this finally branches to loop a few zero P. S s. So this is our destination. So let's also branch. Let's find this routine loop feels Europa as when we take a look at it, we see what happens. It executes this, executes this, this. And then it? S branches two system units to initialize the system. And then finally, it does B I mean it branches to the applications entry point. So this is why we have to make sure we have the main existing in our application because it's going to branch to a label known as Main. If we do not see the label will be created, if we have just assembly language. We have to make sure our assembly language has a main in there so that we can branch. So let me show you something. Let's say I change this mean here to mean to. Now let's build our assembly language program and see a click over here to build. And we have two errors, right, cos we have men, two over here. What does it say in a defined reference to me too? So we have the main two over here. And then let's go to our assembly? S over here. And then I'm going to change this to mean two. And then this is for me to control.

```
 9?    b   LoopFillZerobss
 98/* Zero fill the bss segment. */
 99 FillZerobss:
100    movs   r3, #0
101    str    r3, [r2], #4
102
103 LoopFillZerobss:
104    ldr    r3, = _ebss
105    cmp    r2, r3
106    bcc    FillZerobss
107
108/* Call the clock system initialization function.*/
109    bl   SystemInit
110/* Call static constructors */
111    bl   __libc_init_array
112/* Call the application's entry point.*/
113    bl   main2
114    bx   lr
115 .size  Reset_Handler, .-Reset_Handler
116
117/**
```

```
CDT Build Console [SimplAssembly]
Core/Startup/startup_stm32f411retx.o: In function 'LoopFillZerobss':
C:/Users/Israel/STM32CubeIDE/workspace_1.2.0/SimplAssembly/Debug/../Core/Startup/startup_stm32f411retx.s:1
collect2.exe: error: ld returned 1 exit status
make: *** [makefile:44: SimplAssembly.elf] Error 1
"make -j4 all" terminated with exit code 2. Build might be incomplete.

18:05:55 Build Failed. 2 errors, 0 warnings. (took 2s.94ms)
```

S to be safe. And then click away to build. And as you can see, because I change it to mean to. We can use it to mean to. We can use mine to hear. So if you want to use a different name, you would have to change it from the reset handler. But, yeah, we don't want to do that. Now you understand why we use me. If you don't. Of course you can live it in the questions and answers area. OK. So I'm going to leave this. I'm going to change it back to me so you can even use the word to start or your name. But the reset handler has to branch to that label.

CODING GPIO DRIVERS FROM SCRATCH IN ASSEMBLY LANGUAGE (PART I)

We are going to see a much more practical assembly example with the cube. And what we're going to do is write a GP. I drive by using just assembly code. We are just going to go to the. We're going to start off by going to the datasheet, the manual and the other document and extract the memory addresses. And they're now assigned symbolic names to them and then access these memory addresses or locations using our assembly instructions and manipulate bits. So when a critical project comes over here file and then New STEM 32 project and it's going to initialize the target selector. And I'm going to select my board over here, SDM 32 for one one v t. Um, estimated two for one one should be fine. Just this. I'll make a selection and then I'll click on next. Next is down to oh just drag it up a bit. You can see this next. And then I'll give this project a name, g.P, I oh, underscore assembly. OK. GPI, your driver, oh, brother.

Well, let's just keep the name Sudar. We have the bare metal it in assembly, but they are both bare metal. Okay, I click next over here and then finish. I've said no, but it's gonna open the perspective regardless. Okay. Okay. So I'm gonna close this. And then, um, I'm going to come to I will call forward. This whole project, GPL you on a school assembly. Okay. So this is cool. Like we did earlier, we come to source. We don't need any of this. Um, I'll just delete the main. You can delete the rest. Actually, I think at the end we should try deleting the rest. And let's see if it's affect our project. It shouldn't. It shouldn't. But we'll delete it once we've tested it. Um, okay. So we said we're going to write the GPL. Your driver's, uh, the GPL. You, um. Yeah. Driver for for our board. And we're going to use just assembly language. We already saw this in the um in the. I mean, depending on where you are watching this particular lesson, if you're watching this lesson as part of the estimated 32 Cuba course, we've already seen how to write, um, the bedmate or the Beneteau GPL, your driver, if you're watching this as part of the, um, um, the ARM Assembly course, then perhaps the bare metal lesson once existing since then, of course, is just a bar assembly. In a way, I would just start from scratch. And, um, this will save us a revision if you already know some of this stuff. But I think the differences between, um, the ARM Assembly and the, um, and the and the GCSE that we have to take note of, that is why we have this lesson, especially the directive's some, uh. A number of things changed with regards to the directive, uh, the directives. That is why we are here. Um, yeah. So let's get started. So we start off by we said we said we um we have to enable clock access to the port and then access the data and direction registers to get it to to what. Our inputs or outputs. Okay. Before we do that, we have to create our main dot s file. Right. Click. New this one here. The new file over here is like this. And then I'll give it a name. Men Dot is like this. Okay. Okay. So we said we have to take a number of steps. We have to enable clocks. And they will clock. And then we're going to be talking in the early days when they will clock to Port A.. And then next we've got a search deum the mode we say set P a five two output mode. And then we're right to pay five. So these are the things we need to do. But there's a lot of work involved here. Because we've got to get dim memory addresses of each component. So let's start with what you pay for your ports. Eight, because we need to access UPL. You port A. We need to, uh, because we need to access ports A for its data register. It's more to register and um. Yeah. Because we need these two registered from ports. We need to find a memory address of Port A.. To do that, we need to open one of our documents. We need to open a datasheet document.

Um, we have the data sheet and a reference manual. So the data sheet one is the shorter one to one with about 140 pages. So this is the, um, the datasheet. You can just come up here and then you recognize it. Buy this over here and the number of pages, it's grown so we can find what we're looking for. A two page number fifty four. This gives us the memory boundaries of the various components or simply come to our search arm. Fifty four here. We need page 54. So search 54. Okay, so fifty four here. Gives us the um, the register boundary addresses. So when we search it will tell us these are the cortex M4 registers. It says that this range is reserved. This range is for internal power flows. And when we come over here, GPL you start from zero X Force. You were two two zero zero. So this is the base address of GPL U. E is the base address of GPL. So we have to keep that in mind. I'm gonna copy this over here and then I'll bring it to our project. I call this. GP, are you a GP? I owe a base. OK. This over here. We don't need this other stuff. We just need a starting position to start at a point. So this is my GPA. You are a base. We would also need to get D. We also need these HP. Remember we have the HP. The HP one enabled register is where we used to enable the port. So we also need to access the HP. The HP, the HP is part of the RCC to access HP. You go through the RCC, even in the datasheet to Spreyton RACC underscore HP. So whenever you see a word, whenever you see one word underscore another, the first word or the first characters or the first abbreviation is the base. The underscore is the offset is the same. The GPL you such that when we see GPL you a underscore mode register GPL you a is the base address more drudges. That is the offset. So with this arrangement, each module is the base. This is a base address and the various registers in the module serve as the offset such that we have DGP and we have the GPL. Your base address over here. If we want GPL, you have a data register output data REGISTER that is just an offset from this base address, meaning we simply need to add some number to this to get the output data register. If we want to not register is an offset from this. We simply need to add a number to this, some number to this together. So is the same for airports in the same way we know RACC is written, RACC underscore HP. So if we want to get the HP address, we simply add a particular number to the RCC because the base is RACC. If you don't understand this explanation, please let me know in the Q&A area. So we have to get the base addresses and then we find the offset. So in insane language, in bare metal embedded to see RACC, we often do RACC, HP one, HP one and they will register like this. And then when we're dealing with GPL, you will probably do GPI you a we probably do a GPL you it and then more register and then this, this that we see over here. When we go to the reference module we see that this is written in there like this is written with the underscore is the same thing. When we go to the reference module we'll see that this is written in there with an underscore like this. Right. Where. But more specifically, this will be written with an X to indicate that the same is the same for GPL. You A, B, C, D all the way to H. So I'm saying this bit is the base address. This is the base address if you want to get this is just an offset from this base address. So if you want to get this entire thing, it could be that you just take the base address of RACC plus two RACC plus two. It could give you RACC, HP, one enabler register in the same way. If you want to get the address for the Merge Register of GPL, you say you could put a base address of GPL, plus five. So we just add that to get the address of the mode register. This is what I mean by Bayes address and offsets. So I, I'll just verify for you that indeed in the datasheet to switch in this way. And the reference manual. Sorry. So I'll come to our documentary here. And this is our datasheet house, the one hundred and forty nine pages. I'm going to go to the reference manual over here and then I'll come over here and I'll do control F and then HP will do HP one. And when I hit enter you see that the word starts with RACC underscore. HP. This is for a different, different register. But all of them are offset from RACC. That is why they are written that way. If we do HP enable RACC underscore HP one enabler register. Right. OK. So we have this one. We need the RACC base. The RCC base already knows this one. But you can go and find it out. So the RCC base will be this in order not to spend more time hunting all of them down. I'll be putting some of them in. But when there is something different. It will get Fetcher together. RACC Bass addresses this zero x four zero zero two three eight zero zero. This is the RACC base. Right. So we've got. Did you play a base and then RACC base? We are basically going to be dealing with these two bases because we know we need RACC. HP wants to enable register to enable clock access to G.P.A. you. And then we need GPL, you moad register and then we need GPL, your output data register to set our pin to output and to toggled reality. Right. So what we have to do next is to find the offset that would give us the other registers. So for GPL you also for GPL, you overhear these comments. We'll clean them later. I'm using this as the whiteboard for GPL e. We need the output data register and then we need the mode register. So we would have to get the offsets for this. And then for RACC. For RACC. We need the H h HP one. And they will register because that's what we use to enable clock access to GPL. You put A and all other GPL ports. So what we have to do to get your offset is go to the datasheet puppy for A go to B reference manual. But before we do that, I'm going to create a symbolic name to hold this number here, to create a symbolic name. I'll use the e q u e Q.. You see a dot dot e. Q. Are you here like this? This is a directive. And what I want to do is assign a name for this hexadecimal number. I'm going to assign a name cheaply to o a underscore base to this hexadecimal number such that whenever I want to fetch this hexadecimal number I simply use the name of the assigned GPL you use as a base. Okay, so I'm going to do the same thing for RCC. I'm gonna see dot EKU you here and then I'm going to assign a name. I'll call this RACC base RACC on the score base like this. And then over here we know the RACC base. We said this is it. Okay. Our sign, the symbolic name here like this. This is just a comment. We don't need this. Right. So we've got a symbolic name for this. Then we would have to assign a symbolic name for. We have to be equal to you. Q You over here for G.P.A. You know, we have to do less. Each of you let's do it step by step. I'm going to see GPA, your mode offset. We can do a symbolic name for the offset so we can see GPA as a good register offset. So when we find the offset, we just put it here. We'll put it on the side. We don't have this yet, so we'll feel it. We'll fill in the blanks and then we'll do an EKU for your GPA. You a. Oh, dear. Oh, poor data register offset. And then we don't have this, so we fill in the blank later. And then once we have the offset of this, then we know the offsets, plus the base register gives us the actual base register. So we'll go ahead and do it to you. And then now we can see G.P.A. you a mode register, the actual mode register. And this is simply this will be GPL you a base. It should be GPL. You have a base over here. Plus, keeping you more to register offset like this. And then once that is done, we come in. Then we'll do an EQR for you. And then this you can you will be the um the actual GPL you an output data register. And you know how to derive that as well is going to be this offset plus the base. So for the output data register, it's gonna be this copy. And then we paste this over here. But this has to change to the Otey offset like this. Okay. So after this we would have all the, um, all our registers. The register would be ready. We would have our GPL you a mode register already GPL you and Odey are ready as well. So we will do the same thing over here. Over here we've already found our RACC base. What we need is HP one E and our PS HP one and they were ready stubbies. So we do it. You, you can use, like I said, used to give a symbolic name to the hexadecimal number. We say EKU, HP one enable offset. We do not have the offsets yet, so we fill in the blanks later and we know once we have the offsets, we simply add the offsets to the base, the RCC base to get RACC underscore each one enabled. So we do dot eku you over here. And then we call this RACC, HP one, and they were registered just like it is called in the arm, just like it is called in the datasheet. And this is derived by RACC base plus HP one and they will register offset like this. Okay. So what we have to do is go to the arm, the reference module and find the offset of these various addresses. Right. So we go to the reference module to fetch the offsets. Okay. I go to our documents here. We use the reference module with the one with the pages. So we start with an HP one register offset. So you simply search HP one E and R. This is from the previous search we did. So this is it. I'll click HP one INR and I can see it gives us the offset to what here in the data sheet, the offset. This means it's keeping in mind that we will be doing this type of thing. That is why it's given us the offset. So we simply take this offset from here. So X three zero. That is HP one E and our offset. So this is your X three zero zero X three zero, right? Is that correct? Two X three zero. That is correct. Okay, so next we find the offset for our GPL.

You need more to register. So I'm going to come up here and control F to search and then. Oh, such

```
主 *main.s
1
2 /*Enable clock to PORTA*/
3 /**Set PA5 to output mode*/
4 /**Write to PA5*/
5
6 //GPIOA :   ODR,MODER
7 //gpioa base : 0x4002 0000
8
9 .equ GPIOA_BASE                     0x40020000
10 .equ GPIOA_MODER_OFFSET             -----
11 .equ GPIOA_ODR_OFFSET               ------
12
13 .equ GPIOA_MODER                    GPIOA_BASE + GPIOA_MODER_OFFSET
14 .equ GPIOA_ODR                      GPIOA_BASE + GPIOA_ODR_OFFSET
15
16 //RCC : AHB1NER
17 //rcc_base   : 0x4002 3800
18 .equ RCC_BASE              I        0x4002380(
19 .equ AHB1NER_OFFSET                 -------
20 .equ RCC_AHB1NER                    RCC_BASE + AHB1NER_OFFSET
21
22
23
```

```
 Problems    Tasks   ☐ Console    ☐ Properties
CDT Build Console (Gpio Assembly)
```

motor mode register Malda. Okay. And it's Protus here or click here to jump to this place and the offset I won't register is zero x zero zero. Meaning the first element is the first member. So the offset is the same as the base address. So no problem. We just set it just like you said. So X or you saw X X series. You like this. Now all these are offsets, the output data register offset. There's the register we'll use to control the output. So we search for ADR as well. Come over here. Oh, these are like this. No, I have to clean first. This doesn't exist, of course. Oh, do ya? Okay, so we have this G.P.A. you port data register. Oh, do ya. Click this and the offset to zero x one four two x one four two x one four. So we put that over here like this. Two X one four. Okay, so we have this right. So we can clean up our comments. We don't need to help make these comments again. Enable clock. We don't need this. Yeah. We don't need it. We know what to do. This was just to tell you what we're gonna do to remind you. Okay. So we can, um, put our directives. We can, um. We can start off by just putting some directives, the C.P.U we use in the code, take some of them for here and then our code area is down here. We can start our section code over here. That section of text over here like this. And then once that is done, we can, um, we can create a war, a global export. So we'll see it go global. And then we call this main. And then over here would have our main label made like this. Okay. I think we look good so far. Yeah. We know. Missing anything. Okay, so this is it with our registers. We've assigned symbolic names to our registers and the next lesson we start. Right. Our subroutine to initialize the GPL U. E. And then to Tokyo with the LDA. So this is all the rest. No. See you later. Just bear with me. If sometimes I'm explaining too much or perhaps I'm explaining it and it's not clear enough. You can, you know, leave it in the questions and answers area and I'll get back to you. But this is very simple stuff.

CODING GPIO DRIVERS FROM SCRATCH IN ASSEMBLY LANGUAGE (PART II)

We went to the datasheet and the reference may not get to the memory locations of Iowa registers of interest, and then we assign symbolic names to them. And this lesson, we will go ahead and stop right in the initialization, you know, subroutine for what you call your driver. So when, of course, that when our application starts, we start from demesne. Right. So as soon as we enter the main, we're going to branch into a subroutine that will create. So over here, I would see our center a bit like this. OK. So we started from Maine over here. As soon as we enter Maine, I'm going to want to see B.L. Branch to the subroutine that we shall call. We shall call this GPL. You are in its G.P.A. underscore in its just bear with me as I find a right indentation to use. OK. Just bear with me. I think we are good here. OK. So as soon as it starts, Bill, GPL, you, GPL, you in it. So let's implement this. This label, GPL, has you in it. Can we do this to implement a label? OK. So first I'm gonna be putting some comments to show what this looks like in C language. So in C we would do it, not in Matosi would do RACC and then we'll access the HP one enabler register. It would be one E and R. And then what we're gonna do is add this to the GPL you enable which is your X zero one. Right. Zero X or one. The reason I'm clean in this is, um, I just remembered it will be better if we created a symbolic name to hold this. So we are going to create a symbolic name to hold this um this as well as the bits for as well as the bit for 10 and the bit for certain to output mode in the motor register. So we can see dot eku you over here and then I'm going to call this GPL, you enable GPL, you e e n and GPL you eat and basically means shift one two, position zero. And um, we can um come over here and do another one. EKU you and this we shall use to set our GPL you gpl u five. g.P I will put a pin five to output so I'll call this, I can call this Moate register five more to five out. And we do this because we know what we do. We just shift one two position number ten like this because we have to set a bit ten in the register. One together is to save us output and then we can have early on we can have a symbolic name though. Ten on the ality would do eku you LCD naledi underscore on and then this. We simply know we set bitta number five to one to ten on the LCD. We can do LHD off if we want. And I know you will guess what that is set in bits five to zero. Simple as that. So not only have this symbolically, we can copy this and then. Okay. So in our comment we know to enable GPL, you put a we do this in C language. Okay. In assembly, what we do is load. Load operates and then right back to memory. So we're going to load this into a register, RSU, we're going to load this. We're going to load the address. So I'm gonna start off by saying I use the yellow cups with zero commas. And what we want to load is one enabler register. RACC, HP, one, and they registered this one here. We want to load it into our, you know, one, this means load the address of, you know, HP one. I think I should put comments here, load the address of our RCC, HP one E and R to our zero. And we know that we know this is the address. This symbolic name hosts it. And once we've done this, what we want to do is load the value at the address found in our zero into our one. So what we want to do in layman's terms, we want to get the current content of this register, which is the memory location. This memory location, which is out in these two numbers. Want to get it? Current content of that. And another way of saying dice load value at address found in register eiris. You go into our one because register Ansaru has the address. We want the value at this address. We want to load down to our one. Yeah. If you don't understand this, if you don't understand this, just leave it to the questions and answers area. OK. So I'll just say it as found in our zero into our one. Right. To do this, we do load and then we do our one like this and then square brackets. Ursu. OK. So then our one now would have the current content of the memory location which is the RACC underscore each one and they will register.

```
🔖 *main.s

   8 .equ  GPIOA_MODER              GPIOA_BASE  +  GPIOA_MODER_OFFSET
   9 .equ  GPIOA_ODR                GPIOA_BASE  +  GPIOA_ODR_OFFSET
  10
  11 .equ  RCC_BASE                 0x40023800
  12 .equ  AHB1NER_OFFSET           0x30
  13 .equ  RCC_AHB1NER              RCC_BASE  +  AHB1NER_OFFSET
  14
  15 .equ  GPIOA_EN          1<<0
  16 .equ  MODER4_OUT        1<<10
  17 .equ  LED_ON            1<<5
  18
  19            .section  .text
  20            .globl    main
  21
  22 main:
  23
  24            BL        GPIO_Init
  25
  26 GPIO_Init:
  27            //RCC->AHB1ENR |= GPIOA_EN
  28
  29            //Load address of RCC_AHB1ENR to r0
  30            LDR       R0,=RCC_AHB1NER
  31            //Load vlaue at address found in r0 into r1
  32            LDR       R1,[R0]    I
  33            |
```

⚠ Problems 🔧 Tasks 🖥 Console ⬛ Properties
CDT Build Console [Gpio_Assembly]

So what we want to do is we want to perform all operations with our GPL. You enable and by performing our operation, we don't change the current content. We just add one new bit and enable its current content. So what I'm gonna do is c take the content of register iris you are it with GPL you enable and start A resorts back

107

into our zero. So I'll see it all over here. Sorry. Take the content off the register. Ah one course after this instruction we'll have it into our one will have the value in our one. Take the content of register one or it's with GPL. You enable the symbolic name here. It's an immediate value. So we use this pound sign and then put a resource back into our one. OK. I'll see you over here. There is no relevant comment here. I think this is straightforward. So once this is done, after this, we should have the right bit arrangement to set the pin. We have to write back to memory. So after this, the contents of our one would have a one new 30 turbit's value. Would that preserve the initial status of the HP one enabler register as well as enable GPL, you put it so well, we have to do next is C store the content in our one at the address found in our zero. yeah. We make an assembly sound like it's just normal English language. We say store the content in our one D address found in our zero. This should be one no exclamation. Goodness. Losing it. So how do we execute this? We use the stall operation. This instruction, we say stall. And then this is the saucer. And this is the destination. Stored content in our one at the address found in our zero. so after this we would we would we would have enabled or would she tell you a clock access to G.P.A.? You put it on. The next thing we have to do is set a wire. GPL your mode. Register one set. You call you P a five to output pin. So next we have to GPL you a mode register and then we want a pause mode five out of it like this. So we start off with Habbo. You post the video and try to do this. Given what you've seen with this, try to do this on your own. And once you've tried, we can do it together. so to do that, we do load. And then we do our zero e course GPL you e underscore mode register. I'm not going to comment this much. And then we load our one piracy row and then we do the all operation, all oh we do our one with mode five out this constant that we created. And then finally we store back to memory, which is the register which is. Yeah. The memory address stored in the register store R one. R zero. OK. Right. So after this we would have GPL you. Put a PIN five set as an output pin. And if you do not understand how this accomplishes that, then please start watching the video from scratch again. Or maybe it's in the Q&A area. But I'm sure by now this is very straightforward to you. OK. Next, we need to turn on the LCD and what we do to turn it on is basically set bits. Number five in the output data register to one. So in some languages, BABYMETAL would do GPL u. Oh. Ah. And then if we want to do friendly programming, we can do this early on. But if we don't care about the other bits, we can simply write this to it. And this vertical line, if you've noticed, for those of you with, um, you know, those of you who can. Yeah. Analyze, you realize that this is equivalent to our operation that we always do here. So if I remove this, for instance, in this example, we want to use this. So we wouldn't need to do it at all. So let's see how this would look in assembly. I would simply load the RC room and then the GPL, you A or D r. Once that is done, I'm going to load ality on into a different register early on here. I'm going to load this into rates that are one. So low register R-1 because early on like this. And once that is done, I'm simply going to store what is in register our one at the memory location held in register ARVA zero one over here in our zero. Right. And once this is done, we can return from our subroutine by doing B LR because we are done with this subroutine because they allow me to return.

```
25
26 GPIO_Init:
27        //RCC->AHB1ENR := GPIOA_EN
28
29        //Load address of RCC_AHB1ENR to r0
30        LDR     R0,=RCC_AHB1ENR
31        //Load value at address found in r0 into r1
32        LDR     R1,[R0]
33
34        ORR     R1,#GPIOA_EN
35        //Store the content in R1 at the address found in R0
36        STR     R1,[R0]
37
38
39        //GPIOA->MODER :=MODER5_OUT
40        LDR     R0,=GPIOA_MODER
41        LDR     R1,[R0]
42        ORR     R1,#MODER5_OUT
43        STR     R1,[R0]
44
45
46        //GPIOA->ODR :=LED_ON
47        LDR
48
49
50
```

Problems   Tasks   Console   Properties
CDT Build Console [Gpio_Assembly]

OK. And then we can use the end directive to indicate with ended.
Right. Okay. So this is our program so far. It starts from Maine and
then its branches to the subroutine. Are you in it? And then when it
enters here, it would it would enable clock access to G.P.A.. You
Port A.. It would, um, it would set GPL, you put a pin five two
outputs pin and then it would set GPL. You put a PIN five output
data register bits five to one. And this would turn on the LCD
because the LCD connected to P five. And then would return from
the subroutine. And this is just to indicate this the end of the
assembly file. So what we want to do is, yeah, we can leave here.
Let's build a SC applicable here to build and let's see how many
arrows we've created. Okay. Right. We have arrows with a symbolic
name assignment. OK. So the reason why that is. Yes. So us you do
this as this becomes your job and you do this, you stop mixing
syntax. The syntax is different in the arm assembler. Over. Yeah.
When you do that, EKU you and you give your new name. You've
got to put a comma here. So let's just put some commas. Let's see if

this fixes the arrows. So I could put comma. I have a comma here and then comma everywhere. Okay. I think I may have clean motor. OK. Come here as well. Comma here, comma everywhere. Everyone gets a comma. Coma and then. Now, let's see what we have a quake to build. Let's see how many arrows we have left. We have four. OK. Was the cause, the C o r one. This is on shifted register required on shift, shifted register required or one d or shift to register required. Is that right? The reason for this error is the lack of farm. I'm not a directive. We're going to add another directive to indicate the syntax we use. And so I come over here and see what the syntax over here and I'll say a unified, unified like this. so let's build and see. Click over here to build. We have two arrows, he says. Let's see. It says on define symbol mode. Five out the C word, five out. Let's see, maybe we have a typo. OK. Over here to return mode four is what five control is to save. Click over here to build. It's in. It's built successfully. Okay. Looking good. So we've reached an energy plan with the driver in assembly. Let's see if it runs. And if it turns on the ality, I'll click over here to go to debug. And then click this and then. OK. It's open and I'll say, okay, over here. It's downloading. Okay, it's done. Click here to run. And my LRB is on. OK. So this is the end of this lesson, if you have any questions at all. Just leave it in the questions and answers area. And I hope you're enjoying the course. This is really simple. If you have any questions, just leave it there. Or if you leave it in the Q&A section and you'll note receive a quick response, you can message me. Just remember the directives, the directives and then the symbolic name assignment and then the rest of the comment states here very step by step. That's all a simulator. So for those of you who are watching this in the Cuban mics can remix Cuba Idee e course if you want to land more ebow assembly programming and how to write drivers for other peripherals like the ADC to Taimur and to land the complete assembly program. And you can take a look at the Amah Assembly programming course. There is part one and part two. And after that, you'll be able to write your complete firmware in assembly. So if you're watching this in the ARM Assembly course, just to show you how to create the project and cube I.D. E, then you already know what I'm talking about. But we are not going to dive deeper into assembly. This is just to show how one would go about creating assembly assembly projects in Cuba. The next one we're gonna do is we're going to take a quote created in the Carl MBK using the arm assembler, and then we're going to bring it here and change it to run on Diesem Cube Idee, which uses the GCSE assembler so that we can see that it's basically the same thing.

CONVERTING KEIL MDK ARM ASSEMBLY SYNTAX TO GCC ASSEMBLY SYNTAX

You may be wondering why the window looks different. so this is a project built in called MBK, MBK five, call you Vision five. And this follows the arm, the directive for Mott's for the assembler. You would see that the arm, the symbolic names are assigned differently. And the directives we have here are different as well. And over here, the main we use on the school, on the school main we don't use simply made. And we know why that is, because when we go to the reset handler, if we come over here and we search reset Honolua oh, just give a quick overview. I'm not here to talk at all. Empty caber. I cannot help it. I have to explain every single thing. Control F or search for a reset handler. Okay. And then I'll hit it. Okay. So with this the resets on like you hit enter twice it will bring you here.

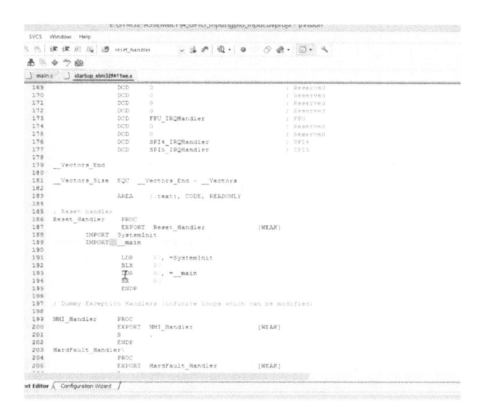

You see its notes on the school on this. Call me. So the starting point is on the school, on this. Call me. That is why in Karl MBK, when we export we stalwarts under squanders called Main. Okay. In SDM 32 Kubi the application starting point is simply made without. At school. At school. Okay, so what we're going to do in this project is just copy everything in the column decayed and pasted into a what is the embedded to Keep Idee project and start changing it life into a cube IDA format. So that's now when you have a project created in column decay you can do to change yourself. And it's as if you've got two items for the prize of one, you know. So let's go ahead and do that. I'm going to create a new project to minimize this. I'll come over here for you. Estimated to project and it's going to load up the target select to. It's loaded. Okay, I'm gonna set my microcontroller. I'm gonna search for it, ASTM 32 for one and, um, I'll get it. I'll click next to grab it. Next over here, I'll give the project a name, g.P. Assembly, call this MBK versus KCC. Call to versus GCSE. Okay, does a descriptive name. You can name it whatever you want. I should point that out and then I'll say next and then finish. And. I've actually seen it. Remember my decision? Don't ask me this again, so click that. Okay. So it would open in a number of seconds. Right. It's done. Open and close this. This is from the previous project to close this. Do you want to save changes? I think. Yes. And so does the previous project. Does the new one column ticket versus GCSE. And then in the previous one, we said we were going to delete everything in this folder and see what we get. So we can do that. And this project would delete everything here because we don't need these files. I'm going to delete them. Let's see what I can use, shift, select all of them. And then I'm simply going to delete everything from the source folder. I mean, call source. And then I'm deleting everything because we write an assembly code. Right. The only thing we need is this over here. Is this dot s file from the startup folder. So now I will call source for this empty. I'm going to right. Click on the file and then I'll call. This may not. S main dot s like this finish. Okay. So I'm going to go to our walk, call you vision and then control A and then control C to copy of Copied Everything or paste over here. And this what we have. Okay. Okay. That's a lot of work here.

```
1    RCC_BASE              EQU    0x40023800
2    AHB1ENR_OFFSET        EQU    0x30
3    RCC_AHB1ENR           EQU    RCC_BASE + AHB1ENR_OFFSET
4
5    GPIOA_BASE            EQU    0x40020000
6
7    GPIOA_MODER_OFFSET    EQU    0x00
8    GPIOA_MODER           EQU    GPIOA_BASE + GPIOA_MODER_OFFSET
9
10   GPIOA_ODR_OFFSET      EQU    0x14
11   GPIOA_ODR             EQU    GPIOA_BASE + GPIOA_ODR_OFFSET
12
13   GPIOC_BASE            EQU    0x40020800
14   GPIOC_MODER_OFFSET    EQU    0x00
15   GPIOC_MODER           EQU    GPIOC_BASE + GPIOC_MODER_OFFSET
16
17   GPIOC_IDR_OFFSET      EQU    0x10
18   GPIOC_IDR             EQU    GPIOC_BASE + GPIOC_IDR_OFFSET
19
20
21   ;Using the bit set reset register
22   GPIOA_BSRR_OFFSET     EQU    0x18
23   GPIOA_BSRR            EQU    GPIOA_BASE + GPIOA_BSRR_OFFSET
24
25   BSRR_5_SET            EQU    1 << 5
26   BSRR_5_RESET          EQU    1 << 21
27
28   GPIOA_EN              EQU    1 << 0
```

So this project, this project I've not spoken about this project. This project is inputs and outputs. This project. This is just like the one we did 10 in DLT on, except that this one allows you to press the push button and when you press the push button, you get to 10 on the LCD and turn it off. So we're going to start off. I'll comment everything out. I start over here and then it's horrible, the control V to pace and then I'll come over here. I'll control it. There should be a way to come in the block. Right. Click and then. See? I'll come to edit to see if I can find a comment block over here. So there's an option here on the source that should be Torgau comment, but it's deactivated. I don't know what it is because it cannot identify this for assembly in a way. OK. We're going to comment on that one by one. So when we write the GCSE version of a particular line, then we comment it out. So we're going to take this first one to the RACC base. Could you try to change this into the GCSE format by yourself in C? So to change this, we know what to do. I'm going to copy the same name here and then we said we use DOT EKU here. The format is not EKU you. And then this is the name and then comma. This is the value we want to give to this name. OK? Right.

So this becomes the new value. So then this also we know what to do, dot EKU, you know, and then we fetch this name and then comma. Does the value we want give it? OK. We know what to do. Comment to tell. And then we see dot eku you. This is the name comma. There's the value. We want to give it to them. OK. So I'm going to post the video. Incomplete the rest cause this is repetitive. And you can do it. You know, you can try to do it yourself and compare it with the outcome I get. So. Right. I've changed the format of the symbolic names. Yeah. It took me about three to four minutes. OK. So this is it. We have all of them. I've kept the original call you efficient code in comment form. And when I touch the project to the video lesson, I'm going to attach the original call. You call your vision project as well. So that if you have a call with your vision installed, you can try both. So it's all being commented out. Right. And then we've used the format. Next, we have to do so. So over here. Yeah. Two extra directives. We have to include the DOT C.P.U directive. I'll come to the top of the fault here. Dot c.p.u. And then I'll give the name of our cortex M4. And then the Syntex we use in Syntax. We use it in a unified way. OK. So once that is done we come down here and this is where we continue. Over here, the directive here. All of this has to change. This is the call to your vision directive. We can indicate the thumb if we want to indicate that we're using the thumb. This we simply do dot thumb. And we don't have to indicate the entry point yet. The word export becomes. Global without un, a global in this area. Here is what we would call the Dots section, but a section like this. And then the section is dot text to indicators for it for code. And this thumb is not even compulsory. So we can take it out. So after we've done this, everything looks good. And then there is one last directive.

```
 "main.s
76 //BTN_PIN                    EQU        0x2000
77 .equ BTN_PIN,0x2000
78
79 //BTN_OFF                    EQU        0x2000
80 .equ BTN_OFF,0x2000
81
82
83
84                      AREA         |.text|,CODE,READONLY,ALIGN=2
85|                     .thumb  //THUMB
86                      .globl    __main
87
88  __main
89                      BL        GPIO_Init
90
91 loop
92                      BL        get_input
93                      CMP       R0,#BTN_ON
94                      BEQ       turn_led_on
95                      CMP       R0,#BTN_OFF
96                      BEQ       turn_led_off
97
98                      B         loop
99
100
```

```
Download verified successfully

Debugger connection lost.
Shutting down...
```

Over here we can align if we want, but we will skip that. And the end directive becomes thought. End like this. OK. So after we've done this, let's build and see what errors we have. Click over here to build. It's Beurden. We have 12 arrows. so the reason we would have the arrows is even I forgot. So. OK. This man has to change. Remember, we pointed out that the reset handler looks for Maine and the Maine doesn't include underscore so Maine house to be written like this. A man has to be written like this. And another difference is that in calling vision, when we write labels, we don't. Let's see. Should I wait? The reason I'm holding back is I just deleted the stuff. I said I was gonna keep it without deleting it. Mm hmm. Okay. I'm going to control it easily and just not delete and keep. Just bear with me. I think this will make your revision easier. So we said this comment, this out, this we don't need us. Well, and this part does say this, but does this export? This becomes Dotts global dot. Global without a global, and the name should be the main course, they reset. Handler looks for Maine and this bar does this area. We said we call this DOT section in our assembler over here. And then this section distorts text and remains the same. So we see a dot text over here. so this is where we end up with from this site or just a line the old guys together. OK. This is what it came with. This is all new stuff. OK. So because this is the global label here has to be made. And one other thing over here, over here in the GCSE assembler, when you write a label, you've got to put a call on there. So everywhere we see a label, we've got to put a call on, put a call on here and then a call on here and then a call on here. Call on here. And then this, a line. We said we can keep it out or we can use dots, a line. I think there's a directive dot a line. And this is the end of our GCSE. Like this. And one last thing. Over here in our assembler, we use Slusher Losh for comment. We don't use semicolons in call assembler. We use semicolons to indicate comment. Over here we don't. So the comment I don't need to keep them there seems to. Oh, just fix the comment without preserving it in its initial format. Right. Do we have any more comments? We do not. OK. We have some over here. Do we have any more? We do not. Do we? We do not. So now let's see what we've got. Click over here. It's Beurden. We've got two arrows. Okay, so safe. Let's see one arrow from her. To fuse Europe? Yes, it's OK. It's in this function. OK. This will have to do with our starting point. So let's go and look out to the starting point to the global main and then section is the text. And then we have our main over here. Then we have our branch over here. And then what do we not have? We have everything we need. And then let's see C.P.U

Coatex him for. It should be fine. OK. OK. I know what is happening. So you remember the files were deleted when we started. Our principal had a lot of files. One of such files or one of those files is the system in its file. And this subroutine loops to that. There's a system in it. So I'm just gonna copy from a previous project. If we go to this over here, if we go and find our loop fields, you, VSS should be down here. This is a research handler. It brings us here. And then it jumps over here. And then it goes to loop fills you OBSS loop fields you OBSS require a system in IT system and its existence in one of the files were deleted. So I'm gonna go to our board GPO Assembly project, go to core and then copy the system. And it's the. I'm going to copy these three files system as dictated to X X, but see, I think its counterpart is the. There's this one here. I think it would have been better if the guys at S.T. put these false in the setup so that we wouldn't need to find it in our application source files. In a way, I'm going to start off by copying these three. I think these three should be required. So. Right click copy and then I'll come to our new project. This is our new project, GPL, your assembly CO, MBK versus GCSE in our source forward. All right, click. And then I'll paste it here. Let's build and see. Click over here. OK. The arrow disappeared. No, we've got no warning. Um, I'm sure we just need one of the three, but we have the three. We can keep the three. If you are more curious, you can go delete. And the other two deleted two at random and see who has the system in it. Right. But we're moving on. Okay, so, Nonno, we've downloaded Anana with boats. Let's go to the debugger. I'll click over here. So like this. And then. Okay. And then I'll say, okay from here. OK. It's done. So we can run our code. It's done. They're working. Okay, so click here to run and it's run in. But when I pressed my board. Nothing happens. Uh, no, I was pressing the wrong key. When I pressed that, it was pressed, um. The black button. Sorry. Bother when I press, as you can see where my hand is on it. The lid is on when I lift my only gross off where my hand is on its own. When I live on my own, it goes off. So this is how we can convert. Call your vision assembly project to our cube IDC assembly project. And this same project should work in any form of GCSE assembly project. So if you are a Clipse GCSE assembler, they should be able to work. They use the same syntax. So that's all the rest. If you have any questions or talk, just live in the questions and answers. I really feel fine and of course, useful.

CODING A HARDWARE TIMER TO GENERATE PRECISE DELAYS

So I'm going to create a new project and this project is going to enable a hardware timer to provide us with delay, basically. So I'm going to select my board. If you have that this call you select the disk will help the new clothes. Also, like this double click. And then I'll do the usual stuff. So first, start off by cleaning everything here. Clipping out. And then this time, Hobaugh, you post the video and initialize the RCC to what we often initialize it to, as well as the, uh, select a zero wire for the debugging. Okay. Once you're out, you've done that, you can impose. And then we do. Right. The usual stuff. Here. RACC, HSC, ojars. Bypass. And then lo LSC. Or see you ceramic crystal. And then. Okay. Once that is done. Okay. We said we're going to initialize a time. So we come to timers. We've got a number of times we're going to use the timer too. So click a time or two over here. So once you click, if it doesn't open, you've got to expand it from here. We need to select the clock source of the time. That's very important. So when I use the internal clock, I'll click over here to select this. And before we forget, we said we want to delay, so it would be nice to use the delay to talk to our lady. So we are going to enable all ality for the output. So P a five. So LCD. Right. Click over here. Keep your output. And like always, we'd rename it or call it ality. Like this. Right. So we've got to figure out what time I hear the unit, et cetera.

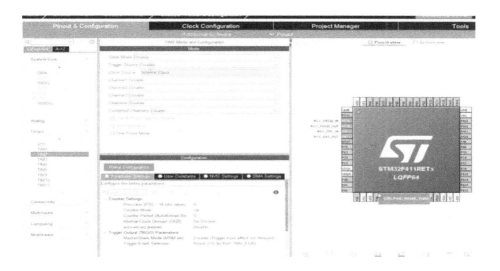

But before we do that, let's take a look at the, um, the clock frequency of all time. Of course, we know how to perform this type of configuration. I'm going to come to clock configuration over here. And we said we are using our two. So, all right. Here we have the. The default clock, 84 megahertz. And then when we come here, we get a clock for the various peripherals. It says MPB to time our clocks is at eighty four megahertz and then EPB one per four o'clock. And then there's EPB one timer clocks. And then there is EPB to appear before a clock. Right. So the question becomes, is there a timer EPB to Taimur or APB one Tyber that we need to find out? Right. So to find that out, we can go and take a look at the data sheet of the reference of the microcontroller, not the reference manual. This will help us. There are so many documents out there. We can take a look at the, um, the data sheet and then that will tell us what. OK. I know the answer to this. I can just move on and, you know, and then see, OK. This is what time I. It's connected to this puzzle. But I think I should show you. So we have to divert a bit. Let's go back to our best friend, Google and get the data sheet. All right. This the most practical course you would ever take. So we need SDM 32 F for one one this time, not reference my door data sheet. It's a different document. Okay, let's see who says PDAF. Estimate three to four. OK. Oh, come here. It doesn't say PDAF, but it might lead us to the PDAF. I'll put PDAF in the search PDAF over here. This is a reference to my No. We need a data sheet. Okay, let's come to the S-T Website. But for one, one, no problem. Thank you very much. Let's go to Resources. Go for a few. OK. So if we were using call you vision, call you vision has a tap for all the documents you would ever require for a particular microcontroller. But that's not a case we use in Cuba, Max, in Cuba already. So we've got to find this. Okay. So we can try another link. No, this is not official stuff, I'm going to post the video, find the appropriate link, and then we open it together.

Could you believe the thing was at the top here all along? Here's the link. We're looking for a STEM 32 resource data sheet. Okay. Right. Click open over here. Okay. So what we need here is a block diagram that tells us about the bus connection of the microcontroller, how the various peripherals are connected to the bus. Okay. Yeah, we go. This is what we're looking for. Page number 15. And, um, zoom in. So this diagram here is very important. This tells us which bus connects to which peripheral. So in arm, there are basically two buses, four connecting the C.P.U to the other peripherals. And they are two because they have different current characteristics. One is faster than the other. We have the HP bus, which is known as the Advanced High Peripheral Bus. And we have the APB bus, which is I think known as advance prep for a bus. The APB is a legacy version. It's older. HP is newer. And the HP allows us to access the various parts or peripherals at a higher frequency. So the APB has a lower frequency compared to the HP. And you can find this out actually as it is written here. Over here. Let's see. It says APB, too. Who are we dealing with? Let's see. Which microcontrollers this esteemed. Three to four. One one. Okay. So this is HP, one hundred megahertz. HP 200 megahertz. APB 150 mega hits, it just so happens that over here we have an APB also with a 100 megahertz, but often. A HB allows for foster access so you can have the same pair for which you can have a single pair for all. And you can either access that single pair for it or by HP or APB. So when you act, when you want to access it faster with less clock cycles, you should opt for the AHP. But if regular speed, regular frequency is what you want. You stick to the APB. So that's the difference between the two. So we said we want to know where our time is. Are we dealing with where it is connected? So to know where a particular pair is connected. Which plus it is connected.

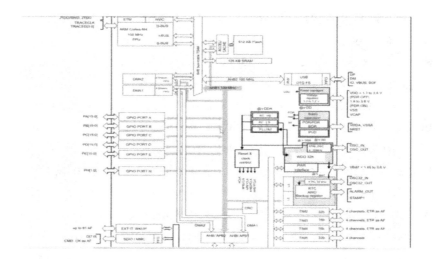

You just need to follow the arrows like it is said to be an investigation. Follow the money. This over here. We follow the arrows. So, for instance, we've got G.P.A. reports. When you see there's an arc connecting keuper your ports e to this other bus here and where you take a look at the name of the bus. It is an HP one. So if we want to know where G.P.A. ports are connected, it is connected to HP one. And in fact, all the GPL uses are connected to HP one bus. OK. So let's run the same experiment for our time. We said we work with time or two. When we take a look at time or two over here, we see the arrow connecting to time or two when we see the other side of the arm. What does it connect to? It connects to APB one. So APB one maximum frequency is 50 megahertz. So as you can see, time two is APB. One frequency is connected to APB, one bus. And we find this in the data sheet. No, the reference nor remember the reference manual or what, 800 pages. This one is just a little over. Or maybe, you know, a hundred and a half pages. One hundred and forty nine pages in total. So let's save this as well so that the next time we require it, we wouldn't go looking for it. Okay. It's downloaded. I'm going to minimize this. So timer two is connected to APB one bus. Okay, so when we come over here, given our current configuration, let's see, it says APB one time a clock. So our APB one time a clock currently is 84 megahertz. Eight people, one time a clock is what we use. You can put. Yeah. Let's see this again. We cannot debug all of these together. OK. So the reason I'm back here is because it says fifty megahertz, Max. But Cuba, Max here is telling us it's set to its default frequency at 84 megahertz. You see it before. So it turns out they're 50 megahertz. Doesn't apply to the time. As you can see, the APB, one bus, has other peripherals connected to it as well. We have the eye to see three eyes to see two Aspey, three Espey to another of another pair for us. We have the, um, the ROTC, the real time clock as well. So there is this part over here, the card. Yet it says the time is connected to APB to uncloaked from timeX clock up to 100 megahertz whilst the time is connected to APB one clock from timeX clock up to one hundred megahertz. So this implies that our time is clocked up to one hundred megahertz. That is why we could have time to two on APB bus, which says 50 megahertz max here. But in Cuba the default is set to eighty four, which is within the range. If we take this sentence here into account. OK. So. Right. That being said, um, where are we? Back to Cuba, Max. And I hope you find this useful rather than me just telling you it's APB, one bus and then we perform the divisions, so. OK. This is APB, one bus, and it's currently clocked at 84 megahertz. So our goal is to bring our timer into the millisecond unit. It's time. Currently it's eighty four megahertz. Mega implies a million. Eighty four megahertz implies 84 million. This means 84 million. Cycos, uh, executed in a single second. That is, warheads apply to Kerans in a second. That implies up implies a second. So meaning 84 megahertz means 84 million. Cycos in a second. So we know in one second it gives us eighty four million. Therefore, we can deduce that. One millisecond would require eighty four thousand. Course, we know a thousand milliseconds gives us a second. Eighty four million Cycos in one second. How many psychos in one millisecond, 84000 psychos.

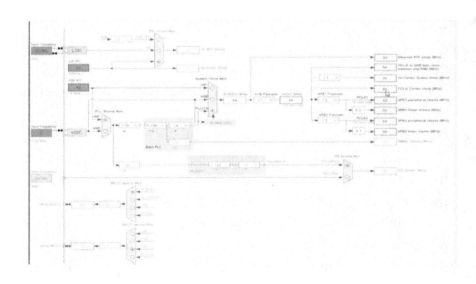

Right. I'm gonna come over here and then our time as a priest killer, I'm gonna put it to 4000 here. It's you four with three zeros. One, two, three. So what happens is this pre-schooler value would divide the time of frequency by this preschooler value. So our time frequency is currently at 84 million. And then we divided it by eighty four thousand. When we'd performed that division, we would have 1000. Then we've brought it to the millisecond range. That is what we're doing here. Leave a comment in the Q&A section. If you do not understand this. So now our timer is in the millisecond range. What we have to set is the time as the counter period, the counter period. This is what would determine the time out. When should the time out? OK. So we have milliseconds. Let's see. We want 10 milliseconds every 10 milliseconds, we'll put 10 over here because. Oh, I forgot this one here. Oh. Forty eight thousand. One, two, three. We need to hit enter. so now our timer is in millisecond range, one millisecond range. And what I mean by one, we derive that by the. The. Sorry. This. Should it be? Forty eight thousand. I'm all over the place. Eighty four thousand just to show you. We went through this. Eighty four million divided by the eighty four thousand gives us 1000 APB. One is at it for me. Go ahead. Which means 84 million to divide that by. Eighty four thousand you get 1000. And this has brought us from second to milliseconds. Cause a thousand milliseconds gives us a second. Right. So then our timer is in milliseconds. When I come here. Oh, I see. The preschooler value, it has to be, he has to be. He has to be sixteen, um, a sixteen bit value. So that is why when we put eighty four thousand there, we're not quite getting it. Let's see. I'm gonna see whether indeed our clock is what it is. Right. Um, our clock looks fine. Yeah. So, okay, this accepts a 16 bit value for it. Um, it's input, the highest number you can enter is sixteen bits. So we cannot enter it in four thousand. See, the largest sixteen bit value is sixty five thousand five hundred and thirty six. That is what that is.

Why when we enter eighty four thousand it doesn't accept. So okay we can all use that as a preschooler. So okay we experimented together. So rather than bring our timer down to millisecond range, we can bring it into, um, ten milliseconds range. Tens. Tens of milliseconds. So each unit, rather than being a millisecond, will be 10 milliseconds. And, um, let's see how you would get this. So remember, we set our clock, which we have over here is the same. Oh. If the datasheet information. No, what we collected is accurate. The information we interpret if it's accurate. And given what we see over here. Oh. EPB one time a clock. It could be one time a clock is. Eighty four megahertz. If this is indeed the case this means eighty four million. And this further means eighty four million psychos are executed in one second. That is what Hertz implies. Hertz implies a second. So. Eighty four million cycles executed in one second. So the question becomes one or the number of cycles executed. And one second, is it four million? How many cycles will be executed? And let's see, one millisecond. Okay. We know a thousand milliseconds makes one second. Therefore, that value is eighty four thousand. So the question is further asked. Eighty four thousand for one millisecond. Then how many cycles do we think will be executed in ten milliseconds. In 10 milliseconds. Actually, um, we can avoid all of this complicated explanation just by bringing our war time down for the range. OK. So I'm gonna change the time frequency here from it. Eighty four gigahertz so that I do not have to start using ten milliseconds as units. And that's very important. Is good that you see this entire process. I could have just, you know, stop this video and then figure it out. What a simple explanation. And they shot a fresh video that moves straight forward. But I want you to appreciate some of the experimentation that goes on. Well, you are dealing with a board and there is no example. And you've got to sort of write it by yourself. So what I'm gonna do here, over here. You're the one timer. The system has set it to eighty four megahertz. I'm gonna put it to forty-eight megahertz. Right. So I just had this. Forty eight megahertz. A lot of things have changed as well. Our system clock has changed from its eighty four megahertz to ninety six megahertz. Right. And then other peripherals of change. But time is the only one we are interested in. So now our timer is at forty eight megahertz, meaning forty eight million cycles in a second. In a single second, forty eight minute cycles. Therefore, in a millisecond. Then we'll have forty eight thousand cycles so we can simply go and then divide a while. Thirty eight to make ahead by forty eight thousand. To bring our time into the millisecond range. So I'll come over here. Okay. We have forty eight thousand here. This is our killer. The killer is used to divide the time of frequency. So with this preschooler we would have forty eight million divided by forty eight thousand. And when we get there will be 1000. Right. So now our time eyes are in the millisecond range. So the day count period is. When we want the time, our tool kit, if we want a timeout, too. Okay. Every 10 milliseconds I can pass 10 over here. If I wanted to. Okay. Over here, every hundred millisecond I can pass one hundred if I want every thousand millisecond. Which means every second. Then I can pass 1000 here. Right. And I hope you appreciate the um. The process, the brainstorming that you know we've done together. Or do you know. Yeah, sure. You've been brainstorming along remotely. I should say. So this is what we are going to keep. We could have, you know, kept our 84 million. And then used other units that would fit into our sixteen bit value. But we can just bring the clock down. And then we can use this if you don't understand how to use the pre-schooler in the current period. Um, you can leave in the Q&A section. Right. So another thing we have to do is to trigger the election. And over here, we're going to keep select updates, events so that you would keep updated. So what are three things we did? Is the preschooler the. The auto reload over here. It's just 10. It should be 1000. The auto reload, which is 1000. And then the update event. Right. Over here, we can set the auto reload preload also to enable. Yeah. Let's move on.

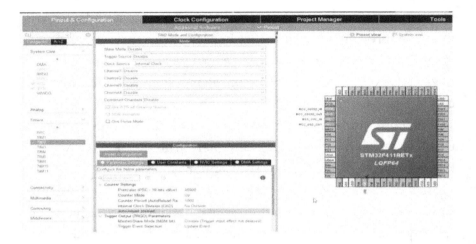

Once this is done, we come to NVC and then we enable a timer to interrupt globally like this. So now we're ready to generate our code. We come to the project manager or select my two chains. It's the cube idea. And then we can give the project a name. Call this time delay. Right. And then a click here to generate a code. Once this is done, click open project over here. So this project or just clean up a bit. So, that's what we have. So that's our main function. This time we initialized upl you and then we initialized time to us. Well, the definition of this function is down here, Terma. And this is basically the selection we made. This is our pre-schooler value. If we want to change it, we can change from here. This is the period we set as well. If we want to change that. That also can be changed from here. Right. Okay. So let's see. What we have to do is first start our time. I interrupt. Let's go to what time I drive up and see the functions available. I'll click over here on Drivers Hall. And then the source over here. I'll click how time I do h o t i m this one here. I'm dot c.. Over here I should say that I will click this open in a large file. Scalability mode has been turned on for. Okay. I'll say yes. Applying clues. The file is very large. It says so. Click over here to see the outline. Over here, it says the outline is disabled due to scalability, MOD click options. Disable ed, pass in. This is what disables the hotline. OK. So let's not spend time here. We're looking for a function to help us start the, um, the timer. First, we've got to start the timer interrupt and then we proceed from there so we can do it manually by finding it. Oh, we can go to the, um, the reference manual we downloaded. Okay, so let's look for it next time. I'm not going to open it. Scalability. OK. So this is when the time-based generation starts in interrupt mode. So the whole time bathes in it. So this is the function we pass the time we pass the address of the time, a handler argument and then it returns the time a status typedef. So I'm gonna copy this controversy over here to copy and then I'll come to Main and then over here after we've initialized the time, are we going to the time line defined by here, time out to a.T.M to sort of copy this and then pass it over here. Right. So we have this next, because our timeline is set as an interrupt every second as we configured, we said the time should be OK. Every second. So every second a block of code in the D callback function is going to be executed. What we need to do next is find the header or the structure of this callback function just like we did. For what other interrupt example for GPL? Your input is interrupted. We had a callback function and then we put out something like a block of code inside a callback such that whenever the interrupt occurs, our piece of code is executed. We've got to do the same thing here whenever the interrupt occurs. The piece of code that we want to execute would execute. But this time to interrupt that or caires is triggered by the time event. Whereas in the GPL, for example, the interrupt was triggered by that, a rising edge or the fallen edge of the switch. Meaning when we press this switch, something changes from high to low or low to high. And by that detection, we trigger the interrupt. But this time, it's going to be triggered by time every second. so we go back to our time as a module. The function is called a period, a lapse of time, a period elapsed the C. It's over here. Line four thousand eight hundred two very quickly. You can just control F and then you search for a keyword just like we do, OK? So it? S also has the weak keyword here. And when we explain what we have. By that we keyword to what we have to do is copy this callback function and then reimplement it. Now what we. OK. So if he has a spirit loves to call back in non blocking mode. Right. So I'm going to copy this controversy. Come to Main and then paste this over here. I'll just paste that. You can paste it anywhere. And then in here we can talk about ality. If you have an algorithm that you want to compute every second, you can put it over here. If you have other things you want to do every second. Basically do something. Whenever you have a callback, you can pull whatever you want to do. Over here, we happen to be using LCD for our sort of computation. We're using the LCD to be like a war complex algorithm that is supposed to be executed when interrupt.

```
    while (1)
    {
    }
}

void HAL_TIM_PeriodElapsedCallback(TIM_HandleTypeDef *htim)
{
    /* Prevent unused argument(s) compilation warning */
    UNUSED(htim);

    //Do something...
    HAL_GPIO_TogglePin(LED_GPIO_Port, LED_Pin);
}

void SystemClock_Config(void)
{
    RCC_OscInitTypeDef RCC_OscInitStruct = {0};
    RCC_ClkInitTypeDef RCC_ClkInitStruct = {0};

    /** Configure the main internal regulator output voltage
    */
```

```
                   from ../Src/main.c:22:
../Drivers/STM32F4xx_HAL_Driver/Inc/stm32f4xx_hal_tim.h:1788:19: note: expected 'TIM_Hand
HAL_StatusTypeDef HAL_TIM_Base_Start_IT(TIM_HandleTypeDef *htim);

make: *** [Src/subdir.mk:33: Src/main.o] Error 1
make: *** Waiting for unfinished jobs....

00:54:06 Build Failed. 3 errors, 0 warnings. (took 1s.411ms)
```

OK. So in here we can torgau the LCD by seeing how on a score GPL you should be Cupps all on a score GPA. You score torgau pin. And then we need to find the um deport. The early DGP, a port. I don't want to make his Pelin mistake. So the first argument is the port. And then the second argument is the pin, which is simply the lady pin. Right. So this is all we have to do so quickly to boot. Well, here. And then we've got some errors. Oh, I still have the weak keyword here. Okay. Click here to build. You still have errors. See? OK. OK. Over here. We had to pass the address, not just this small, I had to bring The Ambersons sign all time base. If you take a look at the function, the function takes the address. So I went to see if this would fix all our problems. OK. We've got problems fixed. Why not run it by clicking here? OK. Says Arrow Initialise in Besty Link. Okay, we'll take a look at that. I reconnected my boat. I'm going to click here to go back to the debugger. You know, click here to run. And as you can see, my LCD is toppling at a one second toco rate, just like we set our timer configuration.

CODING A HARDWARE TIMER DRIVER FOR OUTPUT COMPARE FUNCTIONALITY

We are going to see how to program the output to compare functionality of the timer and what output compares meters as you shall see us execute in a block of code. When a particular timestamp arrives, we can basically have, um, let's say, four different functions that we want to execute. We want to execute one every hundred milliseconds. And let's say we want to execute another one every five hundred milliseconds. A third one every four hundred milliseconds. So are these particular timestamps. We can execute our particular functions and we can achieve that by using the output to compare functionality of the time as we want to see how to do that. In this lesson. So I'm going to create my new Cuba mixed project. Right. So this my new project, I start off by Clarinda and topping out, Claire helping out. And then the regular stuff system call says the buck over here, serial wire on the RCC or bypass the high speed external Lopez crystal resonator like this. Okay, I'm gonna enable our LCD for this experiment as well. P five over here on the set STPI you output. I'll rename it too early. Right. So to demonstrate this, because I don't want to be connected, extend or LCD in extent or things to my new clipboard. I'm going to use that discovery board in this experiment because the discard report has for Eltis and I can configure all four LCDs for outpoll, compare such the one to time auto or kiss that particular LCD is just toggled. Right. So I'm gonna change my board. I'm gonna come over here. I'll say no. I'm going to change to the Discovery Board.

And another reason for the Discovery Board is it has more peace. All right.

Here we have 64 pieces by the Discovery Board, and 100 pins, although he's the same microcontroller in a bigger package. Right. So I'm going to change it. And like I said, the same microcontroller should work the same way across the concept. Everything is the same. So there shouldn't be anything but just for my demo, for me to demonstrate to you how output to compare works. I need, you know, a lot of multiple pins which have access to times. So I'll do SDM 32 for. One, one. Oh, come over here to MCU selectable, and then I'll search or search the board. SDM 32 for one one over here. And then this is estimated to have been discovered. So if you have just a nuclear abort, you can just watch a lock. And I'm sure you would understand this. It shouldn't be an issue. So we go through the same process. So when we get to a part where the, um, the nuclear hasn't got enough pings, we can use the disco sense. If you know how to program the SDM 32 for one, one is the same, is the same whether you have a pancake with a hundred pins or a package with 64 pins. You can see this is desperate. We've got 100 pins here. And the disco has more things we can play with, more LCD, et cetera. So I'm going to start over here by Claire and Claire and the pin out. And then do our standard stuff, come over here says Zero Wire and then RACC. We are still gonna bypass this and then this CHRISTOULAS later. Okay. So our Eltis are connected to PD. Fifteen people, fourteen PD 13, MPD twelve. The Discovery Board has four Eltis. I'm going to set all of these Eltis, all of these pins of the Eltis to be hot to be in the outputs. Um Yelp compared mode. So we just use an LDS example here. If you have the nuclear board and you want a particular thing to or care during the time, or let's say you have a particular, uh, let's see how the buzzer like a speaker that you want to make sound every 50 milliseconds and then every two hundred seconds you want to start a DC motor. In every 400 seconds, you want another output. You can connect those outputs to the corresponding piece. But I'm gonna use an OLED show here cause I have to do this cool boat, lightning round, so I'll come over here. Then I said this to time for S.H. for a speedy 15 and then time for then Tyber for an MPD twelve. So we've got all of our four entities. Right, that we have on the Discovery Board. Okay. So now we have to open the timer module and enable them as output compared with dealing with time off here as we see time for. So time is for us using Chernow's. One, two, three, four. So there is open channel time for here to expand it. click over here. So Channel one. I'm gonna select. Output. Compare. It's basically this one here. And then Channel two, article compare. Channel three, article compare. Channel four, outspoken pay as well. So we've set all of our four channels here to compare. Next, whenever we're using the time, we've got to provide a clock source. I'm going to click here. Internal clock. So now we've got to set the parameters of our time as so offers divide by forty eight thousand.

And then over here, the counter period 1000 like this. Now we've got to configure each channel. So we've got Channel one here. We have to set the demo. You click over here. So we want to toggle a lot. We wanted to toggle when the counter was on. So the pose, let's say counter one or channel one, we can say 200 M. S, we can pass 200 over here. Remember, this is the counter reload help inside out a thousand times, which is one second 200 M. S. We can change Channel two also to toggle on March and Channel two. We can also see maybe something like 500 M. S. And then we have to know three. We changed that also to talk alone much. And then. 750 E.M.S.. And then we can say Channel four should go every second. So I'll pass 1000 here. So then we have one fifth of a second half a second three fourth of a second and then one second. Like this. And then we can see articles comparing preloads. We can just enable this, enable and then enable. So these players will be talking about the respective time stamps. Okay. So it's like controlling Hardware's different hardware devices connected to different players at specific time periods. Right. So once we are done we can generate the, um, the code. Right. Okay. Minimize this. Come to the project manager. I'll give the project a name. Toma output. Compare. Then I'll leave everything the same click over here to generate before I generate. I have to select my Kubi D actually. Okay. No, I'll click to generate. And then open a project. So there's our project. Oh, do the cleanup. Okay. Right. So this will or may not see CFR looks like we've got a wild time, a handler. We use time before we know that. Right. And we enable how and then system clock GPL you and then time of for. So this time a four in its function. This is the code generated for us, given the um, the options we chose as well as the channels the day period or the post we search for the channels. If we want to update that we can change from code. Over here we said two hundred for the first channel and then Channel two we said half a second. Which is five hundred. And then three fourths a second. And then one second. Right. So output comparisons are actually very straightforward. The only thing we need to do is start the timer functions. That's all we have to do. So let's go to a what time module and see the function we need in order to start the timer channels. So come to drive us over here. All drivers and then source and then time at C, it's gonna say it wants to open in scalability mode. Oh say do you want to change scalability settings. No I do not. And um the C. Okay, so the function we're looking for is the output to compare thoughts. So over here, this function is whole. Oh, see if it initializes the timer output company according to specialized parameters. OK. This initializes the article comparison. OK. So there's the function we need: start the timer output, compare signal generation it takes to document. The first argument is the apparatus of the arm, the time of the time, a handler. And then the next argument is Cherno. So we need this and we're gonna call this for each Cherno and it returns the, um. Yeah. The status typedef. Copy this. And then come to mean. So we can simply paste on here and the first argument is, oh, what time is it? This one here? That should be the address of it almost on here like this. And then the cherno. So let's start with China. We spend time at a school, Cherno. It has to be all Cupps TIAA. And the school, China. What can the school want? Okay, so we have to do this two, three and four times. So over here we just change this to China. To China with three. And then channel four. Like this. So that's all we have to do, actually. We can build. It's appealed successfully. Let's debug it. So I just clicked over here to debunk you. Okay. Okay, so click here to run. It's running, but nothing is happening. Oh, I see what's going on right over here. Our preschooler has to be four thousand eight hundred. I'm going to come over here. Worth the time I have. We don't need to go back to Cuba, Max. We can just change from here. Right. So I've just changed it. Okay. I'll click over here to build. And then click here to go to the debugger. And then click here to run. And as you can see. We have our ladies Torkel in India, all during which we are configured. However we miss one. We have four channels. However, we have just three of them. Torkel in um. Let me see. Right. So this is our Cuba next generation. And the reason we have just three ladies blinkers, that's Channel four. We've not changed the mode over here.

TimerOutputComp
TimerOutputCo
Thread #1 [n
main() at
Reset_Har
C:/ST/STM32C.
ST-LINK (ST-LIN

```
26
27
28
29   void SystemClock_Config(void);
30   static void MX_GPIO_Init(void);
31   static void MX_TIM4_Init(void);
32
33   int main(void)
34   {
35
36     HAL_Init();
37
38
39     SystemClock_Config();
40
41
42
43     MX_GPIO_Init();
44     MX_TIM4_Init();
45
46     HAL_TIM_OC_Start(&htim4,TIM_CHANNEL_1);
47     HAL_TIM_OC_Start(&htim4,TIM_CHANNEL_2);
48     HAL_TIM_OC_Start(&htim4,TIM_CHANNEL_3);
49     HAL_TIM_OC_Start(&htim4,TIM_CHANNEL_4);
50
51     while (1)
52     {
53
54     }
55     /* USER CODE END 3 */
```

Console Progress Problems Executables Debugger Console Memo
TimerOutputCompre Debug [STM32 Cortex-M C/C++ Application] ST-LINK (ST-LINK GDB server)

Download verified successfully

The mode has to be torgau toggle on much just like the others. But I failed to change the mode. That is why it is like this. So I'm going to change it in code. So over here. Time off for. Let's see. We come down here. We'll see mode over here said, oh, see mode. Okay. So O.S. mode time in a search over here. So I'm simply going to copy O.C. Mode Tokyo cause O.C. Torgau is the mode for everyone. Either that or I can simply delete this line. And this is important that you understand this because it's a structure right over here. We said the O.C. Mode or C mode member to Tokyo. So anything that we write applies or C more to toggle applies to everything until we change the mode again. So over here we changed it from oh

140

Seymour to Tokyo. So I can simply delete this without change. Want to help so that all of them would have also moved to Tokyo. Right. So I'm going to come out and then they will again. Click over here to build. To build. It appeals successfully, quickly to go to debug. Okay. And then click here to run. I can see. No, we have all four LCD torkel in. Yeah, totally. At the rate that we've said it's using in the upper house, the polls that we set in that specific order.

CODING A HARDWARE TIMER DRIVER FOR COUNTING EVENTS

We are going to see how to configure the timer to count the okay rules of the event, the occurrence of an event could be the press of a button, the detection of the edge of a signal, etc.. This is often known as the input capture mode of the timer. And a mode such as this one is very important. When you are dealing with some sensors, an example of that sense will be the ultrasonics central. And for those of you who are not familiar with the, um, the mode of operation of the ultrasonic central, well, what happens is that you have, um, you have an output piñon, an input pane, and basically the output sends out a signal and then the signal would have to travel and then it would hit an object and bounce back. And then when it bounces back is going to be detected by the input spin and then the time it takes to detect the signal. The pretense is used to compute the distance of the object. It's a very simple principle. And if we're right in the, um, the drive off or on Ultrasonic Central, we'll be using inputs capture all the time as a counter to capture when the signal returns. So without talking much, let's just get into it.

In this example, though, we are going to simply detect the price of a war button on the board. Well, I'm sure you'll be able to apply this principle in your everyday project. I'll double click over here to get started. I'll say no. Over here. A quote, a pinata by clicking pinata of a hit clip in out say yes if I hear. And over here, we can make the Hawaii experiment a bit more interesting, such that when we are able to count the number of times the events will be cast, we can blink on an entity to do that. I'm going to set out what Ellie Dippin here you output like this. Um, actually, I think we, um, we can see input's capture later this time, we're just going to use time as a counter. It's a different configuration compared to input's capture. But there are some overlapping similarities. Okay, so this time we are basically going to sort of capture the, um, the the, the, um, the press of the button. So let's do it. And you understand what I mean. Come over here, timer. And then also let time one over here. Then Luxor's or Select ETR, which is an external clock source. iSelect, ETR. Over here. ETR to extend or Luxor's and everything else. I'll leave it the same. See? so Peter, twelve, ETR two. OK. For our club configuration here, we can leave everything the same. Even if you have the Air Force, your board doesn't matter because our club frequency is going to be based on Dippin. Because, um, our time out here, our time off, which is going to be the, um, what ETR here is a different pin from where our push button SPC Fit and we're going to connect pieces fit into Pier 12. But if we had our button here, it would be fine. But because we don't. We're gonna. Can I get it? If I hear I'm gonna set the, um, the counter period here to five. I wouldn't set a preschooler counter period is basically just going to reload or to reload at five. This is the value to which the auto reload happens. So basically, when we detect, say, five, if you put ten here, we can auto reload at ten such that when the event occurs ten times, you can do an action. In our case, when we detect five presses, we can, um, sort of toggle on the LCD. Next we go to the end, VIC searches and then we're going to take this one. Hit the update. Interrupt. Over here. Now we can go ahead and generate a project, I'll come to, um, January two right here, and then I'll give the project any time a counter. And then also light the torch and SDM 32. Cuba makes, uh, Kubota e oh.

Click over here to generate. We can open a project. So over here, we simply need to implement a Kobuk, all the selections we made have been included in our time. And it's a function over here. So to find a callback, we can just go to the, um, the time a module or come to drive this over here. Hold the driver and the source and then t i n c follow. Give me that. And um, I would just do control f and then I'll search underscore week to jump to the callback. The callback we're looking for is something like a period elapsed callback. It should be here somewhere. OK. It's over here. He loves cool back. Oh, copy this. And I'll bring it to the main let's see over here. I'll close this from here and then. A patient above the main function over here and then cleanup within here. And we said one day when it lapses, we want to talk to the D. I remember the period is going to elapse after with the press of a button five times after its content. Five courses we set the auto reload to five. So here we can simply say GPL you we can see how GPL you toggle pin. So say how on a GPL you are at a school. Torgau pin and then pass the port GPL, you then GPL, you on this call pin on the score five like this. Once we've implemented our Kobuk, we have to make sure we've

144

started our time over to interrupt or come down here and say HRO on this call. Time on this call. Start. He has to be bass. So I'll say I am bass. Serve with the bass on the school, starts on the school I teach and then we pass the stress of the time I handle h t. I am one like this.

```
main.c          stm32f4xx_hal_tim.c
40  }
41
42  int main(void)
43  {
44
45      HAL_Init();
46
47
48      SystemClock_Config();
49
50      MX_GPIO_Init();
51      MX_TIM1_Init();
52
53      HAL_TIM_Base_Start_IT(&htim1);
54
55      while (1)
56      {
57
58      }
59  }
60
61
62  void SystemClock_Config(void)
63  {
64      RCC_OscInitTypeDef RCC_OscInitStruct = {0};
65      RCC_ClkInitTypeDef RCC_ClkInitStruct = {0};
```

Problems   Tasks   Console   Properties
No consoles to display at this time

Okay, so we can build in c o click over here to build. It's built successfully. And then, um, we can go to the debugger or click on the bug over here. So like we said earlier, our external trigger is set to be at 12:00 and we want to, you know, use the button so we have to physically connect. P a twelve and P.S. 13 using a jumper wire because we know our pattern is connected to 13. Um, so we can, um, come over here. Let's go back to our user guide and take a look at it. Where was P twelve. It's about. Oh. Open this up a bit. Um. So this is a twelve over here. We have to put a jumper wire here. One side of the jump, a wire and can make the other side two pieces, 13 over here. Right. Once we connect to the two things, we can simply run over here, we are still in the pogo. And as you can see, when I press when I press five times, it would be Torgau, one, two, three, four, five. And then he came on. One, two, three, four. OK. So what happens is sometimes you may realize that I press three times and then it goes. This is. This is because of a deep bounce. When you press a button, you might think it's the you know, the signal has been read just once. But sometimes you press a button and the press is recorded three times. This can be eliminated using a filter, which is to write or write in a bit of code to get rid of typos. But yet we're not looking at this now. So I'll do it again. One, two, three, four, five. It's my own. One, two, three, four. Because I press too much.

CODING A HARDWARE TIMER DRIVER FOR GENERATING PWM SIGNALS

To configure our time or for PWI. I'm going to create a new project. You project over here. Or select my brought over here. ASTM 32. Four one one. So let's let it pan out or come over here. Claire Penult. So basically, GWM is an output, will you speed up your home to drive things like servo motors, DC Motors and even LCD? So when we set a pin, when we set it up to him, he has to be connected to a pin such that the output that we want to drive can be connected to that pin. So if we want the pin that our LCD is connected to, which is P five, if we want the pin to have Peter OBM, we have to verify that that pin can also be configured as a timer. Because Peter B.M. is a timer. We use a timer to create P2P. So Peter five is where the ality is. If you want to nominate a different pin, certainly you can use a different thing. But to generate Peter, the PIN has to have a timer capability. And when we click PE five, we realize that one of the options is timer to channel one. So I'm going to select this one over here. So we're going to select five to save us time on Channel one. And then we're going to perform a well fed, a configuration or click. Time is over here. And then time to set a set of others. And then we can, you know, with a configuration. So we start off by enabling the clock source. We're going to use an internal clock. And then the channel we use the fourth time or two is Channel one. So we've got. So like Channel one over here. Click the dropdown for Channel One. And I'm going to select Pete OBM Generator, Pete OBM. What is it? Pete OBM generation Channel one. Each one. Right.

Now we need to set a clock configuration or come to the clock configuration tab over here and over here. This is the default clock. When you select nuclear abort in your setup, there's the clock. You come with. But my point is the SDM 32 for one one, ASTM 32. It's written here for one one. The other versions of SDM 32 F, whether it's the Air Force zero one and that one has a default clock of 16 megahertz. Because I don't want us to have any hiccups. I want people to be able to run this code with the F one one and the F zero one. I'm just going to set this to. I'm going to change this to sixteen so that we all have the same clock and you don't need to have issues because you may have a different clock. Right. So trying to set it to 16 is searching for the perfect arrangement. Okay. Once he says 16, then everything here becomes 16. There's one thing I'm going to set APB one per four o'clock here to 216 that will change this. It's 16. Okay, I can get 16 for APB, one perfect clock, but the rest change, I'll come back to 16 over here. I see sometimes you get exactly what you want, sometimes you do not. 16 again. So this setup looks fine. We just have to make sure our time up, our timer, um, clocks are the same. So I have my EPB one time clock, 60

148

megahertz APB to a time, a clock, 16 megahertz. I think time or two is connected to a TV or two. I don't quite remember. But we have both of them at 60 megahertz. So there shouldn't be an issue. You know how to find this information in the, um, in the user guide. We saw that already. So let's move on over here. We can use one thousand as the pre-schooler 1000. But to be more precise, because we come from zero 1000 becomes one one one like this because you count zero one, two, three. But in order not to confuse you, oh, just per 1000, just know that the more precise way is 1000, minus one for the count up period. We can, um, we can put sixteen thousand over here. So like we explained earlier, you first divide by the preschooler and then you divide by the yump to count up the period. Right. So next we have to come configure the duty cycle over here. The word true cycle is now used. What is used instead is the polls. We know the duty cycle is often written in percentage form. So what a duty cycle is. The, um, the percentage of the posts, uh, is the um, basically the duty cycle. This is our counter period. If I take this count up period, which is sixteen thousand and I pass sixteen thousand to the polls, this will mean this is one hundred percent duty cycle. If I pass half of this value this will mean then it is 50 percent duty cycle. If I pass a quarter of this value it would mean it is twenty five percent duty cycle so you can pass one hundred fifty percent or 20 percent.

Well we can start off by just passing 50 percent or pass eighty thousand here like this so we can go ahead and do a January type project or click over here. General Project. I'll give it a name. Time Paedo p.m.. And also like to chain steam theory to cube ideas and then generate code over here. Click here to open the project. So there's a project to finish the cleanup. So all we have to do is start our timer with Peter. You. Come down here and call the function hall. I'm a school teacher. I am in school. Start learning to bracket . Suddenly it's time to learn. Then we passed the Cherno TMM channel to Channel One which we use and channel on a school one like this. Okay, so we can build our project or click over here to build. There is an arrow here. This function is wrong. It should be the whole time paedo p.m. start. So I have to put Pedo Beom over here. Let's build again. Click over here to build. It's built successfully. Let's debug and click over here. Okay, click here to run. And as you can see, the lady is totally.

CODING A HARDWARE TIMER DRIVER FOR GENERATING PRECISE INTERRUPTS

We are going to see how to configure our SDM 32 microcontroller for time interrupt. Let's get started. I've created a new project and cleared all pin out. In this example, we simply going to use time. Materne We've got a number of times. Oh, just select time or 10 from here and then expand this. And then for time to attend, all we have to do is select, activate for other times we would have to select the Channel one, Channel two, if other times I can, to what are connected to multiple channels. But Time ten is simple compared to other times. So all we do. Yes, click active. And to make the experiment interesting, we can enable our GPL you for the LCD so that we can toco the LCD for this P five, this word new clue. It is connected. If you're using a different board, you can use it to discover your LCD. So I can look to the around PD 12, 13, 14 and 15. So select the new clue early. So this is GPL, your output like this. And the clock configuration here in order to allow this example to run on all of the F four boards with almost no almost no customization or change. I'm going to set the clock configuration, which is the default for the estimated two four zero board, minus four one one. If I select this is the default that shows up. So I'm going to select HSR here. And then this will become sixteen and I'm going to pass here sixteen so that we all have the same clock. Even if you have Air Force, you're at one. Right.

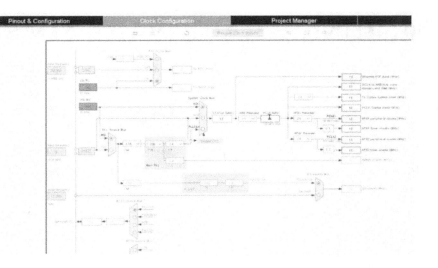

So as we can see, a sixteen Mucke maximum clock and all of our Air Force here have 60 megahertz clock, including our timer. That will be used. So we would apply pre-schooler to this 60 megahertz if we wanted to bring down the clock frequency. So now we can go ahead and configure our timer or come to penult here and then Time or 10 is selected. I'll explain this and then I'll come to the parameter. Stop over here. So over here we can scale down our time. I remember our time. A clock is 16 megahertz. If we divide 16 by 1000, we get, um. If we divide 16 megahertz by 1000, we get 16000, which is sixteen kilohertz. So I'll come here and divide by 1000. But because the count starts from zero to right to 1000, you have to put nine nine nine because you can't zero through nine nine nine and this will give you 1000 steps. So what we left with now is sixteen thousand. So we can further divide this to get. We want to scale down our clock to one second to sixteen thousand. I'm going to divide the 16000 by sixteen thousand, which I'll pass up to this count up here. Right here. So if I pass sixteen thousand here. Now my clock will be out for one second. Our clock frequency is at um. What we saw was sixteen megahertz. And we started by dividing the 16 megahertz by 1000. So 60 megahertz means 16 million. We divide 16 million by 1000. We get 16000. So when we get here, we divide sixteen thousand by sixteen thousand. And then we end up with one, which is one second. So I said, because we count from zero 1000, we have to write nine hundred and ninety nine in the same way. Sixteen thousand. We have to write fifteen thousand and ninety nine. Fifteen thousand. Nine hundred and ninety nine. Like this. Right. Over here, we can enable you to preload. And because we will use an interrupt, we can come to NVC here and enable the interrupt for all time. We said we're doing time. I interrupted an experiment. Right. So we can go ahead and generally tell the code. I'll come over here. Generate code.

And then I'll give this a name. Time to interrupt. Timer on the score. Interrupt. And then also later to change the to Kubota e an hour click here to generate. So that's the project of cleaning up a bit of the comment. So that's what we have. And if you're going to look at our timer in it, it's got all these elections. We made our period. Our priest. And then all of them. And if you go to the, um, the I.T. is competitive for I.T. Dossie file, you realize the uninterrupted love was created for our time. There should be an interrupt handler down here for a timer. It's a timer one up to time 10. I RCU handler term one up. OK. Right. So we can start our tolima. We started time off with an interrupt and then you know when we always deal and we interrupt, we've to implement the callback function. So when we start the timer we go to the um the timer module, which is the time that C file and copy the callback function and bring it here to implement it. So we go into the C hole on the score. T I am on this call base on the score start on the score. I.T. We start with an interrupt. So we need to pass the address of the time. A handler which is h t i m 10 like this. So we can go and fetch our Kobuk. Oh, come over here to our drivers and then haul the driver over here. I do not see fall. Where is it? It's over here. And I'll say no. And I'm going to search on the score, on the score. Which keyword? And this will show me all the callback functions available and I'll find the appropriate one. We don't want this one. We want, though, the callback that would deal with periodic laps such that the time period that we set, when it passes, when it's elapses, we want to do something. Both want to experiment with other callback functions. Certainly you can try them out.

```
void HAL_TIM_PeriodElapsedCallback(TIM_HandleTypeDef *htim)

/* Prevent unused argument(s) compilation warning */
UNUSED(htim);

}

__weak void HAL_TIM_PeriodElapsedHalfCpltCallback(TIM_HandleTypeDef *htim)
{
/* Prevent unused argument(s) compilation warning */
```

So over here we have period half complete callback and then we have period have we have period elapsed, half complete callback and then we have period elapsed callback. So if the period that we set, if half it's in the middle and we want to run that particular block of code. We can use this callback here. But if the period is completely a lapse and we want to run a block of growth, we use that period elapsed callback, which is a copy from here. And I'll come to my middle C file over here. And then I'll put it up here and we know what we want to do. This period elapsed in our experiment. We are simply going to talk about a lower LCD. But like, you know, in the interrupt service routine, you can do whatever you want in there. So basically it is a classic to do somethin. So over here, I will do something. It's not on our rhythm, it's basically talking in the early days. So I'll see how in school to peel you on this score. Period. Lost. Um, sorry. Hall underscored GPA. You, uh, it should be toggled. Goodness, I'm losing my mind. And then there is GPL you. And then we know that in the GPL you pin five over here. This is where a one nucleo LCD is connected. If you're using a different board you've got to select the appropriate port and the appropriate pin. Um we can go ahead and build our projects, our clinic over here to build. It's built successfully. We can go to the debugger, click over here to bug. Okay. And we don't need anything from the watch window or the expressions for you. Oh, we have to click here to run. And my LCD is blinking, and I hope yours was blinking as well. It's totally up to one Hertz rate, which is one second rate, just like we said, a wire timer. So this or the rest full time. I interrupt, like I said, and the interrupt, you can do whatever you want at the rate of the period, the time period. As you said, if you want a block of code to execute every second, you can write to that block of code here. If you wanted a block of code to execute every five seconds, every 10 milliseconds, every hundred milliseconds, you can set the time a clock appropriately and put that block of code in the period elapsed callback. And in the same way, if you want a different block of code to execute half this period we saw that there is that period that has elapsed callback to that would allow us to execute something when it is half of the period we set.

CODING AN ADC DRIVER FOR SINGLE CONVERSION MODE

We are going to see how to convert the ADC using our Cuba mix when it creates a new project. Come over here. You project. And then I also liked my port. So we are going to see different methods for initialization and the ADC. We first going to see this single mode conversion and then we're going to see the continuous mode conversion. After that, we are going to see how to crigger the ADC conversion using a timer. And then we're going to see how to sort of configure multiple ADC channels and use the DMA to do that. So come over here or select SDM 32 for one one. Then I double click this. Gopin. So we start off by clearing the penult. Claire Penult over here. Then I'm going to set up the core. Over here, we're using the sewer wire. And then RCC over here is going to bypass this. Then we're gonna use the crystal. So our estimate there are two for one, one has just one ADC module. So we can come over here to analog. And there's just an ADC one. However, this single ADC module gives us 16 channels. Right. So I'm going to select zero here for input's channel zero. Okay. And in this experiment, we can leave everything here on the parameters set. We don't need to change anything. Right. So we can generate our code now. So we just came to the project manager over here.

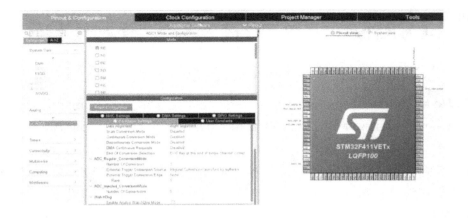

I'm going to select my two chains as SDM 32. Cube E. I'll call this project ADC underscore single mode conversion. Once that is done, click over here to generate and we can open our project. So this whole project I double click here to open. Open the main door to see fall and then clean up a bit. So now the first thing we have to do is start the ADC to do that. We go to the ADC module to see the function out. Allow us to do that. So come over here and find the ADC. Don't see fall. So I hear. See? So we have the function for initialize in these initialize, and as well, the one we're looking for is the start function we can search by doing control F and then we can simply search ADC underscore start. And this is it. So there are two versions: there starts with an interrupt and there is just start. We miss this thought. This is ATC stops with the one above should be ATC start. This is it. OK. So this just takes a pointer to the ADC Hondo, so I couldn't copy this and take it to our main see. So after we initialize the ADC, then we start the ADC. So this takes the ADC Hando, which is up here. Clean this. This or ADC one, Hunda.

```
28
29
30  ADC_HandleTypeDef hadc1;
31
32  /* USER CODE BEGIN PV */
33
34  /* USER CODE END PV */
35
36  /* Private function prototypes --------
37  void SystemClock_Config(void);
38  static void MX_GPIO_Init(void);
39  static void MX_ADC1_Init(void);
40
41
42  int main(void)
43  {
44
45      HAL_Init();
46
47
48      SystemClock_Config();
49
50
51      MX_GPIO_Init();
52      MX_ADC1_Init();
53
54
55      HAL_ADC_Start(ADC_HandleTypeDef* hadc
56
57
```

Project Explorer

- ADC_SingleModeConversion
  - Includes
  - Drivers
    - CMSIS
    - STM32F4xx_HAL_Driver
      - Inc
      - Src
        - stm32f4xx_hal_adc_ex.c
        - stm32f4xx_hal_adc.c
        - stm32f4xx_hal_cortex.c
        - stm32f4xx_hal_dma_ex.c
        - stm32f4xx_hal_dma.c
        - stm32f4xx_hal_exti.c
        - stm32f4xx_hal_flash_ex.c
        - stm32f4xx_hal_flash_ramfunc.c
        - stm32f4xx_hal_flash.c
        - stm32f4xx_hal_gpio.c
        - stm32f4xx_hal_pwr_ex.c
        - stm32f4xx_hal_pwr.c
        - stm32f4xx_hal_rcc_ex.c
        - stm32f4xx_hal_rcc.c
        - stm32f4xx_hal_tim_ex.c
        - stm32f4xx_hal_tim.c
        - stm32f4xx_hal.c
    - Src
      - main.c
      - stm32f4xx_hal_msp.c
      - stm32f4xx_it.c
      - syscalls.c
      - sysmem.c
      - system_stm32f4xx.c
    - Startup
  - Inc
  - ADC_SingleModeConversion.ioc
  - STM32F411VETX_FLASH.ld
  - STM32F411VETX_RAM.ld
- InputCapture
- InputInterrupt
- InputOutput
- TimerDelay
- TimerOutputCompare

Problems Tasks 🖳 Console Properties

No consoles to display at this time.

So take this with Pasos, like you went to this function and post the address over here like this. Over here like this. Right. So this will start with an easy one. Now, the next thing we need to do is pull for conversion. So we need to get a function down, allowing us to pull for conversion when the conversion is complete. When I store the resort in a variable. So let's do it. So let's go to what ADC module. So let's search for a plan for conversion. Control F and the P or L. L for conversion o. Like this. Okay. So there is this function hall ADC poll for conversion. It takes the ADC Hondo and a time out. We can copy this if you want to read more about the function. You can read the brief here. Pool for regular conversion complete. Right. So this parameter timeout value is in milliseconds. So is the timeout amount. I should say. Copy this. And then bring it over here. So we place our pool for conversion here. The first argument is the ADC handle, so HTC One, HTC One over here and a time out, we can give it time out of one Emmas. That is fine. So now that we've bought for conversion, we have to use a third function, which is to get the conversion or stop putting in a comment here. Number one, you start the ADC. Number two. Pull for conversion. Then number three. We get to conversion. Okay. So these are the three steps. So let's grab the third function. I'll come over here. It's known as a value function. So control of okay over here gets value and we can read about it. 0

```
1508    return tmp_hal_status;
1509  }
1510
1511  /**
1512    * @brief  Gets the converted value from data register of regular channel.
1513    * @param  hadc pointer to a ADC_HandleTypeDef structure that contains
1514    *         the configuration information for the specified ADC.
1515    * @retval Converted value
1516    */
1517  uint32_t HAL_ADC_GetValue(ADC_HandleTypeDef* hadc)
1518  {
1519    /* Return the selected ADC converted value */
1520    return hadc->Instance->DR;
1521  }
1522
1523  /**
1524    * @brief  Regular conversion complete callback in non blocking mode
1525    * @param  hadc pointer to a ADC_HandleTypeDef structure that contains
1526    *         the configuration information for the specified ADC.
1527    * @retval None
1528    */
1529  __weak void HAL_ADC_ConvCpltCallback(ADC_HandleTypeDef* hadc)
1530  {
1531    /* Prevent unused argument(s) compilation warning */
1532    UNUSED(hadc);
1533    /* NOTE : This function Should not be modified, when the callback is needed,
1534             the HAL_ADC_ConvCpltCallback could be implemented in the user file
1535    */
1536  }
```

Gets the converted value from the data. Right. You start off regular Cherno. This one just takes the ADC handle. So argument and then it returns the value returned to you in 32, which is the ADC value. So put that in here. And then I'm going to pass our ADC one Hondo here. This plus one thing. The address is like this. And then some cool on over here. So this function is going to return the ADC value that you would read from Channel from the ADC one. And we've configured only Channel Zero. So I'm going to create a global variable to hold the resort. You end thirty two 30 to underscore t, I call this sense of value. Then over here, sense of value is going to have the return of the get value function like this. And with these steps we can keep them in the infinite loop. Cut them from here. Push them over here like this. Okay, so now we can test all the boards. We need to connect a sensor to ADC Channel Zero and then we can read the volume from the watch window. We can read a sense of value from Watch Windu. We can use a potentiometer as our sensor in this experiment. So by 10 and the knob of the potential meter, you basically change in the analog reading. Remember, the potential meter has three legs. The middle leg is the one that goes to our ADC pin, which is P is zero for ADC Channel zero. And then the left leg can go to ground and then the rightmost leg can go to the VCT, which is the voltage source. So you can connect your potential meter Mido leg to the ADC, pin the left one to ground and then the right like to eat up five votaw, three point three vote depending on the board you are using. And if you're using the nuclear connection to the FIVE-FOLD. Yeah. So we can build our project. A click over here to build. To appear in. Well, we have an error somewhere. What does it say so value on declared? Oh, I've got a typo here. OK. Click here to build. Okay, to build successfully. And then we can click here to go to the D-Box you. OK. These expressions are from a previous project. We can delete them. So now we're going to add a sense of value to the expression controversy to copy and then control the fee to paste over here, and then I'm going to click here to run the code. It says Target is not available. Okay, so I'm going to take a look at my debugger, right? So, um, let's go to the debugger again. Click over here. It's open. Right. So if we run this, that's gonna tell us that the target's not available because we're using the, uh, we use the wrong window. This one is called expressions. But to monitor, well, global variables, we have to use the live expressions, video, uh, window so we can come over. Okay. Escape the debug view. Sorry about that. Now go again. I'll click on this bug over here. So I'm going to close this window. This window is called Expression's, I'll close it and I'm going to come over here to the window and then sure window and then I'll select live expressions. You should be here somewhere. This live expression is the issue. Yes, they have the same icon. That is why it's a bit confusing. So if you want to tell your global variables, you use the live expressions. So over here, my global variable is added. But let's see if you started. You had no global variable. I'm trying to clean it. To other globals. For a while. You can just copy the name of the variable and click on expressions over here and then paste the name. So I have this other twice. No problem. So, um, yeah. So to run our code. Click over here to run. And this is the ADC value, and this is based on the current position of my potential, Meeta. And I'm going to move the potential meta. I say move it. You see that the value goes down. I've moved it to the right. Most positions. I've moved it to the direction towards the, um, the direction of the pin that connects to ground. That is why we record at a very low value. I'm going to move it to the opposite direction, the very end of the opposite direction. And as I move, you see the, um, the ADC value increases. So this is how to configure the ADC. And then we shall go on and see two other examples, at least two other examples which regard ADC configuration.

CODING AN ADC DRIVER FOR CONTINUOUS MODE CONVERSION

We shall see how to set up our ADC for continuous conversion. We've already seen how to perform a single conversion. The single conversion is good for every day. No more low speed projects. But if you want your conversion to happen rapidly or if your project requires rapid conversion, something that is very fast, such as digital signal processing, then the best or the better solution. Among the two is the M, the ADC continuous conversion mode. Later on, we shall see how to incorporate the DMA. So let's go to Cuba, mix and start off by creating a project. And then we go to the IDC to write the code. I'll select my board over here. You can use it at a nuclear or the disco. It should be fine. So clear. Oh, PS, like I always do. So we are still using the P is. I'm going to say that as an ADC pin by clicking over here, it's ADC one input's zero. Okay. Okay, so let's configure the ADC first. I'll come to the system clock and just do the normal setup over here first. I'm going to use them. This a wire over here and then RCC like the clocks, the. Artist. I just keep this or keep these disabled. You can, you can. Whatever choice we make here would reflect in the clock configuration. Let's just bypass the high speed external. When we start using the when we get to the part about. About the USB devices, we would no longer be able to bypass high speed Extel would start and enable it.

But thus far we can afford to bypass it. Okay. So once this is done, we can configure the ADC. Um, I'll come over here. The analog stub, my computer's running a bit slow. A click on a log over here. Did you see one? And we would need to arm. We would need to scale down the ATC clock. So let's go to our clock configuration and see what is the current clock of the ATC. Click over here. Clock configuration. So from the microcontrollers user guide that we downloaded, if you check, you realize that the ADC is connected to the APB to us over here. So over here says APB to pay for a clock. It's 48 megahertz. Therefore, this is the clock for our ADC currently. Forty eight make a hit, as we see over here. If we keep everything here the same. So, no, no, we know this. We can go to the configuration of the, uh, the ATC. We know its clock is 48 megahertz. Right. So if I come over here for ADC configuration, um, if I come up here, we can decide to keep the clock at 48 megahertz or maybe we think that is too fast and we want to slow down the clock. So we are given the option to select a divider over here. We can divide the clock up by two, four, six or eight. So if we divide by two, the forty eight megahertz becomes twenty four megahertz. So the default here says divide by two. So I'll just keep that over here. I wouldn't change it. Next sense, we are working with continuous conversion. We came over here. Continuous conversion mode. It says disabled. We're gonna change that to enabled. OK. And the ADC resolution, if we want to change it, we can change it, we have options. We can select six bits, eight, 10 or twelve bits. I'm just going to keep it to the twelve bits and you can rella. You realize that the higher the resolution, the more Crock's like was required to complete the conversion. Such the six bits requires nine ADC clock cycles and eight which requires eleven, ten requests. Thirteen and twelve requires fifteen. So if we keep this then it's going to take 15 clock cycles for a single conversion. Also, we have the option to align the data, we can leave this the way it is, right? Alignment is good and we can come over here. Also, If we had multiple channels, then we'd have, um. We'll have, uh, other Ronke over here. We'll have multiple ranks, Ronke one, two, three, et cetera. And we'll be able to select, um, we'll be able to select the arrangement in which the conversion should. Okay. What do we want? Channel ten to be sampled first or Channel One, et cetera. But of course we have one only we have just one under rank. Over here. And this is rank one. And we can select the sampling time. Sampling time. Can either there be three psychos over here or we can go all the way to four eighty cycles so we can choose for eighty cycles. So because we already mentioned up here that the sampling time is, um, uh, also depends on the, um, the resolution over here. It says fifteen ADC cycles for twelve pits. So whatever we select down here for sampling time should be plus that 12 bit. Right. So there's four hundred and eighty Cycos plus the twelve pit it takes plus the twelve bit it takes for twelve plus the fifteen cycos it takes for the twelve pit. If we were using um um if we were using a ten bit it takes thirteen Cycos. So Timbits has a constant of thirteen,

thirteen Cycos. If we select a sampling time or for eighty then it becomes four eighty Cycos plus the thirteen Cycos for our ten bit. Right. So that is why we have to select sampling time as well. Now we can generate our code. We can, um, we can come over here to the project manager or select my two chains before I forget this. The SDM 32 Kubi d e. I call this project, um, ADC on this call to a continuous conversion. Like this. So we can generate a project. Once we've given it a name and selected the appropriate to chain quickly by here to generate. So like we did in the other lesson, we have to start the, um, the ADC like we did before, and then we create a global variable to get the ADC conversion and store it into it. So let's do this. And this mode, we don't need to keep all the ATC related initialization in the while, one infinite loop. We just need to call the get value Indiewire one loop. That is what is supposed to continuously occur to get a value by the ATC start code that can be called outside the infinite loop because we want to execute that just once. We need to execute that just once. Whereas in the other example, in the single conversion mode, we need to always study ATC. So that's another difference between the two in terms of initialization. So we can start it over here. Over here. Number one, start ADC and we use the same API we use before toll on a score ADC on a score start. And this takes the ADC handle as an address to the ADC handle as its only argument, which is a HP, ADC one course, the ADC Modulus ADC one. Right. And um, we will create a global variable here, which I'll call you into to underscore it. I'll make it volatile. And I'll call it a sense of value like this. Right. So once we've done this, we can get a conversion. So I'll come over here in our infinite loop. That is where we get a conversion to get conversion. I call this. So all we have to do is store the resort and sense of value. We use the pole for conversion, just like we did before to get this. So how? See how on the scroll ADC it is like this. And then pole for conversion. And it takes the um, the ADC handle and the timeout. So each ADC one is the first argument in the timeout of one. Emmis is fine.

and the timeout. So each ADC one is the first argument in the timeout of one. Emmis is fine.

```
*main.c
25
26
27  void SystemClock_Config(void);
28  static void MX_GPIO_Init(void);
29  static void MX_ADC1_Init(void);
30
31  uint32_t volatile sensorValue;
32
33  int main(void)
34  {
35
36      HAL_Init();
37
38
39      SystemClock_Config();
40
41
42      MX_GPIO_Init();
43      MX_ADC1_Init();
44
45      //1. Start ADC
46      HAL_ADC_Start(&hadc1);
47
48      while (1)
49      {
50
51          //2. Get Conversion
52          HAL_ADC_PollForConversion(&hadc1,1);
```

Problems Tasks Console Properties
No consoles to display at this time.

And this is going to return the ADC value which will be stored in our global variable, which we named a sense of value like this. Okay. So this is all we need to do actually. So just two steps. We start the ADC, we get the ADC, we continuously get the ADC in our infinite loop over here like this. Okay. Actually, over here we have to simply use it to get value. We need no pool for ADC conversion. That is the key difference between the two. So over here, how ADC on this gets value. A simple cluster I wrote got converted here. And then I came up with the wrong function. So this is it. We start the ADC and then we get the ADC value as simple as that. And the reason this works continuously is because it initializes it to be continuous mode. Right. So I click over here to build a project. quick over here. And it's built in. We have two errors. Um, let's see. I think it's from our news. OK. This one here. OK. There's a mistake here. And I can know the mistake because whenever you are using the whole library, when you first use the keyword, all you have to do is add the name of the module you are dealing with. So if it was a function that deals with a timer, it would be hard to underscore t I am for timer. If it's a function that deals with less than an ADC, it has to always be hard on the score ADC. So of course I made a mistake in typing this. There should be an ADC score over here. And apart from that. Um, this gets value because we are using continuous conversion mode. It takes just one argument. It doesn't take a timeout cause it's gonna be continuously converting. And, um, we can actually find this function. We can find this function in our ADC module. I'll copy the function name as I've written it. And then we're going to go to our drivers over here, just like we often do to verify the name of the function. And then I'll come over here, hold the driver, ADC Dot. See, it should be up here. It's gonna be too big for the kids. Not so, um, let's see what we can view the outline of. OK. Let's search or do. Control F and then paste the name of the function here. And this is the function name. OK. Indeed. And it gets one argument. It takes one argument and it returns the ADC conversion. So the process gets the converted value from the data register of regular Cherno each ADC pointer to ADC Hando type structure.

And the return value is the converted value. So, okay, we look good. Now we can build again. I'll click over here. It's built in. So it's done building those schools to debug, I see, click over here. Select this, okay? Okay. So that's my live expressions window. If you don't have this live expression, it's opened, you can come to the window, show you and then you select live expressions. It's somewhere here. This is it. You click here to open it. So I'm going to copy ADC volume control, see to copy and then I'll double click in here and then I'll paste it. So now this is inside the live expressions. So I'm going to click here to run the code or click it to run. And this is my ADC value and I'm going to move my potential meter, which we are using as the SENSOR. And as you move, as I move, you can see the ADC value changes. So if this were to be a light sensor or the ADC value will be changing accordingly based on the amount of light you received. If it was a different type of sensor such as temperature or pressure, you would work the same way. Okay. So that's all there is for this lesson if you have any questions at all. Just let me know.

CODING AN ADC DRIVER FOR INTERRUPT CONVERSION MODE

We are going to see how to configure our ADC to work in interrupt mode. So I'm going to create a new project over here. I'll select my microcontroller. It is the SDM. Thirty two four one one. You can select it at a nuclear discovery port. Anyone is fine. Oh, just select this. I say no. Over here. And Eau Claire dippin out by coming over here. Note Claire Penult. And I'm going to select PSU to be my ADC for this experiment. Close this. Come over here quickly. This. PSU becomes a DC one input's zero. So we can go ahead to a clock configuration, we know what ATC is. Can I go to the APB with us? Um, so the board I selected, I selected a nuclear if not changed in it, then this is the frequency it's giving me the default frequency. Um, APB to is currently at 84 megahertz. You can keep this the same or you can just change it. I'm gonna send this to 60 mickum uh, 60 megahertz, which is fine. If you're doing something that requires more frequency, you can certainly change it. Um, let's see. So the reason I'm setting it like this is because some of you may have the estimate that two F four was zero one boat and that one's default frequency is 60 megahertz. So I want us to keep within the same format so that we can all try it on different versions of the F forebode. So. OK.

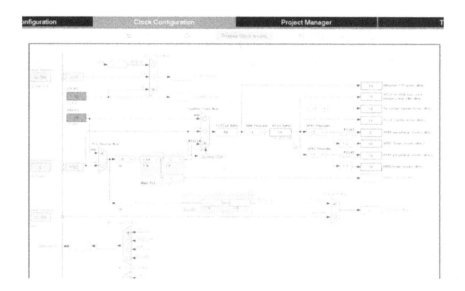

And my AP two, which is the, um, the, um, the bus for the ATC is also at 16 megahertz this fine. I'll go to pan out in configuration and click the system view over here. And once this opens, I'll click the ADC and I'll configure the ADC. OK. It opened over here. So click here to expand it. I've come down here probably to certains and no krunk this port. And over here, the clock preschooler is telling me that is dividing my clock source by two, which is my 16 megahertz. This has been divided by two, which you end up with eight megahertz. This is fine. Over here. Keep everything the same. And then just change the, um, come to the rank over here. Because we have one channel. We have just ranked one. I'm gonna change sampling time to four eighty or we have to don't actually come to the end, fix certain stuff. And um, enable our ATC one global interrupt such that we'll be notified whatever, whenever a conversion is complete. Now we can go ahead and generate the code or click generate over here. I'll give it a name or simply call this ADC. Underscore. Interrupt. And, um, I'll select my two chains over here. SDM 32. And then keep everything the same and click here to generate code. Click here to open the project. There's a project. It's opened close, this old one. This is it. ABC interrupt over here. No, no. Open this and clean up a bit. Okay, we've cleaned up. So what we have to do is start the ATC. I'll come down here and see how to underscore. ADC, let's call start. On the score, 84 interrupt. And this takes one argument. The address of the ATC Hondo, which is ATC, each ATC one over here. I'll pass that over here. And then with The Ambersons sign here like this. Right. So this starts the ADC with interruption. So because we use an interrupt, we have to define our Kobuk, we need to go to our ADC module, come to drivers over here, source. And then you find your ADC to see fall. And then in there, you find the Kobuk. To find a callback, we can just search for the keyword, because we know we are often pretending. They often start with a word weak. So do control F and then underscore school week. And then I hear this. OK. This is not the one we want. We want the confession complete. Yeah, we go ladies. Conversion complete callback. So I just copied this. And I'll come to my mind or see you fall over here and I can put us anywhere. It's a function so it doesn't have to be within that of another function. So I'll clean the key word here and all of this can be eliminated like this. So what this means is once the conversion is complete, the, um, the program would jump to this Kobuk function to execute one of others on ADC conversion complete whenever the conversion is complete. We'll come to this function. What do we want to do whenever? An ABC conversion is complete. If you want to run an algorithm, you can put it in this function if you want

172

to do a particular thing. If you want to light up an entity, anything, you can do it here. But a more appropriate and sensible thing is to get the value that was just converted. So what we have to do is see how underscore ADC gets value like this. And this takes the ADC Hondo US argument on this. We return the ADC value. But we have to create a global variable to hold it. You underscore to call this sense of value like this and sense of value here. Oh just copy this and sense of value here. You cause this over here like this. Right. Note that over here we have the um. We have the option to use it. We can use it.

```
22  #include "main.h"
23
24  ADC_HandleTypeDef hadc1;
25
26
27  void SystemClock_Config(void);
28  static void MX_GPIO_Init(void);
29  static void MX_ADC1_Init(void);
30
31  uint32_t sensorValue;
32
33  void HAL_ADC_ConvCpltCallback(ADC_HandleTypeDef* hadc)
34  {
35      sensorValue = HAL_ADC_GetValue(hadc);
36  }
37
38  int main(void)
39  {
40
41      HAL_Init();
42
43
44      SystemClock_Config();
45
46
47      MX_GPIO_Init();
```

Problems   Tasks   Console   Properties

No consoles to display at this time.

This local handle here. Oh well. Global undo ADC one. Right. One key thing because when I use it in a continuous mode, when the ADC completes one conversion, it will just run this um Kobuk and then it will be done. It wouldn't run any more conversions if we want to start the conversion again. We have to call haul on the score. ADC on this call. Start interrupting like this. This is key. Without this, the ADC will just perform one conversion and it will be done like this. Okay. No, we are ready to build, let's click here to build and she will have. It's built successfully. We can run our

174

debugger or click over here. It's open. OK. I have to reconnect my board. So we can add our global variable here to our live expression to observe it. I'll double click there and then concurrency to copy and I'll come to live expressions and put this over here. I'll remove these old ones. They are from a previous project. I can simply. I can do a remove or remove all like this. OK. That will click. This new one hit Enter. And then we can, um, click to Run. I'm gonna connect my sensor, which is just a potential meter to P is you. Right. I'm going to click here to run and we can see the value here. So there's the unlock value. And now I've moved it to the opposite direction and this is the value we're reading. So this ADC is in interrupt mode.

CODING AN ADC DRIVER FOR SINGLE-CHANNEL DMA MODE

Let's get started. So we are going to use our P, uh, our ATC Channel Zero, which is P0 of our esteemed 32 F board. So select P if you hear us input Channel zero. It is one input, zero configuration. What I'm gonna do is, um, I'm going to set a clock so that you work for F zero four zero one as well as F one one. If I leave it like this it would work for everyone. But because I don't want us to have all foreseen issues when some other person is using F zero one F for actually it is at four zero one, then I'm just gonna set it to the default of Air Force One. So come here it I and then this goes to sixteen and um I'm just gonna sit here two sixteen as well. I selected it here and then I'm just changing this peripheral clock to sixteen. Right. And it's going to go through that. And once that's done we can come back to the pin and configuration and then deal with the ATC configuration, click ATC over here and then I'll open it from here. See? Click here to open, so. Yeah. Channel zero. How can I go by your parameter settings? So to continuously convert values from the ADC channel using the DME. First we have to set a continuous mode because we want it to be continuous. Let's see continuous mode over here enabled and then a continuous request. The reason why this is like this is because we've got a going at our DNA first. So come to image settings and then I'm going to add select ABC one. OK. So then I go back to parameter settings and then give me continuous requests. Now the dropdown allows me to see a neighborhood. And one last would be within D.M. Hour channel. We have to know so we can increase the number of Cycos a bit. Also like this one. Eighty four cycles. Right. So we can go back to our DMV settings and complete it. OK. Everything here makes sense. We know we are taken from the peripheral and storing it in memory, meaning we are reading from the, um, the ATC, which is a peripheral storing. They read Vudu into memory. We read a value to store it in the memory so that direction is peripheral to memory. Aubagio, we want to make it a secular buffer so that it continues all the time. It doesn't just end when it reaches the end. It's secular. Right. And the data with Yeah.

Is a sixteen bit half word data size, which is fine because we've selected our, uh, ADC because our aid is just running on top of it. So yeah, it's within the largest of bits. Number is four thousand and ninety six. So yeah, this falls within the range of the half word that we have selected over here. We need not change it. Right. So now we can go ahead and generally talk with a click with a huge rate and then I'll give this a name. ATC on that score at the end like this, also added to change is the SDM 32 Kubota E.. Click here to generate. So this is a project of clean up a bit. Yeah. Clean up a bit of the comment. And as you can see, we have our eight is one in eight. And the DMA in it. Right. So over here, we simply need to use the whole ADC starts DME API to start our ADC with Yemi. And we've got to create a buffer to start it. Um, the conversion. So I'm going to come over here and see you end 16 on squatty and then I call this sense of volume. It's a single value. And it's a size of one. Cos we've got this one ADC channel we are working with. So I'll come down here then and then I'll call our function. That is all on this call. ADC on this call. Start on the score, DME, and then the first argument is the handle is the, um, under 40 ADC, which is each ADC one. And then the second argument is the, um, the buffer to store the, um, the ADC value. The name of the buffer is sense of value. And, you know, the size is one. But we've got to typecast this to you in 32. The function expects a you in thirty two point. So you enter thirty two on this call to start over here and put some code on here. So when we run this, we should see our ADC value whenever the sample, the sampling is complete from our peers. You when we connect our senses to P is your what. It's A temperature sensor or hot reaction. So pressure sensor, et cetera. Whenever you notice a new something complete, we should see it stored in this array here. If we want to be notified when the sampling is complete so that we take a particular action, such as run a particular algorithm, let's say we want to be notified that sampling is complete. Today, the sample, we can use a callback function for something like that without a callback. We will still get our ADC value if we want to get a notification when the sampling is complete. Then we can implement a callback function and put a block of wood. We want to execute when the sampling is complete. OK. Right. So let's go and get a callback. We know how to get a callback. We just go to the module we're dealing with is the drivers and then the source we're dealing with is PTC. So we select PD. You don't see far out of here. And then, uh, what are we going to do? A search a week to work on a school, on the school week, and then we go through them one by one. And then there is this Kobuk version, complete Kobuk. This is the notification for completion. The conversion is complete. Even if it's half complete, we can still be notified. So we execute a block of code. Well, we can just use the complete. You can experiment. We have to complete it on your own.

```
16       *
17       * * * * * * * * * * * * * * * * * * * * * * * * * * * * * * * * * * * * * * * * * * * * * * * * * * * *
18       */
19   /* USER CODE END Header */
20
21   /* Includes ------------------------------------------------------------------
22   #include "main.h"
23
24   ADC_HandleTypeDef hadc1;
25   DMA_HandleTypeDef hdma_adc1;
26
27
28   void SystemClock_Config(void);
29   static void MX_GPIO_Init(void);
30   static void MX_DMA_Init(void);
31   static void MX_ADC1_Init(void);
32
33   uint16_t sensorValue[1];
34
35   int main(void)
36   {
37
38       HAL_Init();
39
40
41       SystemClock_Config();
```

Problems · Tasks · Console · Properties

No consoles to display at this time.

So copy this. Come over here. And then, um, I just paste this. Yeah. But we don't have to do anything here. If you have an entity to blink or something to a puzzle to sound, you can do it. I'll just tell you to do something here. Just do something, you know, like this. OK. So we can grow in, um, Londis and then check the expressions to see whether indeed we can see our ADC value when we connect a connected senso. So click here to build our project. It's built successfully. Click here to go to the debark. It's open. This is a project where we can learn everything from the live expression. This is from a previous project. I'm going to add our sense of value here to live expression. Like this. And for those of you using the nuclear board, this is the location of P es u p es you. Is this paying off? Yeah, this one here is P is euro, so you can connect your senses. Oh, here I can just connect a potentiometer. And then just turn it so to the. So I'm going to put a breakpoint in here. My wife, I want to loop. There's the break point and we have this. Yeah, I've connected. I've connected a potential meetup to my peers. You click here to run. And then I'll click again. And I'm going to expand this. And this is our sense of value. So there's so much to quote, forget the ADC for DME transfer.

CODING AN ADC DRIVER FOR MULTI-CHANNEL DMA SCAN MODE

We are going to see how to use multiple ADC channels with a DMA. So I'm going to create a new project or come over here, file a new project. This time we are going to use P, a one, MP or two. So I just said I must ADC Pier one. I said this to ADC in one piece to our side as to ADC into. And also, I should mention, it's not compulsory to always set up the system core that we always do. We can leave it. You only have to set us up if you want to set it all on use. PS as input to PS. So there is an option. I'll show you when we click the code generator over here, OK? And we come to, um, we come to advance setters. Um, we come to the code generator. We come to this tub over here and a code generator. This sets all free pins as analog pins. I should say. So when we set off free pins, using analog pins, it helps save power. The reason why we, uh, we always configure the RCC and then the system over here is so that those pins don't get set as analog pins. So if you want to use set pins as analog pins. So set on using pins as analog pins. Then you always have to set your racc. And this is this. These options are here. You always have to set them accordingly so that the pins will be set by if you don't want to use it, you can leave it to its default state. Okay. So I'm just gonna show you the example where we don't set this. We just leave it and proceed. Um, so we've set in and in one and in two so we can come over here. Clock configuration. Too often we just keep the clock. We don't interact with the timer much. Okay.

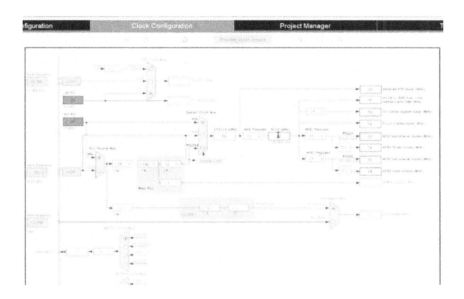

This time I'm going to change the clock to ninety six megahertz. I'll just type 96 over here and then I'll hit enter. Everything else is going to be adjusted. Click okay. Over here. So I'm going to adjust the various parts of the system to enable my HSC. Okay. To be 96, just like I've typed. All right. So this is where we have changed this to HCO, key of change, the Ishioka 296. And he says the maximum you can get to is 100 may go ahead. OK. So now let's go and configure our ADC channels. I'm going to come back to Pinart and Configuration and then select system view and then, oh, click on

ADC. And it's open, but I've gotta expand it from here. So click here to expand it. We use it in one and in two. That is why they are ticked. I'm going to come under parameter settings and I'm going to set them. It is a clock to lessen. We can divide by eight is fine. And we can leave the, um, the resolution the same, so we said in this project, we are going to use the DMA. So we have to enable that. Also, we want continuous mode. So I'm going to enable continuous mode over here. And DMA continuous requests. I'm going to enable that as well. Well, what we have to do is actually enable scan mode or enable con mode over here. So what we need to do is and neighbors can mode. We don't need to enable continuous conversion mode. So just scan mode enabled. And then we have to enable DME. But when you click this dropdown, you don't see the enable option because they expect us to select the DME first in the version four of Cuba. You could have just selected by inversion five. You first have to come to DMA settings. And then you add the DMA. So you click on ADD and then select over here. I'm gonna say ADC one now that I've added it. I can come back to the parameter settings. And then when I click this, a dropdown says enable dia DME continuous request and enabled. Right. So because we have two conversions, we can set two channels. We can set a number of conversions to two. Okay. So now we have two conversions, the two conversions. Therefore we have two ranks. We have run quanti rank two. So we've got to select the ranks. We've got to set up the ranks. So rank basically means which one shall be, um. Which one should be sampled first? Is it channel number one or channel number two? Currently, rank number one is channel number one. We can leave this rank. Number two is still channel number one. So I'm gonna change this to channel number two. So rank number one is channel number one. Ranked number two is channel. Number two, if you have sixteen channels, you'd have 16 ranks and you can arrange them in that order. The sampling time I'm gonna select for 80 over here and then for 80. Over here as well. So once we've done this, we can go back to the DME tub. We've already added a DME demo. We wanted to be secular so they would go back to the top or select Sechler over here and then over here, data with.

I'm just gonna select a word size, meaning 32 bit. Okay. And then this is all we have to do. And if we want to change the priority, we can change from here. But we can leave it for this lesson. So now I can go to the, um, the generated code or click over here. And then I'll give the project a name. Call it ADC Unescorted DME. Multichannel DME. OK. And then also like my two chains. Then a creek generates like this. I'll open the project. So there's the project. It's open. I'm going to clean up a bit. So in the Cuban mic setup, we initialize ADC pins, P1 and P2. So we have two channels, meaning we can connect to send a source to a white board and record the ADC. So to use this and the DME, we can just order the result in an array. I'm going to declare a global array over here. I'll see you in the underscore team because we declared our DMA a data size to be a Web site. What basically means two bits of data size. And I'm gonna call the central values. And because we have two Chernow's, I'll pass two over here like this. So what we have to do is now start the ABC with the DMA. We saw how to just study ABC. Hi, ladies. You start. We've seen how to study a D.C. would interrupt how ADT ADC starts on the score, I.T.. Now, we're gonna start with DMA and we can go to our ADC module to see the function before I write it. So I'll come to dry this or come to haul driver source and then I'll double click on ADC. Don't see over here like this and then I'm gonna search control F over here and then I'm gonna search ADC on this call. Start on the score DME and then hit enter. Okay. So that's the function. That's the function. It says and navel adc DMA request after last transfer and enables ADC paired for each ADC uh and and enables ADC peripheral. Okay. This first line, the second line H ADC pointer basically talks about the argument. The first argument is the arm is the pointer to the ADC Hando. And then the second one is the data. We jumped. Let's see. OK. The second one here, the second parameter. What does it say? The second parameter is the data destination buffer, which is what we've declared a global variable. And the third one is the length of the data to be transferred from ATC peripheral to memory. Okay. So that's the function we require. I'm gonna copy this and then I'm gonna paste it in here. So we don't need a return. And I'm gonna pull comments here.

One start. One here starts in D.C. with DME. Function. Okay. So the first one is, so what, ADC Hondo? The second one is the data buffer, as I point out to you, instead, to underscore T.. So I'm gonna bring our buffer over here. And the second one is the length. The length is just too. Gonna pass this amber over here like this. So in this experiment, you can guess I've got a sense or a potential meta connected to P one and another one connected to P E two. And what we're gonna do is add a wah sense of values, um, array here to our live expressions, window into debug view. And then we're going to turn the knobs and see if indeed we can get the analog reading. So I'm gonna click over here to build and it's built in now. Okay. The reason we have the theory is we don't need to put ampersand here. It's expected of you in thirty two or three. Okay. Now let's build. Right. The ABC. ABC. The ABC on the list. It's ABC one. No, simply age. ABC can show over here. It's ABC one. Click here to build. OK. Now we have no errors, no warning. OK. So before we go, actually let's see the code generated. Course you can see each ADC and HDMI, HTC One over here. And indeed, we can see that there is extra code generated in our ADC. This is our ADC in its function. This is the standard in it. We go with our ADC. Now, if you see we have Ronke one over here, which is for ADC Channel one, run two, which is for ADC Channel two. And there is another function here which initializes the DME. And over here it sets the DMA priority as well as enables the interruptive for the DME. This other function is DME in its function. Right. So we can go to the debug for and see, you know. I'm gonna click here to go to the debugger. DoubleClick this. I say, okay, over here. Let's call it a success for me. Um, let's see. Let's go to our live expressions. We can take this out. This is from a previous project. You can just right click and remove or. And I'm going to add this new one called Sense of values, plural. Okay, so because it's a way we can expand here to see the first and the second. OK. So I want to click here to run. Now, as you can see, we have our ADC one value here. We have them, um. The one connected to appear to this is Channel two.

Channel two is reading three thousand to five one. I'm going to turn the nub of Channel Zero, which is, uh, the knob of Channel One, which is ADC Index zero. Remember, index your index one. And then we have Channel one, Channel two. So index series for Channel one. Index one is which I know two. So I'm gonna turn the potential meter for this index. One. Senseor. Let's see. Okay, let's not change it. I'll take a look at it right away, I wasn't connected properly. Okay, so now the second one is moved to the position of ground. The second potential meter, which is connected to Channel two, tends the wire to the direction of the wire that connects to ground. So we see that it's read in this, whereas the other one tends towards fee plus plus. Now I'm going to turn to the other one. I'm going to turn this one to the position to always be a plus plus mine and I'm going to move it to the opposite direction. Remember, it's a potential meter with three legs. Right. And as you can see, they both have higher values. Now, of course, they've both moved towards, you know, the, um, the DVD, uh, the five foot order, three, four, two lines, basically. Basically, there's a sign. So it's just like the other ADC experiment that we did, um, just turn into a potential meter in opposite directions and based on the direction the analog value is low or high. So this shows how to have multiple channels which ADC. So you can use this for ten channels if you want. If you had 10 channels, then the buffer size, you would be ten. And then you would have an array of 10 elements. And each one will belong to each channel. And you can you can, um, you can take it from the array and process it accordingly, such that if I want to channel one, I can just see, I can just see each one equals sense of values. Array Index zero. And I know this will be giving me my ADC Channel one value and I can take this and put it in the DSP algorithm or whatever. I'll go with them. I hope for further progress. And if I want to Channel two, I know Channel two is looking at the index one so I can just see Channel two you cross. I can just say Channel two because of this. I can just see, um, Johno, too. Index one. Actually, I'll show you how this is, because I don't want to leave it stored in the array like that. Okay. So it's not over yet. I'm going to exit this now. I'm going to come here and then I'm gonna cut this. And this is the. Often when we use DME, the beauty is that we don't have to be read in anything and we don't have to be rude in anything from the wild. Want to say we want to, you know, take this and put it in some, uh, some local variables or whatever. This is Channel one. Channel two. I'm going to declare two local variables here. I'll say this, as for a little, by the way, it's good to set these things, Swiller, too. And then I'll come over here and then I'll declare local to local verbose. That's local because I'm declaring that within the main function, what is outside the main function is global. OK. For those of you who are not aware you are 32 on a score. T, c, h one. C, it's two. So we have two local variables over here. And we say in C, each one equals the sense of the index. You see H two core sense of value index one. Okay, so we'll click over here to build. It's appealed successfully. What do we have here? Okay. So, okay. The function doesn't accept roles at all. Of course not. Okay. We check this out. So our warning is saved. No more warning. What does this one see you in thirty to where it was? Each one said, but not used. See, each one is used here. How come we cannot see it? See each one.

```
46
47        MX_GPIO_Init();
48        MX_DMA_Init();
49        MX_ADC1_Init();
50
51
52        //1. Start ADC with DMA function
53
54        HAL_ADC_Start_DMA(&hadc1,sensorValues,2);
55
56
57
58        while (1)
59        {
60            ch1  =  sensorValues[0];
61            ch2  I  sensorValues[1];
62
63        }
64        /* USER CODE END 3 */
65    }
66
67
68    void SystemClock_Config(void)
69    {
70        RCC_OscInitTypeDef RCC_OscInitStruct = {0};
71        RCC_ClkInitTypeDef RCC_ClkInitStruct = {0};
```

Problems Tasks Console Properties

<terminated> ADC_MultiChannelDma Debug [STM32 Cortex-M C/C++ Application] ST-LINK (ST-LINK GDB server)

Debugger connection lost.
Shutting down...

See each one. Okay, let's build again and see what we have. So see each one, see each one set upon or used or use its variable, but if C, H one is no use, then there should be an error, you see. So this is a bug. It has to be a bug from the cube. I d e okay, we can go to the debug for you or click over here. So we can just otherwise see it, want to see it, too, to our live expression window. Copy this and then I'll add it over here. A copy of this. They're not allowed to see H2 over here like this. So these are the current values. So it's

189

because it's running. And this is the current state of it. Right. So we can get this exact same result that is stored in the two deery the array, because we went out of the debugging, came back, it sells, it says over here, failed to evaluate. We can't remove this. I'm going to stop it. Remove it and add it to the. We just confirmed that we have the same result. I'm going to add our array here. Okay, we are back with it. And you can see the results are the same. So if you have 10 of them, you can take them by the array indices one by one. But normally, when using DNA, uh, DME, the advantage is that you don't spend any process in cycles having to read outside a buffer. You can just rather than read the content of memory and store it in another variable, you can just use the sense of value index to know that that is your channel one, your channel one. So you wouldn't need to do this.

CODING SPI DRIVERS FOR POLLING TRANSFER MODE

We are going to see how to configure the S.P.I. So I've started a new project. As you can see, we can start off by selecting DSP. I come over here. Where do we find SPOG connectivity? We can start with S.P.I one click over here to expand it. I'm going to select Full Duplex. And it's selected the, um, the three pins required is squaddie clock the so when Dendi Mozi, as you can see from here. So I'm just gonna come to clock configuration and then change 260 megahertz so that we all have the same clock, including those with the Air Force. Your reports. So change over here to 16. And I hope I can get 16 on both off my clock buses if I don't. I would have to fiddle with it more. Okay. It would be time to clock 16 if everyone was 16. Okay. We are good. So we can come back to penult and configuration and then I'll come to systems for you over here. Okay. S.P.I, he's already selected. So I come to the parameters set in tab over here and then I'm going to pull this up like this. So over here we can leave most of the options the same. The preschooler here basically is just like a preschooler and a timer. It's the number we pass. Yeah, it's used to divide the frequency. So our sixteen gigahertz will be divided by two and we end up with eight megahertz and the board rate becomes eight megabits per second. I'm gonna reduce this further. I'm going to put it around one megabits per second. Therefore also like to eight over here. Um, yeah, I'm, I'm putting around two megabits so I select eight. If I select 16 is gonna give me one megabit, which is a thousand kilobits per second. So I select eight over here like this. Next, we go to the GPL, your tub and ensure that we are running. We run in at high speed. So the GPA sets is let's see, this is the clock line. Let's see, well, we have maximum, very high.

What is the one we have set at high C? Okay. Cuba makes her set it for us. Very high, very high, very high. And the older version of Cuba makes you. You would have a drop down. You would have another window that allows you to change the speed. But we want them all to be at high speed. We can go ahead and generate our quote or come to the generator over here and then I'll give my project another call this S.P.I pole. Cause we're going to see how to use interrupts and other methods. There's the pulling method and then I'm going to select it to train over here. Steam 32 Kubi the E. Click over here to generate. So there's a project where we can take a look at the generated code. It's very similar to all the other peripherals we've seen thus far. It basically has a handle. And they handle this very similar to these. You are to actually get an instance, the mode, the direction, data size, Klok polarity, clockface, poudre to preschooler, et cetera. So this is it. So we're gonna start off by creating two global arrays. We shall use them as buffers. We show a transmit buffer and receive buffer. And we're going to send data from the transmit buffer and verify that we can receive it in the receive buffer if that works accurately. Then that would confirm the worst setup is working as we expect it to. So I'll see you in eight on the squatty. Over here. And I'll give this a name. I'll call this or call this, let's say T x buffer, because we're gonna have two of them. And then it's gonna have, let's say, ten numbers. And then, um, we can simply say 10, 20, 30, 40 or what is 50, 60, 70, 80, 90, 99. Or 100, because we are dealing with a debate. We can still go 100, right? Okay. And then I can see you in eight on the squatty. And this is the rmx buffer. This buffer would have the received data and it's going to be of the same size over here like this. And, um, once this is done, we can proceed to initialize. You can close this up a bit. We can transmit that data by using deha s.p.i, transmit data. And um, we can receive use in the whole S.P.I, receive um receive data um or you call it. Um we can use that transmit, receive uh API both for receive and transmission. And if we want to learn more about this, we can always take a look at the whole library, um reference mind or we downloaded earlier. All of this is explained and the steps to deal with each and every pair is explained in that document. So simple. How S.P.I. Over here. And then the function is transmitted and then received like this on. The first argument is the handle of the SBI HSPI one. The second argument is the um is the transmitter buffer.

```c
40      HAL_Init();
41
42
43      SystemClock_Config();
44
45
46      MX_GPIO_Init();
47      MX_SPI1_Init();
48      /* USER CODE BEGIN 2 */
49
50      /* USER CODE END 2 */
51
52
53      HAL_SPI_TransmitReceive(&hspi1,)
54      /* Infinite loop */
55      /* USER CODE BEGIN WHILE */
56      while (1)
57      {
58          /* USER CODE END WHILE */
59
60          /* USER CODE BEGIN 3 */
61      }
62      /* USER CODE END 3 */
63 }
64
65 /**
```

Problems   Tasks   Console   Properties
No consoles to display at this time.

So the transmitter for what name did we give it. We said to you X buffer over here. Your xpo for the next one is the R X buffer. We call that uh X buffer. So we just change to our X and then the um the next argument, which is argument number four is the size of the buffer. This is ten. And the, um, the last argument is the time out of past one hundred here, over here like this. Because we have no S.P.I sleeve. We're going to verify our experiment by using something known as the loop back. We're going to connect to the measles when the Morsi line the Mizo stands for. Must that enslave out. And then the Mozi stands for M. Out Slavin. We're going to connect these two lines so that we can see the data transmitted from masters to slaves. Um, it's just known as the Lookback method basically. So we're going to have a jumper wire connecting P. six and seven. And that should be able to allow us to see that our S.P.I configuration is working right. So let's find where P is six MPLX seven are located O come over here. This is, uh, wiping out of the nuclear board. If you have the disco board, you have the pinata right in there. So you need notes, um, sort of refer to any document. But here we have P six, MPLX seven. So we just need a jumper to connect to be a six MPLX seven. I'm gonna do that. We can go ahead and build our project. Click over here to build. It's pulled successfully. Click here to go to the debug. I selected the wrong one. Click here to go to the deponent. Okay, I have to create a new book. I'll come over here. Debug us ASTM 32 Coatex M. Okay. So I'm going to do it at our X buffa to live expression, remember the X parfaits empty. We want to know whether we can receive this data in the Erich's. So I'll put this here like this and then I'm going to click here to run and then I'm going to pause and then see what we have in the X buffer. Got X upon this like this. And, um, we have nothing in the R X buffer. When I run again. Pause. We have nothing. I stopped it. Nessy. If the true causes of this, if you find nothing. It could be that the decompiled is optimizing in a way to values or you've not connected your jumper wire properly. So we can disable the optimization first. I just realized the problem is from my jumper wire off. Yeah. I'll fix that. So let's see again. And then, um, I'll show you an image of my setup, a click over here to debug a few. Okay, so we can put a breakpoint here. You can basically click here. Click the line of the wall one to place a breakpoint. Right. And then we click to run so that it would stop at a breakpoint. This is our expert Paphitis. This they receive Buffa. I remember they received barflies empty. So if we expand now to receive Buffa has the content of the T x buffer to verify that this is really the S.P.I transmitting the information. I'm going to take out my jumper wire and run again. So I'm gonna pull out my jumper wire. And I'm going to terminate and relaunch. Opened in. Let's see. We still have our break here. I'm going to click to run. No, there is no jumper wire. Let's see. The oryx barflies empty. Showing is very true, meaning no data is received from TXU to Rex. And then we're doing this, like I mentioned, using a method known as the loopback where we've connected the Mousie and Mizo. With this, we can verify our S.P.I configuration without requiring a particular S.P.I sleeve.

CODING SPI DRIVERS FOR INTERRUPT TRANSFER MODE

We shall see how to configure our S.P.I for interrupt mode. So we will do exactly what we did. So come to connectivity S.P.I one. I'm going to enable the most duplex US food here. And these will be a neighborhood for us. Okay. And then I'm just going to make sure our board works with most of the F four boats out. I'm gonna change this to 16 so that I can get my EPB one timer clocks 60 and an APB to term a clock 16 as well so that those with the Air Force, you shouldn't have any difference. Okay, now we can go to the, um, the configuration of the S.P.I. And then I click over here, parameter sirtuins. And this time we can reduce the frequency even further by getting a larger and larger preschooler to use a preschooler such as this over here. And we're doing this because we're using the um, we're using the interrupt. And we don't want to sort of miss some of it. We don't want to, uh. Yeah. Miss some of the data that comes.

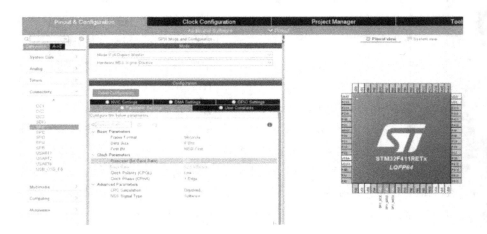

So we reduce drastically the frequency of the S.P.I. And because and because we use an interrupt, we have to always enable the interrupt from the MVC certains over here. We can go ahead and generate our project or come over here. I'll give the project a name. I call this S.P.I as a call interrupt and then, um, isolate it to change over here. Skew the mix. Click generate over here. So those are projects we do like we did before, we're going to create the Eriks buffer and a T Expo for the T Expo for the data. It's going to transmit it. And we expect to receive in the X buffer. Right. So we've defined it the same way the R X buffer starts off empty. Once that is done, we can, um, use the same API, but this time would interrupt that we used earlier. We use HARL S.P.I transmit, receive. This time we're going to use Harlette, S.P.I crunch me to receive an interrupt. Let's do so. I'm going to come down here after S.P.I has been initialized. I'll see how underscore s.p.i. And then on this call. Transmit like this then. And then receive. And then over here I t for interrupt. And then the first then is the address of the handle, the SBI handle which is H s.p.i one. HSP won't like this. And then the next is the um the Bufford has the data to be transmitted. We call it this t x buffer. And the next argument is the buffer to store the received data. We call in this R X buffer. And the data size, which is 10. This time we don't need to pass the time out because we are dealing with interruptions. Right. So n as you would know when we are always dealing with interruptions. We've got to find the callback function. So let's do that now. So we go to the module to find a callback. I'm going to drive us over here. And then source. And then what I'm looking for is the S.P.I to see. And then like we did. We can control F and find the weak keyword. Because they always start with weakness. And what we're looking for is the um, transmit receive complete callback. If we want to do a callback only when the receive is complete. We can take this one if we want. Just transmit complete. We can take the other one. But we want both our 60 X callbacks. So I'll copy this from over here. I'll come to Main over here. Then I'll paste this in here like this. And everything in here is going to be wiped off like this. Okay, so we have to delete that, we could cue it from here. And over here, we don't need to do anything in the Kobuk if we have something to do. We can put it here, but we don't have anything to do. So is our classic to something. If you want to blink on LSD, you can blink an LCD. We didn't set up the LCD, so this is classic. Do something. One other thing we can do is just put an infinite loop here that will do nothing. Remember, this callback is only you know, the process only jumps here whenever this received, when never you know this receive and transmit it s are 60 X.

So it doesn't mean we're going to be stuck here forever. You know, it's a background thread. Um, actually, I'll take this out. Shouldn't be teaching. This is not a good will front in this example. If there is something we want to do here, we can, um, do it here. Um, let's see. Put a counter here and counter. Then we can basically do the counter. Plus plus. Plus plus here. Okay. Now we have something we can work with. Remember we still um we are still doing the loop back. So you've got to connect the P seven and P six with a jumper wire to demonstrate this. I'm going to click over here to build a close to this fully. I'm gonna go to the debug click over here. This one here. And then okay, over here. Over here, we still have a while. Let's see. We cannot break points here at home. That's mean. Just click over here. We have a breakpoint. I'm going to add our counter to the Yum, to our expressions when two US will pull a counter over here like this when I click here to run. It's, uh. Um, oh, I ordered two expressions, I should be added to live expressions. I'm going to clean this. So I'm going to add two live expressions and I'm going to add our experts here. Remember, we've run once. That is why we see an account to us then. This is our receipt for Lissie. And indeed, we've received the data. We can try that again. I'm going to relaunch, terminate and launch again. Okay, it's Lodin. AK. And we still have a break point here. Well, we have heard this expression. I'm going to click to run to see. We have two other expressions again. This is frustrating. Stop this. Oh, just remove all evil and then add our X buffer. Oh, that will counter. Which is up here. I added our XPO for it. I'm supposed to copy this. Oh, you're supposed to copy this, sorry, but the computer is a bit slow. so we came to one because we had just run again. OK. And then, um, I know you get a point so you can take out the count, uh, take out the jumper wire and you realize that our console, our counter one to count is a duplicate of a counter won't count. And then our experts are empty. So we like a mission in this hall. S.P.I T XRX Complete Kobuk. If you have a block of code that you want to execute, one of the SBA transmits and receives data. This is where you do it. Over here we simply count on a variable. And equally, if you have a block of code that you want to execute only when data is received by the SBI, such as you want to take that data and pass, pass it and pass, it could mean taken or taken out spaces and commerce and created into something. You can execute that in a callback as well. Over here we just put in a counter. So that's all the rage from any questions at all. Just leave it in the questions area. As you can see, the difference here is basically transmit to receive, which I t which means interrupt and then you just need to put this callback function. We can leave it empty if we want. But it has to be here. We can leave empty. Right. But I'm just using this opportunity to increment a counter and then, um. Yeah. Like we said, the S.P.I trick we are using here is a loop buck trick, um, such that our experiments want to depend on a particular sleeve. But later on we'll start dealing with some other peripherals that require S.P.I communication. And you would see how practical the S.P.I setup is. But this order is for now.

CODING SPI DRIVERS FOR DMA TRANSFER MODE

We are going to see how to set up the S.P.I with DME functionality. So I've created a new project, as you can see over here, and I've cleared all the pins. And when I select our S.P.I, I'll come to the connectivity S.P.I one like we did earlier. And then I'm going to set up a foremast. A duplex mode over here is foremast. A duplex like this. Okay, I'm going to set a clock two sixteen so that all of us with a four would use it equally so 16 over here and everything will be readjusted. So now we can go back to always pure configuration. OK. Come two systems view over here. When I open this, I should see S.P.I spilling over here. I've got to open it by clicking here. Okay, I'll come to parameter certains over here, okay? We can keep the pre-schooler off, too. That is fine. We don't need to reduce it further. So what makes this project different is we've got to go to DMA settings and at the Yemi. So I click add and then I'll select S.P.I, our DMA and then. Oh, add another DMA over here. 40 x. Click over here, S.P.I, DME, like that. So now you can go ahead and generally talk code. I'll come over here, generate code. I'll give it a name. S.P.I, dma p I underscore d m a like this. And then also a letter to change the M 32 Kubi d e and then a click generated over here like this. So this whole project. So we do like we did earlier. We start off by creating our Rixon T x buffer. I'll just put this here. We initialize the T X buffer to have some data and we expect to find that data into our X. If you want, you can take a look at the code generated by a Y. Cuba makes elections is basically the standard S.P.I code generation to get out with some third generation for the DMA and setting the DMA interrupt and DMA priority. You can take a look at that. And again, if you want to see more about this, you can take a look at the DEHA preference module we downloaded earlier. Let's go step by step, um, step by step, um, information on how to deal with each of the whole API. So over here, I'd just like to interrupt an example. It's exactly the same API, except that the last word is DMA. So the API is whole, underscore, S.P.I, underscore, transmit and then we have received. And then the first argument is the handle of the um, of the S.P.I, which is H. S P. I want the second argument is the um it's the T X buffer.

The next argument after this is the R X buffer and then the data side. We don't need to pass the arm. We don't need to pass out. This one we have to Artemia at the end of the DMA like this. Okay. So with DME and interrupt you, we always have to find the, um, the callback function to implement the callback would require. It's exactly the same callback we used for the S.P.I interrupt the project um as the receive uh transmit complete callback. So we can go and fetch it like we did or come to drive us over here. Hard drive a source. And then what we were looking for is S.P.I dot C over here and I can just search the weak keyword. And it would take me to a control F and then I hit one, two, three, four, five. So this is our 60 X complete callback and copy. Put it up here. And like I said, this Kobuk, you just do something in it, do something first. You delete the key word and you can just do something, you know, like this. Earlier on, we were just incrementing a counter variable, but we can leave it empty so it can go ahead and build our project or click over here to build. To build in, then we can go to the debug, click over here or select this. And then I say, okay, over here. And I'm going to add my ah ex buffa to the live expressions to see if indeed we received the data when I put a breakpoint over here. That's the main function. Over here, man, I'm just going to click here to put a breakpoint here. OK. When I click it to run, it stops over here. Sorry. I want to put a breakpoint at the wall. One loop. No, the main function. Goodness. Over here. Like this. So click here. And then it stopped over here. So let's see if our Poffo has the data. It has to have and indeed it's working.

CODING UART DRIVERS FOR POLLING TRANSFER MODE

We shall see how to create a you are to drive by using our SDM 32 Cubitt mix and the Kubi e of creating a new cube next project to apply here. As you can see, I'm going to start off by clearing the piano. Quick over here. Clap your note and click. Yes. Over here. Like this. And then this is my microcontroller, the SDM 32 for one. And you might have a different version. SDM 30 to Air Force, your one and you may yeah. You might have a different development board as well. You might have either the nuclear or the disco board and the differences between the two, because what happens is we are going to configure you out onto a microcontroller. But before the microcontroller is able to talk to our computer for testing purposes, we need um, we need a USP to, to um, to you to convert. Now if you have to discover a port you need an external USP to convert. But if you have the nuclear abort, the nuclear port does not require this. So let me show you what this converter looks like. If you have a disco ball you can just go to Google and search USP to FTD converter. And. Different types. Different colors. But what is important is they often have our X and T X lines and we can make the R X line of the connect of the converter to d t x line of our microcontroller and we can get t x line of the converter to the R X line of our microcontroller so we can jump a. Yeah.

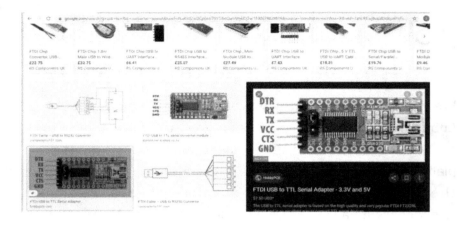

And then this side connector USP and then the US because Dell Computer, such that we can be able to send data from this from our microcontroller to our computer. Again, this is just for a disco board. The nuclear power does not need this. Right. So you can order one. If you have a disco board, you can simply search USP to F converter F. TDA is a very popular company to create this type of solution. That is why your name is there. Um, so let's go ahead and um, write the um that you are to remember, it's a twisted arrangement if you have the chip the way you can. Actually microcontrollers that t x of our microcontroller connects to our X over here and then our X of our microcontroller connects to T, X or Y here. And then you connect the ground to ground and then you connect the PCC to the five foot. We don't really care about DTI in S.T.. S fine here. We don't care about those things. The reason why for the new CLO, we don't need to connect in an extend or um chip is that it's been enabled for us through the um, the same method that we flash code into the port. So P two MPLX three are the U. We can use it on the nuclear board. That does not require us for X then that does not require us to have an external converter. So we're going to use these in our experiment. Nonetheless, I should point out that the uh other us more uh are you out modules are available on our microcontroller list. Take a look at it over here. We have you say one. You said two. You said six. Meaning we have three different sets, modules. And the reason it is written, you said here, is because the full name of the art that we are dealing with, its full name is actually used in the use that stands for Universal Synchronous asynchronous receiver transmitter. When we are using it in asynchronous mode, it becomes your art without the s such as the universal asynchronous receiver transmitter. So that is why we often see you Art. But when you check over here, it is written the way you use it. So let's say P to a click on peer to and see which you artist connected is. You ought to. I'm going to enable your art from here. Click this over here and mode. Oh dropdown and select asynchronous. This what I was talking about because we want to set it as a you art if we wanted it as you sort Synchronoss we select this one over here you art and you realize that as soon as I selected my T Exline, which is P two in my our X line, which is P three, I've been selected automatically right now. Let's take a look at clock configuration, often to generate the you are clock the um it requires precise clock configuration. So the clock source Martis yet in our high speed internal RC, um it's, it's precision is around one percent. So that should be fine for us. I'm going to select H. S I over here. You see the radio button was. Yeah, I've just clicked over here to select HSA, so I'm going to be using this clock source over here. And what I'm going to do is I'm going to verify, um, I'm gonna verify the clock for my use of that one to make sure that. Um, I know exactly the clock.

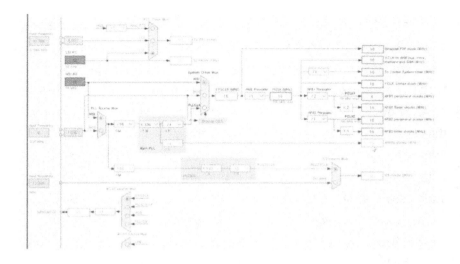

Um, so to verify the clock for the particular pair, you have to check the, um, the past. The perp is connected because over here we have the clocks of the various buses. So I'm going to go to a datasheet and take a look at the block diagram. So what is the block diagram of our data sheet? We don't look at this earlier than we are using. They use it to model. It's connected to APB one, right? It's connected to APB one, as you can see over here. This is APB one. And then this is us two. Okay. And we said the Artosis word is connected. Okay. And you can find this on page number fifteen of our wall of our data sheet. And the data sheet is that documented? The 149 pages. The other document has over 800 pages and it's another one with a thousand pages. Right. So I'm gonna minimize this. So we said it's APB, one APB, one lessie APB, one time a clock. That, um, is sixteen megahertz. And then we have APB, one per four o'clock is at eight megahertz. What I want to do is set APB one per four o'clock to 16 megahertz as well. And the reason I want to do this is because those with the, um, the F zero one, um, SDM two board, they have their default frequency set with this at sixteen megahertz because I don't want to have any problems between EF four one one and F force you or one. I just want to make sure it follows the Air Force Rule one so that people with that board wouldn't need to change anything. Because often when I take SDM thirty two courses, I realize some people still have Air Force Rule one. And there are other changes that are required. So because of that nowadays, I just make sure the code is sort of fixed for Air Force One. And then we run it on air for one on one. Right. So I'm going to change this here to 16. This is eight people. One pair. Four o'clock. We can verify that again because we talked for a while. You said two are connected to GPP one. And when I said this to EPB one. Okay. Once that was done, I said 16 hits enter. It's gonna change a number of things. Okay. Luckily, we've got everyone at 16. Okay. This is the exact configuration of the Air Force or one. Okay. We can continue with our configuration so we can grow to be um and configuration. Stop over here and we click on that parameter certains over here and over here. We can set the bar straight. And this is fine. We can keep it within here. The same actually the board rate one hundred and fifteen thousand two hundred. You can change it to nine thousand six hundred, et cetera. But we can keep this pretty. These are default settings, so we really need to change nothing here. If you want just it to be half duplex, if you want to be a receiver, only a transmitter, only you can change over here. That's data. Um, data direction. Right. So we can leave everything the same. We can live by oversampling the same. This is calibrated to what you call it. This determines the speed of the data sampling.

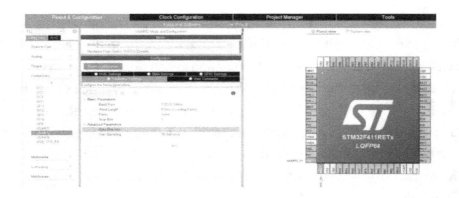

And this takes into account the frequency at which, um, why you are prepared for it. Run it. And we know that 60 megahertz. I wouldn't touch it. Nathan, here we leave this the way it is. I can generate it by coming over here. And I'll give this a name. You Art Paulin, because we're going to see how to do this would interrupt as well as DME. So just give this a descriptive name. And the two changes estimated to Kubi D e and I'll click over here to generate. Mm hmm. So there's a project to clean up a bit. Um. So in this experiment we are only going to see how to transmit data where you are. So I'm going to create a buffer without data. I'm going to create this array here, which I shall call a message and a message shall hold this sentence. Hello from Cuba, Max. And then, um, we are going to use you all. You transmit API to transmit this data. And then, um, you can find the information about the API. Of course, cointel you auto C file or go into the reference manual of the whole drive a library. Oh driver and library I should say. So I'll come over here and see how you underscore your art. Underscore. Transmit like this and this. This function over here takes arguments. The first document is the handle of the U. At the address of the handle which is h h. You ought to be using your auto module as it is defined up here. The second argument is the um, the buffer that has the data. So we call in this message. We've created this character as a record message. The third argument is the size of the data to be transmitted, which is 30 over here. And the last argument is the time out like this. Okay, so if we, um, if we don't do this onto a board and run, we expect to see this message sent over. You ought to another device which is receiving it because we want to monitor the, um, the receive side from our computer. We need to download a special program that can, um, sort of receive you, uh, you are data from an embedded device. So we need a program such as Terra Tim Party or any of those zero terminal programs. Let's go to, um, Google and get one. A very good and popular one, which I use is the terror term. This is what it looks like. You can just try to download it by clicking on this first link here will provide a download information. This is a terror term. So I've opened this first link in this tab over here. When you get here, we'll tell you where you can download it from. It says, to download the available page from OCD and download the page. So you can click over here like this. And we are brought to this page so we can scroll down here to download it at the X or the zip file. You can just click on terror to hyphen for dot e XY to download off clicked here. You can see it's downloaded because I've downloaded this once, I have this as number one. So you can just double click and go. And he stole it. Go through the wizard and install it. Perhaps I should just show how that is done. I suspect this is straightforward. You shouldn't be an issue. OK. So this is it. Oh, double click to start the installation and then Umbro here. So once you've read the license agreement, you can click over here, accept. And then you can leave everything else the same and go on to the next. And then if you have a different language, you can select your language over here. The next. And then you can create shortcuts, et cetera. Then next. And then you can just click install.

But because I have it installed, would it proceed? Just cancel this. Yes. I want to cancel. Okay. I'll close this. So let's build a project. This whole cube IDC project I click here to build. It's Putin. We have no errors. What does it say? Over here? It says we are passing. Argument two of the whole. Okay. So the reason we have a warning here is because it expects us to typecast this to a U. Eight pointer. So I'll put it, Brocket, you end it on this Quartey stuff over here. That is why we have this warning. I'm going to click here to view it again. The warning disappears. So I'm going to click here to go to the debugger. I'm gonna select this. And I'm going to open my terror term when you open terror term. This is where you find you can either use it for, um, TCAP, IP connection or serial. What we are using is a voice, the serial connections or so like this radio button here in the dropdown here, I see my SDM 32 board. Yeah, this is the name it has. You might find a different name here. But one way to know which one your board is, is to disconnect your board and come to this dropdown. If there's a particular one for two missing, you can take notes of them and then you connect your board and come back here. If you see it as a neocon port, then that is the new device you just connected. So I'll come over here and then select this. Com three and then I'll say, okay, over here. Then this window, nothing is showing this because we're not running from our debug. I'll click to run. And our system is running now. Let's see what the track team is feeling. Nothing is showing here. It just showed, you know. And the reason why that is, is our board rate is not aligned. You know where you set up, we're using a board rate of one hundred and one hundred and fifteen thousand two hundred. But the default setting here is ninety six thousand or nine thousand six hundred, I should say. So I'm going to change the board rate by setting up a zero port and then this nine thousand six hundred dropdown. I'll click here. And then also like this is the port rate. We set our microcontroller to work at Click. Okay. Over here. And I expect our port to stump speech in some data. We may need to research the port. Click this. Oh, we can't even, um, escape that debark view, since the framework is already flushed. I see it's connecting back to the deep of you. Okay. You saw it. Hello. This is it. And the reason why it appears is because we haven't had it in a while, you know what? Infinite loop. So we can do that now. I'm going to take a while to transmit. I'm going to cut this and put it in the wall. One loop like this would keep transmitting the same information. And I'm going to repeat my project. Click over here to be at. It successfully earned an hour click here to go to the Depok you. And then click here to run. Oh, you know, you don't always have to run your code and debug for you once you come to debug. You can exit the debugger because the fermoy is going to be flushed into memory and you can check. But, yeah, we can keep this open. Let's take a look at it. And we have this running. The reason it is a bit like this is because we need a delay. We have to put a delay there to make it flow smoothly. We are even lucky that it is showing in, um, data at all. Sometimes if you don't put a delay there, um, it gets stuck. So I'm going to put a bit of a delay here. Oh. See how. Hall underscored DeLay and, oh, just applied, uh, s mistily here like this. I'm going to come out.

And then I'm going to click here to build. And then I'm going to go to the debugger by clicking on the bug over here. Once that is done or click here to run, let's see what terror I'm showing, I can see this is it. It's printed in print and with Tenements Diddley, we can increase the font size by coming over here. Edit I see. Well, we can just go to set up and then no phone to here and then Fonte. And, um, we can select size 14 and I'm going to choose this font, Lucita, and then. Okay. And as you can see, we have this bigger.

CODING UART DRIVERS FOR INTERRUPT TRANSFER MODE

We are going to see how to configure our SDM 32 you art for interrupt mode. So what I'm going to do is create a pin out of a new project, as you can see, after years to collect a pin out. And then the other time we use that, you are Temotu to this time less use. You are too much of one. And remember, you, art module one is no hasn't got the, um, the V1 capability. If you use your automotive one or your nuclear board, you wouldn't be able to view it on Terra too. You would require the extent or you are to be a converter in order to view it. It just happens that our You are module two is connected to the debugger which allows us to view it. So this time we're going to use module one and this time we would use this opportunity to try to receive a function as well. And what we're going to do is we're going to tie the transmit and the receive pins of our microcontroller such that we can create a loop back. The data we send through the transmit, we receive it through, they receive a pin. And this will verify that we've configured both our Rex and T x. So come to connectivity over here and then I'll select you at one. And once I've selected it, I'll open this. And then now enable it as asynchronous mode. And then this will show the pins involved here. It's A ten and P in nine. So to create a U. A loop back. We know this is the R x receive. And is the T expen. So what we can do is take a jumper wire, connect to P eight nine and P a 10. So we connect a pin here such that what is transmitted from P in I will be received from P A 10. And we can verify that what we transmit is received. Right. Next we go to a clock. I'm going to go to the clock set in here and then I'm going to select it. As I am the source from

213

this multiplex up here. Once that is done, I'm going to make sure my pass is 16 megahertz so that those with the F one FS Air Force, your one would just use the default settings or hit enter here. And then everything will be adjusted accordingly. Next, we go back to the PIN and configuration tab to continue our configuration. I'll come to systems for you here. I'll click with you at one, you know, expand from here. Let's see. Yes. To be expanded. Okay. And over here. keep everything the same. We want to receive and transmit the other part. We wanted the same.

But because we said we'll be used and interrupt, we have to enable global interrupt for the U. The USA. So click over here to enable global interrupt. Now I can go ahead and generate the code. Come over here, generate code. I'll give this a name you art underscore. Interrupt. And then also to change over here. SDM 32 cube idi e. And once that is done or click over here to generate. So this is a whole project of cleaning up, a bit of taken out most of the comments over here. And then you can inspect the generated code. It's almost the same as the one we saw for you to pull in. The only differences are, um. An interrupt handler was created in the underscore I don't see followed by here because we enabled global interrupt. So if you open an estimated four X X underscore, I don't see you feed C D. Do you not interrupt the handler included here. As you can see, you use that one I RCU handler. Right. Okay, so we'll come over here. Well we have to start out. Were you transmitting? Receive which interrupt. And then we implement the interrupt callback whenever we use it in the library. We know when you use interrupt. You've got to implement the callback function. So. Right to find the callback function. We know the trick. We go to our Trivia file and then we find the, um, the type of callback we want to do. We want a callback for data received complete or we want a callback for data transfer complete. We want a callback for data that has received complete meaning if half of the reception is complete. All of that is there. And we can find that out by going to the driver. So go to drive us over here. The driver, the source and what we're looking for is that you art or use that dot c file over here to return. You asked to see a double click. And we know the, um, the callbacks always start with the underscore week keyword. So we can simply search the control F to open the fine window.

```
 81     RCC_ClkInitStruct.APB2CLKDivider = RCC_HCLK_DIV1;
 82
 83     if (HAL_RCC_ClockConfig(&RCC_ClkInitStruct, FLASH_LATENCY_0) != HAL_OK)
 84     {
 85         Error_Handler();
 86     }
 87 }
 88
 89 /**
 90   * @brief USART1 Initialization Function
 91   * @param None
 92   * @retval None
 93   */
 94 static void MX_USART1_UART_Init(void)
 95 {
 96
 97     /* USER CODE BEGIN USART1_Init 0 */
 98
 99     /* USER CODE END USART1_Init 0 */
100
101     /* USER CODE BEGIN USART1_Init 1 */
102
103     /* USER CODE END USART1_Init 1 */
104     huart1.Instance = USART1;
105     huart1.Init.BaudRate = 115200;
106     huart1.Init.WordLength = UART_WORDLENGTH_8B;
```

You press control plus F and then you type on the score week and then you start looking for it by hitting enter to go to the next one. So this is the um, transmit complete callback. And trust me, to have a complete callback. We are looking for a complete transmitter. We need this. We're gonna implement one callback to transmit complete information. And another one to transmit half complete. There should be a callback, a single callback for both transmit complete and receive such that it's gonna be you at T X are x complete callback. But we are using t x separately and RACC separately. So let's get to our X version. O continue by looking. So this is the R X complete. I'll copy this as well. Right. So I'm just gonna clean this up. We don't need the content here. We don't need any content here either. And then the weak keyword here can be eliminated. Okay. So for this experiment, we went to create two buffers, just like we saw earlier in the earlier example, we had a buffer, which was basically, um, an array of characters. And then, um, the buffer had a content halo from Cuba, Max.

This time, we are simply going to create an array of numbers. And this we would send from one buffer and expect to receive it in another buffer using our T X are X looped back because we are going to use a jumper wire to connect our T X line to the R X line, such that when we send from T X, we expect to receive an X and we expect what we receive to be available in a while are X buffer. So I'm going to come over here and create two arrays. I'll see you at eight. And this Quartey and then I'll call this T x buffer. And it's gonna be an array of size 10. And over here, I'm just going to put numbers. Start off by saying, um, 10, 20, 30, 40, 50, 60, 70, 80, 90 and 100 like this. And then over here, I'm going to see you integrate. And there's Corti. And this is going to be the ah X buffer. This is going to be the receive buffer. And it's a size of 10. But this one is empty. We expect to find data inside this when we run our code. Okay. And remember, the callback function is just the function for doing something. Basically, if you have something you want to do when data is received, you do it over and over here, do something as well. But over here, because we don't have anything special to do, we can simply increment a counter variable or come here and create you. X3 to underscore T accord is our X counter. And then I have another one called X counter. These are global variables. And then in the Eriks callback, I just increment the ERIKS counter. Rick's account plus plus. Like this. And then over here to X.com, two plus plus. And we will observe these counter variables in the expressions window like this. Okay. But you can do any elaborate stuff. You can pass on the data. Perhaps if you receive data, you will not pass it through an algorithm such as delete the comma process, CSP file, et cetera. You can do it in the callbacks and um. Yeah, depending on the type of data. If it's not text then it's an actual signal such as um maybe ADC values, you may want to clean it up, et cetera. All of that you can deal with using callbacks. Okay. So once that, uh, once we've implemented our callbacks, we can go ahead and start the, um, the ADC stats, the you ought I should say. So let's start. Are we going to set out where you are to receive an interrupt? We're going to see all of you on the scroll. That's the name of the function. And you can find this in the, um, the driver fault, which is that you are but see all the um the whole reference manual. So this is what you are to receive on the score. Eighty four, interrupt, receive, use and interrupt. And the first argument is the outrage of the you are to handle which is you are one over here and then the buffer for the received data. Where do you want to store what you received. Want to store it. You know. What did we call it? Quantity over here. Eric's buffer. I'll copy this R x buffer over here. And then the next one is going to be the size, which is ten. So pass this over here like this, following this. The next

218

one is going to be the transmitter. So over here, receive which interrupt. Now transmit. Oh. On a scale you art transmit on the school I.T.. And then the first document is the U to handle U R to one. The second one is the T X buffer. And then the size is 10. So we're going to take what is in the T X buffer, which is this content, and then transmit that. And because we're gonna connect a jumper wire, we're going to connect our ex ante X line using a jumper wire. What is transmitted or what is sent through the transmitter we received on the receiver pin and stored in the receiver or our X buffer.

```
44   void HAL_UART_RxCpltCallback(UART_HandleTypeDef *huart)
45   {
46   //Do something...
47         rx_counter++;
48   }
49   int main(void)
50   {
51
52       HAL_Init();
53
54
55       SystemClock_Config();
56
57
58       MX_GPIO_Init();
59       MX_USART1_UART_Init();
60
61       HAL_UART_Receive_IT(&huart1,rx_buffer,10);
62       HAL_UART_Transmit_IT(&huart1,tx_buffer,10);
63
64       while (1)
65       {
66
67       }
68       /* USER CODE END 3 */
69   }
```

Problems Tasks Console Properties
No consoles to display at this time.

So now we can go ahead and arm and build our project. But before we do that, we have to create the loop back. We spoke about what this was helping over here. We said we're going to connect our X and T X lines. So we've got to connect P 18 to P in line if you're using the Discovery Port. It's written on it. So, you know, look at your P it and MPLX nine, which I use in a nuclear. You've got to check the actual pin out, not what is written. What is written is based on the art we know. P note. So this is a new clue. Actual pin out and then know we're looking for P in nine MPLX 10. So this is P in nine over here. This is P nine and this is P a ten. So we've got a connection to jump a wire from here.

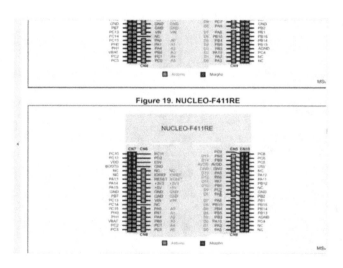

Figure 19. NUCLEO-F411RE

One leg of the jumper wire here and the other one here. And this would create a loopback connecting T, X and I. Right. Click over here to build my project. It's Putin, it's pretty successful. Click here to go to the debug. So what we want to do is check out our ERIKS buffer to our live expressions and see if data is received when we're right, when we run our code. We can also check out our extensive X

220

counter to see what it is going to send us once. Oh, yeah. Let's see. When I remove this, this is from a previous project. Remove all and I'm going to come over here are X buffa. Remember our X barflies empty. No X barflies. The one with the data. But we've created a loop back. We've connected Ericsson t x so we expect to receive at our X. Okay. And then I'm going to take my R X counter as well or another over it. I'm copying by pressing control see. And then we can see T X can't control see to copy double click control V to paste over here. And then I'm going to put a breakpoint at my wild one loop. Remember we are using interrupt so we don't um. We don't have to implement anything here. I'm simply going to double click here to put a breakpoint here. Then I'm going to click here to run the code. And Tehran and it stopped over here. We can take a look at it. Nothing was sent. Nothing was sent because I can see the Erickson T x counter being, um, zero and zero. So let's see where the issue is. So the issue was from my jumper wire. If your jumper wire is not tightly connected to the P, a nine and a 10. You might not see the, um, the receiver and transmission happening. My hands are literally holding the jumper in place. I'm pressing them so that, yeah. You know, they're connected. They're fully connected. Yeah. Because a loose connection would um make this experiment difficult to run. So as you can see, it's because we run once. We've already transmitted the data. You can see our X counter one, anti X counter one, cause there's been a single transmission in a single reception. And this is our X buffer started empty and now he has the content of the T X buffer. So because of our loop back. And we can do this again. Oh, just. Oh, just, um, stop this. And then we start again. And then I'll click over here, come to the bug. It opened in. And then I'm just going to remove everything in order to gain. Because some of them are saying we failed to follow it or just remove or not start off by adding our Erich's buffer to the live expressions window. And then O. A war t x counter. And there is no other way. Ricks counter. Right. And we still have our breakpoint here, which is, you know, well, one loop break point is inside a while, one loop. Um, so click over here. Run. They run. OK. I clicked run twice. And this is what we have. We have our X buffer, our X buffer with data. N t x buffer here one and then our expert for here. Okay. Strange. I don't know what it's because the, um, the breakpoint is in the wall. One loop that is making it work. No, but. Yeah. This is what it is. So it is working out loopback. We've been able to test our ex ante x but let's test this to get. I'm gonna put a breakpoint up here and let's see if that would cause any problems for Kubi D. I wanna come out. I'm gonna stop this and go back to it. We can run this experiment together and see.

OK. So I'm going to go back to debugging. I'm going to take out the break point from here. You see, the breakpoint is put into 11. Let me put out a top here. Let's see when I click here to run. OK. Nothing is happening when the breakpoint is at the top, yet nothing happens. I'm going to take it from the wall one line and put it inside a wall, one loop. So I'm going to put a breakpoint here right now or quick to run. OK. So now we know to make sure the breakpoint is in the 11 loop. It doesn't have to be on the line, but in the loop.

CODING UART DRIVERS FOR DMA TRANSFER MODE

We are going to see how to figure out what you are to work with. The DMA. So let's get started. I've created a new project for Klett. We're going to use our user, Toine, in this example in loop buck mode. And what I mean by loop back is we're going to connect the T X and our X line and it sends you to see that one is better suited for this experiment, especially when you have the new glue board where they use it. That's your debugger. So I'm going to come to my connectivity. And then you saw one over here and I'm going to select it to act. Also, you are two, which is the asynchronous mode. And then down. So like this for me. And then I'll go to clock configuration. Like I said, my clock configuration will always set it to sixteen 16. Isolate H.S. I hear. And then this becomes 16 and I'm going to set this to 16 as well. Oh, hit enter. Right. So we can go ahead to configure the, um, the you. I'll come to the Piñon configuration and then the system's view and then I'll click on you saw one we use and just use one in this experiment. Click here to open it up. Let's see. You have to be open. Okay. And then we don't need NVC interrupt here so I'll leave that. But DMA certains. That's what we need. So pull this up here and then I'll click to add. And then a dropdown comes over here and also like you saw one our X and NDR X the stream. I can choose it at DMA stream to or stream five. I'll keep this the same. And then this is the reception. So this is to receive data. The direction is from peripheral to memory. And we know that course you are receiving from the pen and storing it in memory and then you might use it for something after you start it. And the priority. We don't care much about that. And then we can add another DMA stream for the T x. Also like this and this. Defaults to stream seven.

And then this one T X is from memory to peripheral. Because you write something and then you transmit over the peripheral line. So that's the direction. Right. So it's looking good so far. So now we can go ahead and generate the project. A click over here. I'll give it a name. You art DMA. I'll call you Art. You got on the school, DME, and then also led a toolchain, which is the SDM 32 QAD E and then click here to generate the code. So there's a project to clean up a bit of the comment. This is very similar to our You Art Project standard. You are just that we've got a DMA initialized here as well. And then when you go to the M, the UT in its function, it looks exactly the same way, apart from a line that links that DMA and the You OTS together to show that we are using DME in this project. So yeah, you can take a look at the M, the function is generated and if you want to know them step by step, you can always refer to the m the whole user guide that we downloaded earlier. So let's get started. Remember, whenever you are using the DMA, the DMA uses the callback of the particle out here for your use. So whatever the callback function is for ADC is or time is when you are using ADC with DME. Your callback will be the ADC conversion complete callback. And that is where you do your code. When Aboudi conversion completes in the same instance while you are, the callback will be exactly the same callbacks that we used in the previous you. The project, which is the um, the you to transfer a complete callback as well as the you are to receive complete callback. So I'm going to copy these callback functions from our previous project. Specifically, if you interrupt a project, I'll come to you to interrupt a project over here. We created a callback. We had the um u r t x complete callback in Eriks. I'm just going to copy them Coskata. Same just at this time. The trons added the transaction is going on with the DME rather than using the interruptive lines. OK. So then I'm going to bring our buffs as well, going to Koppio ATX and our X buffer and then we have our X content six counts. I'm going to copy all of that. It's exactly the same. And then passed in the one who knew me and would see Father Y here and then. Now I'll close the old one. Okay. The only difference over here is when we are going to call the receive and transmit function in the interrupt example, we said how you are to receive on this call 84 interrupt.

```
main.c
 34
 35
 36 uint8_t tx_buffer[10] = {10,20,30,40,50,60,70,80,90,100};
 37 uint8_t rx_buffer[10];
 38
 39 uint32_t rx_counter,tx_counter;
 40
 41 void HAL_UART_TxCpltCallback(UART_HandleTypeDef *huart)
 42 {
 43   //Do something...
 44
 45       tx_counter++;
 46 }
 47
 48 void HAL_UART_RxCpltCallback(UART_HandleTypeDef *huart)
 49 {
 50 //Do something...
 51       rx_counter++;
 52 }
 53
 54 int main(void)
 55 {
 56
 57      HAL_Init();                                          I
 58
 59
```

Problems   Tasks   Console   Properties

No consoles to display at this time.

This time we have to see how you are to receive DMA. And we do the same for the, um, the transmitter. So come down here and then I'll see how you underscore you. Unaskable, receive an escort DMA, and then the first argument is that you are Tando, which is each U out one. The second argument is the M buffer, which is the R X buffer. And then the last argument is the size. And then we do the same to transmit all on a score, you add on a school transmit underscore DMA. The first SDM, Hondo H u r to one and then the puffer, which is the T X puffer. And then the size like this. OK. And remember, this is still the loop buck mode or what I've been by loop loop buck mode is that we have connected a jumper wire to our T X and our X line, which is P, A 10 and P nine, so that we can just see that we received the data. Right. click over here to build the project. It's built successfully. Click here for Debug. No debugger has opened. Come to live expression. I remove all of this, which belongs to the previous project room or and I'm going to add our X buffer to make sure to verify that we receive what we say and controversy out of here. And then we can order our X counter as well. And then I'm going to come over here and then put a breakpoint in my wall, one loop by clicking here like this. Okay, then I'm going to click here to run and then click again. You can see our X counter is one. And when we check, we've received the data that we put in the transmitter buffer. So this is you utter with DME and you can use the same method to transmit the data to view on your computer. You can initialize the you out with DME and use your ad. Which is connected to the virtual comports and uses the trout term, which is the serial program to view it.

CODING MULTIPLE UART MODULES

We are going to see how to use more to pull you out modules. We've seen how to use you, too. We use that to transmit hello from Cuba, mix in our first project. And the previous one, we saw how to use a different you out module, which was you at one. We created the R x t x loop back and we were able to use interrupt to send data from the T X to the Erich's. This time we're going to initialize your auto modules and interrupt with both of them. So I'm going to come here for connectivity. And then on the other two, I'm going to set it up for us over here, asynchronous mode and we can get you to hear. And then I'm going to set you to one as well as asynchronous mode. Right. And then we have you at one here and we're going to interrupt both of them. So this is you in one sentence. We had a we at the end of acceptance. OK. Let's deal with this later. Let's go and calibrate our clock to 60 megahertz SUDA all of four boards would have the same thing. I'm going to change this to H. S I up here and then I'll change over here to 16 hit enter. And we all have 16. Okay, so now come to pin conflagration or come to systems view and then I'll select you at or you saw one once clicked. I would expand from here like this. And I'll come to the end, Vic Certains. Look at this. I just drug this open, this is you start one. This is the parameter set and we keep everything here the same. We really don't want to change anything here. It looks good. We want a neighbor to interrupt. So just a neighbor global interrupt here. Right.

This for you saw one or two. The same for you. To know what to use when they were global. Interrupt here. Okay. Once that is done, I'm going to generate my project. I'm going to come over here. And then I'll give the project a name. Cohodas you at. Multiple. And then I'll select my two chains over here, which is the SDM 32 Kubi E. And then I'll click here to generate the code. So this is my project to clean up some of the comments and the experiment here is gonna be similar to the other one. You can inspect the code. As you can see now, we have you are 20, you are two of Sandos and both of them have been initialized. And when we come to a wall in its function, we have seen one in it. Use us two in it. Right. clean these comments over here to shorten the length of the file. Clean this as well. Hmm. And then this. Okay. So I'm going to create my ah ex ante x buffer like I did earlier. The T X has the data where X is empty and we expect to be able to get the data. Oh. So if we inspect our I.T. dot see file, we realize that we have an uninterrupted request handler for use out to us. Well. So we have sought to either. Q You saw one either are. Q Because we enabled global interrupt for both of them. I'm going to copy and paste the code from our previous use of the project. We had the callback while you ought x complete callback and then we had how you got our X complete and we had two global variables that we were using to count the number of T X and the number of our X, so I've put it here. So now the question becomes over here, the local parameter is h you at. How do you know whether r x is complete? Okay. Don't use that one. Or use us two. In the same way. How do you know where the T X completely occurred in the U. S. One or you said two and solved it. We can use an if statement to check if h you are T equals one then we no use that one completed. If it was then we know it's you who said two. So two. Dennis, do you remember the um you said this over here is a structure and the structure has different members.

```
34
35  uint8_t tx_buffer[10] = {10,20,30,40,50,60,70,80,90,100};
36  uint8_t rx_buffer[10];
37
38
39  uint32_t rx_counter,tx_counter;
40
41  void HAL_UART_TxCpltCallback(UART_HandleTypeDef *huart)
42  {
43      //Do something...
44
45          tx_counter++;
46  }
47
48  void HAL_UART_RxCpltCallback(UART_HandleTypeDef *huart)
49  {
50      //Do something...
51          rx_counter++;
52  }
53
54  int main(void)
55  {
56
57      HAL_Init();
58
59
```

The member, the member that keeps the module name is known as the instance. And this literally is that you are to register that base address as we see written here. So we're gonna check the instance of the instance, because your attitude in that is you add to or you said remember the word you utting use that are used interchangeably. And I will explain to you why these two words exist. You know, Synchronoss, asynchronous by Fey using just the asynchronous is simply you, art. Okay, so we're gonna check if the instance is of you ought to or you add or you add one and then we take the appropriate action. So I'm going to see over here if this logo over here, if this and then member instance, because it's a pointer, we use the arrow operator if instance because to let's see, use that one. What we want to do is. To put, do we use that one related to something specific you want for you said one and then we can do. Also, if I can copy this and put this over here, because you said so then you do you start to relate it to something. So you're working with two, you sort of mojos and you have a block of code that executes for the data that, you know, is received from USA one. And you have a different block of code to execute for the data that is received from USA two. So you put that you saw to one in this, um, if block here and you put a user one in this block. We can do the same. We can actually copy exactly the same thing and then put it in our, you know, what we call it in our T X and this global this is something that is outside the if statement. This is just for the T x any such reception. We can have something that will be executed, but if it's coming from use, that's one. We can have something else that will execute. Only when we receive from the user that one. And we can have another block of code that would execute. Only when it's received from USA two. So that is how our code looks currently. So we can start a while. You saw it interrupt like we did earlier. I'm just gonna paste those two lines here. This is for starters. Um, you said one hour breaks and then you start to use one T X. So we just took a look. If you saw one. No. Um, so if we run this, the results in the live expressions window should be exactly the same. But we can make this a bit more interesting by starting with us. Well. But let's see, are we going to use the same buffer if we want to run the same experiment, the same Loop Park experiment with you said to then we need to connect a jumper wire.

```
67                  //Do USART2 related something..
68          }
69
70 }
71
72 int main(void)
73 {
74
75     HAL_Init();
76
77
78     SystemClock_Config();
79
80
81     MX_GPIO_Init();
82     MX_USART1_UART_Init();
83     MX_USART2_UART_Init();
84
85     HAL_UART_Receive_IT(&huart1,rx_buffer,10);
86     HAL_UART_Transmit_IT(&huart1,tx_buffer,10);
87
88     while (1)
89     {
90
91     }
92 }
```

Uh, we need to connect the user said to our ex ante experience, just like we did for user one. And then, um, we can do it. So I'm just gonna copy this and then paste it here. And then I'll change this to you. Set two. And then you set two here. OK. So we have this as well. And then, um, what's gonna happen here is I'm gonna create another buffer here. I'll copy this and then I'll call this T X buffer to T X buffer here. And then over here we simply Quint's and one to just single numbers. OK. Actually we'll be better if T x buffer one is the one that says single numbers. OK. So now of change. I want two T X buffers. And then we have T X buffer one to X buffer to our X buffer one. Our X buffer two. And I'm going to change the data we are sending over here like this. Okay. And this was sent in okay.

Right. So if we run and we go and check out our X bar for one and our expert for two would see that they would both receive the data. We can create. So you can think of these, um, control variables. There's global contessa's us just telling us what's on our X has arrived or T X. Now let's create custom ones that will tell us specifically. I use that one. Our X arrived in the USA too. So I'm going to have our X counter one over here. And then T X counter one. And then our X counter to T X Konta two. So what I'm gonna do here is over here in my outer X, if it's from USA one, I'm going to count T X, counter one. And if it is from two to X Konta to you like this. And then in the Erich's I'm gonna do the same thing. I'm going to add all of this to the live expression's window if it's from one one. If it's from two to remember, this one just tells us that, you know, on our excess or kid, regardless of whether it's one or two. And this one is specifically for one and this one is specifically for two. So let's go and run this current good. I don't have a jumper connected to the R, X and T X of my use out two. So we don't expect you to count anything because there's nothing going on there. After we've verified that X only is being shown to count, then we know the R X bar fights working and then we add the um the other part for the, the um the to the user too. So I'm gonna go ahead and build. Let's see. So over here. So I'm going to change this. We renamed this to buffer one before up before one over here and then before two and then two over here. Okay. So click over here to build. It's a building. And then we go to debug by clicking over here. Right. So I'm going to remove this. And then once I've removed it or added all of our new clothes. OK. Let's go up here. Are you sure you want to remove this? I want to remove from live expression or remove everything from here. Remove all and then we go up. We're going to take T, X Buffa one, T X. We know the content of T X, we need not check T X, so our X before one, which is for use that one. Then we're going to go to our X counter to see whether you know, you saw one received. And then we are going to go to um r x puffer too. This is for you Saaz to remember currently you said to look back. It's not connected or not connected. There are two jumper wires for use. So we don't expect to see anything transmitted and then we're going to do um counter to our X counter to which will be for use out to our X counter to over here. So I'm going to put this over here like this. And then I'm going to put a breakpoint in my code for a while. One loop inside here. Point, break point. And then I'll click here to run. And then a click to run again. And I can see where X.com to one has been incremented to one. And our X for one, it has the content. One, two, three, four, five. And our X buffer has nothing because we have not connected the Erickson T X line. So nothing has been received. So the essence of this is that we know that our firmware can identify where the, um, the interrupt kid wreck's counter wants is just for use out one. That is why we have this. Okay. In our X counter to nothing, OK. It is still zero and then it's about five two zero. So I'll leave it up to you to connect to the jumper wires to connect our X are X and to X of sorts too. We can verify that from here when we come to penult we know it's p a two MPLX three. So all you have to do is go to our. Our datasheet is over here and finds P a two and a three, so there's P a two MPLX through this P two, P A three.

```
        tx_counter2++;
    }

}

void HAL_UART_RxCpltCallback(UART_HandleTypeDef *huart)
{
    //Do something...
    rx_counter++;

    if(huart->Instance == USART1){
        //Do USART1 related something...
        rx_counter1++;
    }

    if(huart->Instance == USART2){
        //Do USART2 related something...
        rx_counter2++;
    }
}

int main(void)
```

Actually, let's do that together so that we make sure there are no unforeseen problems. Cos I've not tried this before, so I'm going to connect, not a jump away from P A to B A three. I've already connected P in Olympia 10. That is for the U at one. Are we doing the same for you at two? I've done my connection. I'll minimize this or minimize this so we can um. We can stop and then go back to debug. You can see what we have. Click over here. It says, failed to evaluate our export for one. So I'm going to remove that and put it back. Sometimes this happens or removes this and our export for one again. Where is it? This is our X buffer one. This is where they receive data from, you know, USD one will be stored. So a new expression over here. Hit enter. And we still have our breakpoint inside you while one loop. So click here to run and then I'll click again to run. Let's see, we have our X counter too, which is those who are X counter one is one. Let's see. Why are X counters to sue? But we can verify Eric's buffer to see what we have with our data. Okay. Nothing has changed here. Let's see. Right. Okay. So we're not seeing anything here. And this could make sense because remember, our you ought to it's the same line that we use for debugging. So perhaps the system is not allowing us to, um, sort of create a loopback using our. Said to which is the same line that our debugger uses. So, um, we can, um, we can stop this experiment. A better experiment will be maybe to send data from one use out to another, use it and check the serial monitor whether we can see it. Since you said to her success, to the, um, the internal USP to, uh, use that converter. We can check what we send from the user we want to use it to. We can communicate between the two. Rather than apply the, um, the loop back method for the user to as well. And as we can all see from here, we know that, yes. Our callback function recognizes. Which you said happened just that. Yeah. The Lookback method over here. This tricky method, perhaps it's not the best method for use out to because it has been used as I want debug line as well. And I hope you understand this. So I'm gonna stop this. But certainly you can try. And if you see an anomaly as to why this is no, um, behave in a way you should behave. You can leave it in the Q&A section for all of us. Yeah. So what I'm going to do is I'm going to open the terminal and send some bytes and see if we can receive that to user two. So everything is the same. I'm not changing anything in the code. I'm going to debug fuel over here. It opened in. And, um, all of these years failed to x, uh, to, um, fail to evaluate expressions, so I'm gonna remove all of that, remove all, and then, um, I'm going to go to our r x buffer to see where this is running to someone else. Lo uh. Okay, here we go. Because I had the previous projects I may not see files open as well. And then, um, so are X Buffer to come over here at this hour, X two, which is for us. You add to our exposure to copy controls each copy and then over here to paste and then I'll take the counter as well. Contrast to copy and paste as well. It says, cannot evaluate this. Let's see. I'm going to repeat what my project cost. Come over here, remove or stop this. For a bill, it's my project, I'm going to add X buffer to, again, our expert for to. Controversy to copy that expression. And then I'm going to add our X Coulter controversy to copy. Old expression. So this is for you, sir, too. I'm going to open my eyes to terror. Click to open it, and I'm going to select my comfort here. I know you saw, too, is my S.T. link virtual COM PORTS or so like this? I'll say. Okay. And then I'm going to go to set up to set the correct ball straight, cause the default here is no what we set or select this then. Okay. And then I have my code run in. I have the um I've not started running but a breakpoint is still inside the wall one loop. Let's see. This has to be opened. This is it. This outbreak points, so click here to run. And it's run in a quick year. And I'm simply going to type something into something that is received here. Um, we have received something. And I just type something and you can see because I type something. We have our X counter too, received here. And let's see what I typed. I just type some random stuff. Right. so we are working with both users. Now we can check out why you said one is still working. It's not like it has stopped. So I'm just going to copy this and add user to one X for two expressions just to show you that it's still active as well. And let's see if we can see you see that one is to send in the data. That got sent. Right. And I want the reason why I was. Oh, are you sad, too? It's not showing. Well, we sent it because we no longer use the T x profar for you to remember. We have taken out my loopback jumper wire so well Gore received in USA two is the random stuff that I typed and we can see you saw it. You said counter showing that yes, we've received something. OK. So that's all to use Mojo's. And then, um, the um. The lesson here is that in the callback you can basically use an if statement to um, to find which you site has just transmitted or received data and run the appropriate block of code to this or the rest.

UNDERSTANDING THE USB CAPABILITIES OF DIFFERENT DEV BOARDS

We are going to see how to develop a USP device. Or we are going to see how to develop USP devices using a Y ASTM 32 microcontroller in the same experiment, which will be used in the Discovery Board because the Discovery Port has this extra USB port over here that would allow us to use a white board as a device. So basically, if we can't figure out the board as a mouse, we would have to connect a USP here and then connect it to our computer so that we can be moving the disco board as if it were a mouse. The new clue hasn't got this, but the code you learn here would work exactly on any board. Remember, the microcontroller chip is where we are programming.

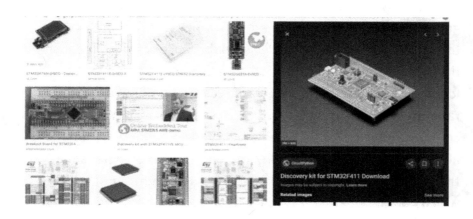

The reason why the new clue cannot be used in this experiment is just because the new clue hasn't got this metallic fin here to allow us to connect or USP. But internally, if we flush the cord onto the new two DSP pins, which are normal GPL, Europeans don't forget to save us USP Moonen. If you buy your own SDM Pettitte two for one one microcontroller this chip and you flush the quote out, we are going to write if you flush it and then you sold everything including a USB port to it. And what I mean by USB port is just this metallic thing. If you saw it out, it should be able to work. But for our experiments sake, we already have a disco ball to house all of this sorted. So we'll be using this, right? So in the next lesson, we should go ahead and configure our USP. Our disco board works as if it's where it mounts. We're going to see how to create a USP HIIT device. HIV stands for human interface device. And this human interface device is going to be a mouse.

CODING USB DRIVERS FOR HUMAN INTERFACE DEVICE (HID) - KEYBOARD FUNCTIONALITY

We are going to see how to develop a USP H.I.G.H. keyboard using our Cuber mixing cube idea. So I'm going to create a new project. I'll click over here. You project or select my port over here. SDM 32, a four one one. And then also like this. We start off by clearing open out. Click over here, clip in, out, I'll say yes. Over here. I've said it to, oh, gee, by coming over here, multimedia, um, actually connectivity, USP, LTG mode. It's a device only. Now we've got to set a clock. I'll go to the UN system, call RACC, and then high speed KI which is HSC or select Christo's large ceramic resonator. This is based on the setting of my board. I'm using the SDM 32 F for one one for each board. Okay, next we've got to go to middleware and it's like the class. I'll come to Mido Middleware over here. And then you s.b device class for FSD IP. We want to do an HIV device, a human interface device. Okay, so now this arm does well, although we've done it similar to what we did when creating the HIV mouse. But to create a keyboard we have to do exactly the same thing and then change the P I.D. number so that our computer will identify what microcontroller is a keyboard. Well, here I'm going to change the PDA from two to three. One, five, two, two, two, three, one, six. So I click over here and change the five to six. Okay. I'm also going to initialize our push button so that we can use it in our experiment. To be a zero is where the push button is connected to on my or my disco board. Where P is you. I've got P three over here. This is P is. You said it to GPL. Your input. Like this? No, we can go to the clock conflagration tub and you can see we've selected the HSC here, the high speed external, and then it's set to ninety six megahertz, which is quite high. I'll leave this the way it is now or generate the project by coming to the project manager over. I'll give the project a name. I call this USP underscore. H.I.G. underscore. Keyboard. And then I'm going to select my two chain SDM 32 to IDC and then I'll click generate over here.

So this a project, this, I mean, see fall, and then, um, as we saw in the setup, we did exactly what we did for the, um, for the most project. So the way this is going to act as a keyboard will be through some manual changes that would do to the code. Here we start off by changing the report cites the report, the end and point report. Size is different for the mouse and the, um, and the keyboard. So we go to a USB device, H.I.G. dot each file to change the to locate the USB device, H.I.G. dot h file. You click on middleware you USP device library class H.I.G. include which is I n c and then you find the fallen open. So like we said, the default, if you um if you set us up in Cuba makes that default is setup for mouse. So we've got to change it to give us the keyboard. Right. OK. So this is where it gives us the end point size, which is two x zero four here. I'll post a comment. I'll see. Change to zero x zero eight four keyboard. So this is going to be the first change we make. We apply. I'll just change this four to eight. OK. Next, we have to change the interface protocol to keyboard. Now, we can do that in the implementation file of this same file. This is the head of our USB device on a score, HIIT dots each. We've got to go to the DOT, see Falin perform this change. I'll come to the source over here. USB device on this score. H.I.G. dot h. And then I'll scroll down. We've got to locate the descriptor. Should be down here somewhere. We are looking for this over here. USP, H.I.G. Configuration, FSD Descriptor. Remember, we are using a word device in FSM mode, not an H.S. mode. If we were using an HST mode it would come to the HST descriptor. Which has a configuration descriptor. But because we've set it up for effort, we'll come over here. What we're looking for is to change the, um, the protocol from mouse to keyboard. And there are comments here describing what each line over here does. When you come down over here to line number one hundred and sixty one interface protocol. Zero is none. One is the keyboard. Two is the mouse currently by default. It is said to two. I'm going to change this to one for the keyboard like we are told to do over here. Now we've got to change the, um, the, uh, the. Report descriptor. We've changed. Thus far, the configuration descriptor is known as another one known as the. The report descriptor. This war tells the, um, the computer. This is a mouse. When you receive this. This is a click. This is, um. This is right click, left click scroll wheel, et cetera. We've got to change it for the keyboard.

```
0x07,                    /*bLength: Endpoint Descriptor size*/
USB_DESC_TYPE_ENDPOINT,  /*bDescriptorType:*/

HID_EPIN_ADDR,           /*bEndpointAddress: Endpoint Address (IN)*/
0x03,                    /*bmAttributes: Interrupt endpoint*/
HID_EPIN_SIZE,  /*wMaxPacketSize: 4 Byte max */
0x00,
HID_FS_BINTERVAL,        /*bInterval: Polling Interval */
/* 34 */
};

/* USB HID device FS Configuration Descriptor */
__ALIGN_BEGIN static uint8_t USBD_HID_CfgHSDesc[USB_HID_CONFIG_DESC_SIZ]  __ALIGN_END =

0x09,  /* bLength: Configuration Descriptor size */
USB_DESC_TYPE_CONFIGURATION,  /* bDescriptorType: Configuration */
USB_HID_CONFIG_DESC_SIZ,
/* wTotalLength: Bytes returned */
0x00,
0x01,   /*bNumInterfaces: 1 interface*/
0x01,   /*bConfigurationValue: Configuration value*/
0x00,   /*iConfiguration: Index of string descriptor describing
        the configuration*/
0xE0,   /*bmAttributes: bus powered and Support Remote Wake up*/
```

Um, so we've got to locate it first. So this was the March report Descriptor, HIIT, Mones Report Descriptor. This information here encapsulates what it means to be a mouse. It encapsulates the essence of a mouse. So this shows what this computer is able to know. This is a mouse and how it should sort of translate to information. So for a keyboard, there is a different set of numbers that you need to use. This can be generated from the, uh, the USP Web site. And you can also get it from S.T. to people at SD Microelectronics. Um, so I have this file here which has that descriptor for USP, um, for keyboard. This over here gives us the same, the same um, the same thing for keyboard. So I'm gonna copy everything here. Control a and then control. See I'm going to touch this to the lesson as well and I'm going to paste this here. Right. So once I've pasted this here, we can delete the first one. We can delete the first one. You note that this one is still called H.I.G. March Descriptor. We can change the name to keyboard if we want, but because we have two of them now, we can delete the one for the amount. We don't need it most in this project. So I just deleted it from here like this. Either that or we could have used an if else and just set the mouse to zero. We can see if zero executes the mouse else executes this other block. But this is easier. Okay, so this one over here is the arm. The report descriptor for keyboard. Okay. No, no, we've changed the reports descriptor from most of the keyboard. We've got to change the size. When we come to the dot each fall, the size, the report descriptive size is defined. We've got to change it over here. It set us seventy four. We have to change the size because as you saw, the array is bigger than this one here. It's bigger than the one we deleted from Mount. We have to change this to one eighty seven and um we can um we can rename this too keyboard or if we don't want to make a lot of changes we can still keep the same name. I can see why he has to assess H.I.G.H. Mount reports this group to size. We could have just created a new defined statement and called it H I.D. keyboard report scripter aside and find every word that this is used and then replace it with keyboard.

But an easier way is just to change this. Yeah. No, we can go to our main would see fall and then um and then run the experiment. Basically when we um when we press our push button we want to press a particular keyboard key such that our push-button will be detected as a key by our computer. When I come to mean that C over here and in our infinite loop, we'll check without a push button is pressed. We just see if on a score cheapie I owe on the score we'd read a pin and then the pin Portas gpa you it penis cheapie I o on the school pin on the scores. You read it. This is Piers Zero. If this is set up we checked out by saying GPA you on the school pin on this course set. If such is the state then. We want to do something and there's something we want to do is send a key press, a key basic, just like we did in the mouse example we need to do over here. Well, we need to declare a buffer. We'll see say this time the buffer size is eight. I'll see you in eight. On this score, t in key buffer. Oh, I see. Buffer. And the size is eight like this. Okay, so let's input our data. Um, so we have eight eight spaces. That's the size of our buffer, just like we did for the mouse. I'll come over here. Index zero is for the report. Idee Index zero here. Reports I.D.. Just pass one. And then index one is the modifier. Above zero. Indexed to his T or E m. Index three. This key code data. Actual data that we wish to send. Index four, five, six and seven, equal key data. I'm going to set all of these two zero initially. This is for certain. Two zero two zero. This is five. There's a six set index, six two zero. Oh, set index seven to zero as well. Is six, seven. Okay, so we can send a key. We can send Page down, press the, um, the hexadecimal code for the ISO X forcE. So to do that, we just place it in the key code data. But I'm going to place it at is index over here. So I would say if I were a push button is pressed, then I want to see what keys Buffa Index three equals through X. Through X for E. This is on page down press. And once we've done this, once we've seen Saturdays, we've got to use the, um, the H.I.G. send reports to send a buffer, the top of our content, just like we did for the mouse so we can come over here. The defense argument is the, um, the handle the USB device handle. The second argument is the buffer and then the buffer size. And we know we find a handle in the, um, the device does see fall. They use devices to see. So I'm going to come to the source over here, USP device to see. And then over here, we should have this. I'm going to copy this and declare it. And it may not see us external. Put it up here. I'll put the extend keyword here like this so we can call our function now the send report function. I'm going to copy this controversy to copy, because we need this for the first document of our function. And I'll say. The function is USP D on the school, each I.D. on the school send report. The first argument is the, um, the address of the Hando. Then, the report Buffa keeps both over here and the size, which is eight like this. So what we have to do is to, um, press and release. We know when you are using the keyboard on the computer. If you press a key, nothing happens. You have to press and release it, press it. Did, uh, a press or a key is read when it's pressed and released. You can realize that if you would just drop your hand. You know, depending on the keyboard, some keys. You have to quickly, you know, press and lift your hand. Others, if you keep your hand on it, you might press more. But in our case, we are doing the press and release over here. Um, so once we've done this, we would apply a bit of delay and then we release or C on underscore delay fifty. Yeah. Like this. And then I'll send a release or simply copy this. The um copy this from here. Over here. Paste it over here like this to release me. Basically send no data so I'll pass it over here like this. Okay. Remember, when you press the page down on your keyboard, it screws the arm. It's close to the screen. It will give you a dance crew. Right. So that's the effect we expect to see. And, um, I'm going to build. Let's see. I'm gonna include USP, H.I.G. device, the H over here. So I wouldn't get any arrows. Also include U. S bd underscore HIIT dot h. Like this. Okay. Click over here to build. It's pulled successfully. I'm gonna download onto my board by clicking debug. Selectees. They don't say, okay, over here. Right. Okay, so just exit this since it's downloaded, the download verified so slick successfully so I can exit this and test it out without being in that book for you. So this is our USP keyboard project of downloaded onto the board of Built downloaded onto the board by going through the, um, the debug sequence over here. I'm trying on a different computer because my computer records the video. Um, the fast USB port is being used for an external hard disk. So I'm testing on a different computer. So you can see that the IDC looks, uh, a bit different. And over here we have just the USP, the HIIT keyboard, uh, project. So. Okay. This is our project. And then we said we're doing page down. Page down. Is similar to pressing that down RACQ on your keyboard. So what I'm gonna do is I'm gonna press the button cause we expect this to scroll down the page. If it's working. When I press the blue button on this keyboard, So as I press the page jumps. And now we are at the end. I'll go up and impress again when I press. It just jumps. It goes. So this page is down. So this is how we build the HIIT keyboard.

CODING USB DRIVERS FOR VIRTUAL COM PORT FUNCTIONALITY (TX ONLY)

We are going to see how to configure our SDM 32 microcontroller for USP federal complete communication. And this actually allows the SDM 32 disco board to be able to communicate with the computer as if it has a USP to you. Article that. So basically, we are going to use the scoreboard to send data to the computer terminal as if we were doing that over you. Right. But this time we're going to be transmitting such data using the USB protocol, rather. And like I mentioned, this is, um, USP experiment. The, um, new clipboard hasn't got a USB port for running these units. We experiment. So you want your development board. Should BDM the disco board at this stage, unless you have one of the new versions of the nuclear board that allows, um, the US experiment and also, like I mentioned, all of them have the same microcontroller. If you design your own, you know, your own product, which is to compare it to F for one one, you can flush the, um, the same code in it and it would work the same way. You might need to buy, you know, the metallic USB port. You see the metal that allows us to connect the US. But that's the only thing that, you know, the best, the only thing the disco house in the nucleus hasn't. Anyway, I know you get what I'm saying, so I'll stop talking about it.

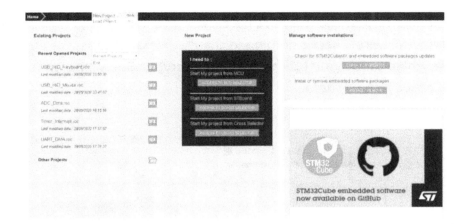

I'll create a new project to buy a new project. I'll select my board here. ASTM three to four. One, one, and then also like that, the school board here and then double click to open or say no. Once it is open, Okello or Pinault click over here. Clippy note. Say yes. And then I'm going to come over here. Often forget what USPS connectivity is. Yeah. So we come to USP, OTTF is then the mode that we want. When I said it to the device only. Right. And we can see a war, you know, D plus and B minus PS activated here. Next, we need to go to the middle and make the selection. I'll come to a middle way over here. Espey device. And then what we want is the virtual import communication device class. Also like this. next up, so a clock configuration. Oh, come to system call over here on the RACC. High speed extends or also like the crystal ceramic resonator and then, um, watch all of this is done. I'll come over here and because I have this red mark by clock configuration, I'm asked what I want, the automatic clock issues to be solved. OK. Yes. Over here. And it's going to sort it out by itself. It ended up with 72. I'm going to increase this to nine two six. You can leave it the same way. What is important is that you've selected high speed to extend all over here to this what we have here. So this is really straightforward. There's nothing to change. We can keep everything as it is your product I.D. and everything. Yes. Just what is supposed to be by default.

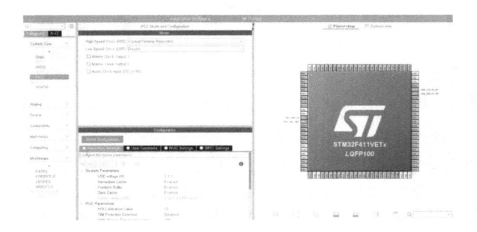

So we can go ahead and generate our projects or come to the project manager over here isolated to change the competitive Kubi. The E call this USP on the score virtual comport. And then I'm going to increase the size a bit. Oh, I don't know, does euro here? Of course, it requires a lot of heat for this project. OK. To be honest, if I saw it. Oh, uh, to be safe. Oh. Increase the stock as well. By including another zero here. And then once we verify it looks good. I'll click over here to generate. A quick over here to open the project, so to transmit data, we need to use the CDC, transmit EFAs function, and we need to keep the data in a buffer like we saw in the two examples. I'm gonna create a buffer to hold the message here. Also, you integrate on the squatty or call this message and then I'll say size of fifty. And I'm simply going to see yellow from cube IDC. And then you line over here. Right. So this is going to be the message we sent. So we can go ahead and send it. Oh, come over here and then I'll use the function CDC on a school cross metaphors. And then I passed the, um, the array, it's called message. And then the size of the array, we can use the screen length function. And then you take the, um, the arena, which has to be typecast. To a pointer. But a string length is found in the string dot h file. So we need to include that up here. Right. Looking good. Let's put a bit of a delay here, I'll delay or post 400 here. And then let's build and see what we've got a click away here to build. OK. This function is not a phone. So we found this function here. The function CDC transmits efforts, we find it in the U.S., we divide CDC, I-F. OK. This one here, CDC. If it's defined here. Right. It's defined in this function. So we simply copy the, um, the head of fall so that we have access to the, um, the functions. Oh, come over here. Paste this. Okay. Control is too safe. Click over here to build. OK. The warning disappears. Okay, now let's test it out. We need to arm. Click the book to download it. And then select this. OK. And then okay, over here. Right. So it's downloaded onto the board. So actually the debugger by clicking over here. So this is our USP federal comport demo, so we can occur right here to build or build mine. And once that is done, we click on the debark and all we need to do is go to the, um, the debugger and then exit the debugger. Because we don't want to debug it. We just want to flush it onto the board and then see what we can indeed communicate to it. Our serial program uses this method. So it says build finished, no arrow, no warning to click here to go to debug. And I'm testing on another computer. Yeah, I'll click over here, debug. And it's indicated here four percent, it's trying to launch the virtual com port debug. so this war we have, so we can just click, we can exit, actually, oh, just exit this because it's flushed onto the board. And I've just connected. Now, you can see my computer has identified that being connected at an estimated 32 virtual compo devices is because, um, running two operating systems on the same computer as us won't be asked. I want to connect to Mac or Windows. Oh, just you wouldn't get this message. I'll get this message. Okay. So once that is done, I'll open Terrytown. And this is a terror term. Oh, come over here, comfort. You see, we have another comfort here. Federal comfort. And when I click okay, let's see where we get. I didn't select it. It's still out. Come one. So, yeah. I've just come to zero ports. Select our virtual imports. That was number 16 or so. OK. And as you can see, hello from Kube, I'd eat just like, um, we wrote over here. And the reason it's arranged this way is because we forgot to put a slush. Ah. But anyway, you can see that we can, um, we can use this as your art. So this is our disco board without any external hardware. We're not using, um, a converter, a USP to FTD converter or any of such converters. So this is how to um to set up the USB device as a virtual import.

CODING USB DRIVERS FOR VIRTUAL COM PORT FUNCTIONALITY (RX AND TX)

We saw how to send data. Using what you virtual comfort in this lesson, we're going to create a new project and then send data and receive data as well. We're going to see our X and T X using the compote to keep the mic setup exactly the same. But because I want a new project rather than, you know, change that I want so that I can upload or attach to a different project. We start from scratch again. So come over here. New project. And then I'll open this, I'll say no. Over here. Oh, come over here. Penult, clapping out. Oh, say yes. And then I'll start off with my USP initialization. I'll come to USP, oh, TGF this device only. And then I'll come to middleware USP devices. What we're looking for is virtual comfort. We leave everything the same. And then we go to our system, core RACC, high speed extend or we use the crystal or the ceramic resonator. Right. Everything else should be left the same. And then I'll come to the clock. Um, let's in fact, let's enable one of our LCDs. I'll quote from Rome, fifteen. I don't know which colitis, but I just said it to GPL you output so that we can turn on reality and I'll rename this to LCD so that we can identify it as well. Okay. And then I'm going to go to a configuration and we have this here asking whether we want to resolve the issues or two particularly I'll click. Yes. Or go out here and it's going to do it on its own. And then I'm going to bump this up to six. You can leave yours. All that matters is you've selected a high speed extension all over here. And I know why you're using the PLL clock.

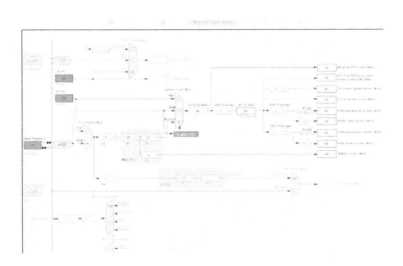

Okay, so then we go to the project manager. I'm going to increase the heap and the stack. Oh. At once you. And then add once you both. Yeah. Yeah. And then I'm going to create a project name. I'll call this USP school. Virtual comport r, x, t, x. And then I select my two chain SDM 30 to Kubi D, E, and then I'll click over here to generate. It's generated on the routes may corrupt previous previously generated projects. I wonder why I'm getting this warning. Hard to say. Yes. Click over here to open the project. Launch. This is my project, I've cleaned up the comment I'm going to build just to make sure everything works because of the warning I saw earlier. it's all good, right? So, um, let's go back to our CDC. I have to see fall and see the functions we have available to us. Okay, let's see. We're looking for the receiver function. There is the USC X buffer effort. This is, uh, this is a buffer. Okay. Looking for functions. CDC, in its efforts, the in it control efforts and, um, receive efforts. OK. So this function is statically defined, meaning it is. It is constrained to just this fall. But we want to be able to access this function in fouse outside of this external fault, such as? Oh, it may not seem far. So one way we can get around this is to create a callback function for this. So I'm going to go to the interface for all of this CDC underscore I see and then define a callback. So to find the CDC, I think I should be able to. Right. Click and go to the, uh. We need to go to the dot h file of this. Yeah, let's see. I'll come over here. That will click. Okay. This did not age four, okay? So we're going to define a new fall here callback function, and when we include this doth fall to any other file, we'll be able to use that for the function. So we're going to, um, use the word keyword so that this will always exist and then we can re implement it in our main dot. See.

So the same week, CDC underscored. Receive Kobuk. And then there's. Which will make it take two arguments. The buffer pointed to the buffer. To be specific. And then the length you end. Two. On a score t like this. So does dot age fall. So this has to exist in the dots. Yes. Well, we can just keep it empty and then put its proper implementation in domain. So, um, this is a new function of copy, the header. The function header. We are coming to reimplement it here. We can keep it up here if we want or just paste this over here. So we have a new function. This function is called receive callback, which includes this to our CDC. I f c for. So what we want to do is call this callback function of ours one of our data received. So I'm going to copy this function name and then come to the water, and receive our CDC receive function here. This is the CDC received. And when it receives the packet, I'll come down here and then call our function. Remember, our function takes two arguments. The buffer is the same as the same buffer that is here.

And then the length, the length here, we can just pass length the address of the length. Oh, we can just see. Yeah. 2.0. We can pass the address. It's fine like this. So because all function is, um, it defines us weak. We've got to do the proper implementation for me. I'm going to copy this and then go to Maine. And this means that you can have your own implementation, remember? And then, um, I'll put it somewhere in Maine. Oh, put it down here. Oh, don't hit hideous. I can put it up here. And then delete the weak keyword over here. So for our experiment, we can simply echo the data back to the transmitter. To do this, we can use the transmit F. S function we saw earlier. Also the CDC over here. Transmit. Underscore efforts. And then we can pass the buffer over here. S first document. And then the length over here. The second argument. So this means whenever we send data, we should see it echoed back to the transmitter. And I hope you understand this. This is just a callback function. The callback function is simply do something right, do something. So if you don't want to see, um, the data I could back, you can disable this and just see reality such that whenever you receive data, just the LCD will be lit. So we can see Harl underscore GPI. And then remember we um, we set one of our early days. We can toggle it. So we say torgau pain and then we can see GPL.

```
31
32      HAL_Init();
33
34      SystemClock_Config();
35
36
37      MX_GPIO_Init();
38      MX_USB_DEVICE_Init();
39
40      while (1)
41      {
42
43      }
44      /* USER CODE END 3 */
45 }
46
47~ void CDC_ReceiveCallBack(uint8_t * bff, uint32_t len){
48
49          //Do something..
50
51          //CDC_Transmit_FS(bff,len);   I
52          HAL_GPIO_TogglePin(GPIO_LED_PORT,)
53
54 }
55
```

Problems Tasks Console Properties

CDT Build Console [USB_VirtualCommPortRXTX]

```
00:12:38 Build Finished. 0 errors, 0 warnings. (took 23s.332ms)
```

You underscore ality, underscore port and then GPL, you the dependence GPL you Ellie Dippin GPL you on underscore early dippin a thing that is PD fifteen with it. So if you have more things you want to do whenever data is received, you can add it here. But we can have the echo as well. Right. And that's going to be our main function is just empty. We're doing it in the Kobuk that we've created. So let's build and see what we have. Collected here to build. We have a number of errors. Okay, so this one here, how GPL you were Togo in GPL, you report. I think the way you play a live report is not spelled properly. Capital letters. Some of them need to be smaller letters. OK. Ellie, DGP, your posts should be DGP, your port. Over here. And then early, Depayin simply added Dippin. Okay, let's pivot again. Click over here. And then the reason we have the warning is we've got to include the USP, CDC. I f dot h. Come over here and see. Include USB device, speedy underscore, CDC underscore I f dot h. Like this. So let's click over here to build. It's Putin. Now, we've got no arrow, no warning. Click here to get it onto our board. So like this. We'll see. Okay. Over here. And it says waiting for the probe of connection. OK. Download verified successfully, so it flush the port. I'm going to disconnect the debugger. And then we can test it out. So let's go ahead and test out our federal comb, our X, T, X over here, we want to test out receiving and transmitting of the data. Um, before we do that, um, let's check what a callback implementation looks good. OK? We said this is a callback. You can do something, but we basically want to echo back what we receive and then turn on the ality. This Elegy pianist connected to the blue LTT of the Discovery boat over here in a mock in a wall made wall one. I'm going to put a bit of delay here. We'll see how all on a score delay. And then I'm going to pass this. Five hundred here. Okay. And then let's go to our CDC dot. I filed this one here. We made a lot of changes here. This is the main change that we made. Let's see. Does OK over here to point to because it's a point to the CDC underscore receiving efforts. I'm going to change this and learn the index. You like this. so we did this and then we have the weak object over here in the same file which we implemented the actual thin and demand dot see. Right. Okay, so it's looking good so far. Let's click over here to download, uh, to build first. So it's building while it's building over here to really capture the essence of what's going on. We need a different serial program.

```
29
30  int main(void)
31  {
32
33
34
35
36
37
38
39
40
41
42
43
44
45
46  }
47
48
49
50
51
52          CDC_Transmit_FS(bff,len);
53          HAL_GPIO_TogglePin(LED_GPIO_Port,LED_Pin);
```

```
Problems  Tasks  Console  Properties
<terminated> USB_VirtualCommPortRXTX Debug [STM32 Cortex-M C/C++ Application] ST-LINK (ST-LINK GDB server)
```

```
Debugger connection lost.
Shutting down...
```

Terror term does not give us this x, t, x functionality in a proper way. So we're going to, uh, download another one known as real time. You can go to Google and search to download real terms. And at this first link once it opens, you just follow the, um, the procedure to download it. And then, um, what you do is you click download and once you click download it opens a page, you will start downloading enough. Download this before. So um. Yeah. So it will start downloading shortly. Right. You just follow the steps to store. So to install, you just simply click next. Keep everything the same. Keep clicking next and then you click to install off, install it before. So I wouldn't go ahead with this, so I'll cancel this. OK. This has finished building. Oh. Click debug to get onto the board. So it's work working from here, you can see getting onto the board. Right. Okay. So we are in debug mode. I'm going to exit because I just need this to be on the board. I don't know. I don't need to debug it. Okay. So now I'm going to open the, um, the real term we downloaded and installed. Oh, open it. It's called real time. OK. Over here. So this is real time. So when we start, we have this quote display because I want to show the echo. I'm going to enable half duplex over here on the do display or enable this import. Oh, come here. This dropdown. What device? My device is not shown here. I'll reset my board. You see, okay, this is my device click connect to window windows, and I have to reset this for it to show. So I'm going to open this again. I'm going to open Real Real-Time again. Open. This is real time. Okay. I said I'm going to set up a half duplex. Okay. And on the porch, I'll drop down over here. USP device. I know it's 16. And I verified that using terror 10. You can also verify that in your device manager or click 16 over here and under send. Come over here. Then I'm going to take it. See our life so that we get a new life. And what we want to send. I'm going to send. This is it. How about that? Or hello from Cuba. Like we did earlier. So then I click send us and we are sending. But when I receive it, I see why that is. Okay. Simply by pressing the reset button. I think we are looking good. No, I just reset my boat. Nothing has changed. So Sandusky well in the yellow is what we receive. Does the echo. Right. If we turn off half duplex here, we really see where we type, so. Oh, turn this off. Half duplex and I'll go back to send. And we saw just one part of the message we're not seeing. TXI. We're just seeing Dietrich's so half duplex would give us all of it, put T X and what is brought back. Right. And you can see the LCD is on as well as Sandusky. And I can see. OK. So this is T X outbreaks and you can see the stats showing up when we send we receive us work where you see the light indicate the activity. So when I click this, I transmit and receive hands. We get two sentences. What is transmitted and what is received. OK. So if you have any questions, just live in the questions and answers area.

CODING ACCESSING HARDWARE DRIVERS FROM MULTIPLE THREADS

Now let's analyze our free Archos config dot h file. Because if you want to change the, um, the settings of the kernel. This is why you do it. So double click here. Free Archos config dot h. And over here, this is where we decide to use various aspects of the kernel. It says over here, config use preemption. One means. Use it. Zero means force, meaning do not use it. So we want to use preemption set to one. We want to support static allocation. This is a two one dynamic allocation. We don't want to use either. Hook is set to zero. We don't want to use the take hook to set it to zero. So if you want to know more about these parameters, I would advise you to free up to, um, to take a look at them. To take a look at my mother. Free ATA's on, um, process source. From the ground up. Um, most um. Oh. If you're already seeing the free Artus for uh for um process source then you'd already know this. The reason I'm saying this is that in free ATA's on um processors from ground up we use the call I do and this lesson might be included in that same course to show people how to use free ARTUS with Cuba mix in Cuba.

```
47  /* USER CODE END Includes */
48
49  /* Ensure definitions are only used by the compiler, and not by the assembler. */
50  #if defined(__ICCARM__) || defined(__CC_ARM) || defined(__GNUC__)
51    #include <stdint.h>
52    extern uint32_t SystemCoreClock;
53  #endif
54  #define configUSE_PREEMPTION
55  #define configSUPPORT_STATIC_ALLOCATION
56  #define configSUPPORT_DYNAMIC_ALLOCATION
57  #define configUSE_IDLE_HOOK
58  #define configUSE_TICK_HOOK
59  #define configCPU_CLOCK_HZ                      ( SystemCoreClock )
60  #define configTICK_RATE_HZ                      ((TickType_t)1000)
61  #define configMAX_PRIORITIES
62  #define configMINIMAL_STACK_SIZE                ((uint16_t)128)
63  #define configTOTAL_HEAP_SIZE                   ((size_t)15360)
64  #define configMAX_TASK_NAME_LEN                 ( 16 )
65  #define configUSE_16_BIT_TICKS
66  #define configUSE_MUTEXES
67  #define configQUEUE_REGISTRY_SIZE
68  #define configUSE_PORT_OPTIMISED_TASK_SELECTION
69
70  /* Co-routine definitions. */
71  #define configUSE_CO_ROUTINES                   0
```

Preview Tasks Console   Build Analyzer

terminated - FreeRTOS_TasksAndMutexr Debug [STM32 Cortex-M C/C++ Application] ST-LINK (ST-LINK GDB server)

Debugger connection lost.   FreeRTOS_TasksAndMutexr.elf
Shutting down...   /FreeRTOS_TasksAndMutexr/Debug - Jun 1
                                                                             2020 2:41:05 PM

                                                                             Memory Regions Memory Details

So if you are viewing free arter from, um, processors from ground up, you already know these. But if you're not you, your view and just kinda makes ASTM to Cuba mix. Cause then you wouldn't know the meaning of these parameters and you could check that other course out or you could just um search the free ARTUS, uh, manual. Okay. So these are where all parameters are. So if I want to use something, we set it here. If we do not, we set it off. We turn it on and off in this file config using mutex because we are using mbewe text to be set to one if we were going to be set to zero. We're not using the sixteen bit tick's. So it is set to zero maximum number of priorities. Seven. The take rate is to 1000 hertz the clock. Hertz is using a system clock. When I use it I hook. And when we come down here we use our cystic as the time base for our ARTUS. Like I mentioned earlier. So yeah. So let's move on with our Y experiment. I'll come back to the main dot CFR. So now, um, we have our system work in a round robin harbor. We talk about LTE. We're going to use our thread. Want to talk about it with reality so we can go to the thread. Function off the one. And at the ality Togo code over there. This is the red one. We have the pre uh, we have the profile. We can comment this out. The profile is good for debugging. We only turn it on when we want to see how things are not working. The first thing you do is you profile it to see if it's changed and meaning the threat is executing. Right. So I'm going to comment out profilers and bring back the delay I had in the thread function when it was first created for us. Okay, common dessert also. So the third one, this was thread function one. I'm going to start off by talking in our early deoxy hall on the score cheapie I oh, on the score, Torgau Pain and our early DP five. So CGP are you a comma qpr your g.p.a. you on this score pain underscore five like this. We can also send some data from here. We can um tell you what I'll say. You ain't eight, you ain't eight on the score t and then I'll call this message and then I'll give it a size of let's say twenty five and then I'll see maybe greetings from the third one. Something like that. I'll put a new line to encourage return here.

```
179         //Default_Thread_Profiler++;
180       osDelay(1);
181     }
182     /* USER CODE END 5 */
183 }
184
185
186 void ThhreadlFunc(void const * argument)
187 {
188     /* USER CODE BEGIN ThhreadlFunc */
189     /* Infinite loop */ I
190     uint8_t message[25] = "Greetings from Thread1"
191     for(;;)
192     {
193         //Thread_1_Profiler++;
194         HAL_GPIO_TogglePin(GPIOA,GPIO_PIN_5);
195
196         osDelay(1);
197     }
198     /* USER CODE END ThhreadlFunc */
199 }
200
201
202 /* USER CODE END Header_Thread2Func */
203 void Thread2Func(void const * argument)
```

Oh increase this to thirty five and then semicolon over here so we can transmit this using our you out. So now we simply see how an escort you out on the score transmit and then you are Tando the address h you two and then the pa voice quote message the prophecies to get an actual size we can count one, two, three, four, five, six, seven, eight, nine, ten. Okay I'll just put thirty five to thirty five and then we can put a time out of one. Okay. Cause we've declared thirty five. It might be bigger than that, although we could include the string dot h and be able to automatically compute the size of the buffer. Uh I'll leave that to you. And uh um one M. S delays too late too. So I'm going to increase this a bit. Once this is done, I'll build. And I'm going to turn it on to the board by clicking over here debug. And I'm going to open up the term terror. Zero program to see what I can view the data. It's like this. This is it. And then you orthopod rate the default. But wait, what are you? What is it? One hundred and fifteen thousand two hundred. Okay, then, um. I'm gonna click play over here. So we have greetings from threat one, the reason it's behaving like this. It's because of our courage, return with courage, return is not. Let's see, I've reset my board. Let me see the same way, okay. I'm going to change this, then this. We have 24 characters in our cities, two to enforce. Well, I'm going to click here to build. It's important that we get it right? Perfectly so that when it jumbo's up, we can know that it's jumbled up because I want to demonstrate what happens when we are trying to use threats to access the same resource. So we need this to show how it's working. Good work and condition. And then when it starts jumbling up text and we no doubt it is not the way it should work in a way.

```
41  typedef  uint32_t  TaskProfiler;
42
43  TaskProfiler  Thread_1_Profiler,Thread_2_Profiler,Default_Thread_Prof
44
45
46  int main(void)
47  {
48
49    HAL_Init();
50
51    SystemClock_Config();
52
53    MX_GPIO_Init();
54    MX_USART2_UART_Init();
55
56    osMutexDef(uart_mutex);
```

```
                                          rt_mutex)};

                                  osPriorityNormal, 0, 12
                                  (defaultTask), NULL);


                                  tyNormal, 0, 128);
                                  ead1), NULL);
```

Debug   Project Explorer

- FreeRTOS_TasksAndMutex Debug [STM32 Cortex-M C/C++ Application]
  - FreeRTOS_TasksAndMutex.elf [cores: 0]
    - Thread #1 [main] 1 [core: 0] (Suspended : Breakpoint)
      - main() at main.c:49 0x8003ffa
      - Reset_Handler() at startup_stm32f411retx.s:113 0x8004562
  - C:/ST/STM32CubeIDE_1.2.0/STM32CubeIDE/plugins/com.st.stm32cube.ide.mcu.externaltools.gnu_tool
  - ST-LINK (ST-LINK GDB server)

You would see what I mean. OK. So click here to run this. Do I have to return to open Tobin? Lucy. You know, I escape from this, then I'm out of the Dybbuk. Of course, we don't need to. We just need to flush it to our board once I'm out. I'm going to press to reset my board. It's strange. I'm going to start to reteam again because it's misbehaving. This is it. This over here. And then zero port. One hundred and fifteen thousand two hundred, OK. Like this. They reset the board. So let's increase the timeout a bit. I'm going to increase it over here to ten. Okay. This is the same. We have the courage to return a new line when I click here to build. It's built successfully. Click here to get onto the board. Okay, it's downloaded quickly here. It's still working this way, too, but I can escape this by simply coming out since it's already on the board.

No, I can go. And take a look at it. Come over here. This is the port and then select the portrait.

Over here like this and then. Okay. And this is what we have. It's a peer, not a one second rate, and my ality is totally at a one second rate as well because we are talking in reality. So this is it. We are sending this message to the U. S. From our threat one. Right. Moving on, no less. Interact with threat to what we're going to do in threat to check if the button is pressed and if that is price. We want to send you a greeting from a threat to us. Well, so come over here. This is a threat function to check if the push button is pressed. We can see how on this call we want to use that GPL. You read Peine, GPL, you underscore read. And then this one takes the port and then a PIN number GPL. You print 13 because it's P.c 13. And we want to check if this is reset, meaning, uh, this push button is active, low by default, it is high. When you press it to activate it, it becomes law. You want to check if it's Lowe's, which upl your opinion on this call reset like this. This is surrounded by an if if this is reset, then we want to send a message and the message can be similar to the one we sent. So just come over here and copy this. And then push this in here and then I'm going to copy this. This message we have here and then I'll paste it here and I'll just change the number one to two. So this creten from third to like this. And just like, well, we have in thread one, I'm going to set Dilli here to 1000 as well. Right. So I'm going to click here to build. It's built successfully. I'll get it onto the board by clicking over here. Okay. It's downloaded onto the board. I'm simply going to escape this and go to Terra to click over here to open. Over here, then. Okay. And then I'm going to set the ball straight through a port. This is all board rates and I'm going to press to reset my board. OK. The boathouse where we sit. So I've not pressed a button yet. So we just get in hello from threat one. So I'm gonna press the button and we have. Hello. From threat to. Okay. Sometimes when I press the button, there's a miss. But we can see it. Okay, so the reason this is work and thus far and there is no conflict is because we have a significant amount of delay between the two. What we're going to do now is reduce the amount of delay. Let's do that. See what we get before we reduce the delay. Before we reduce the delay.

Let's get the two threads to have the same amount of work to do. What I mean by that is I'm going to comment thread one. Libby went out such that they are both doing exactly the same thing. They just transmit this. Right. They just transmitted the message. so when I click over here. It's built in. It's built successfully. And then, um. We get to the debug to get onto a board. Okay, let's download it. So I'm going to escape this and then try it manually. What I mean by my knowledge is actually the way on the board. So I don't need to be in the debark. I'm going to click here to stop it. And then I'm going to. And then I'm going to go to Terra term. Click over here. This is then set up through a port. These are bought right then. OK. Over here. I'm going to press the button when I press the button. We still get it. OK. They're doing the same amount of work. Sometimes when I press the button, I don't get any threat to appear at all cause there's conflict sometimes. OK. So next experiment, I'm going to disable the button, then just let him, you know, run on his own. We just push on it to the part where we realize the system cannot be able to provide us both at the same time. So over here we have. If the button is pressed, transmit the message. So I'm going to just take this out and then put it over here and then comment on this block of code. Switch it up. Are the same. No. The red one transmits greetings from threat one. Always daily this and then through to transmits this was delayed. Okay. This could work as well because that delay is a huge delay. One second real time reporting system. You know, the universe has quite a lot of time to wait. Right. So it's built successfully. We click over here to go to the book. It opens in. It's on our board. I'm just going to exit. I'm going to go to terror term. And then also like this. And then also like the board rate then. Okay. Gonna click to reset the board. OK. So we have the Cretans from thread one, Cretans from thread to greetings from thread to greetings from thread one, two, one, two, one, two, one. We're still looking good, right? So great to reduce the delay amount to 10, Emmis. OK. Going to click here to build. Let's. Click here to go to debunk, and then I'm going to escape the debacle by clicking here. OK. And then to return. Come over here. This is how comfortable I am, so I'm gonna select the board rate. And then click to reset a board. OK. So this is where we get to know, we get into gibberish. This is it, because both of the threads are trying to access the same, um, the same resource at the same time. And because of this, there's a coalition and the hardware, which is the single resource, cannot handle this. OK. To prove that this is what is really happening. I'm going to comment on thread two and keep thread one. Send in its message unless you because it could just be that 10 M. S is too, too little for any threat. So I'm going to comment on that threat, too. And let's just see thread one attempt to send with a delay of 10 M. S. It's built in. Click here to get onto the board. It's downloading. It's done. I'm going to click here to escape and then I'll go to terror by clicking over here. Then I select my port. Then I'll change the board rate by coming over here. She can see through it, one is working on its own with 10 M. S delay. So the problem was we had two threads trying to access the same resource at almost the same time. And if we had some delay, which is 10 Imus and 10 Imus in real life, uh, in our toast time in our total universe, that's a lot of time. But that's the quittin allowed the, um, the two different threads to access the same resource. So we solve this problem using Ammu ticks from the music we created earlier. Right. So I'm going to enable the message from the thread again, cause we can use, you know, with the aid of the mute ticks or just do controversy over hand and controversy over here.

CODING ACCESSING HARDWARE DRIVERS FROM MULTIPLE THREADS USING A MUTEX

We are going to see how to access a single resource from multiple threads or tasks by the help of a new text when using mutex. There are two functions or two API. We need the, um, the new tax give and the new tax take or the semaphores take and the semaphores give me Texas, that type of semaphore. So, um, I'm gonna come over here. This is my third one. You can think of the mutex as a key, a single key to the rest room or the toilet or the um the restroom. I know you get what I mean. So if you want to go to the restroom, you pick up the key and then you open the door. When you finish using it, return a key such that the next person can pick up the key. Open the door. And when there are different issues in it, they return. So we are going to use them. Ex semiformal take to take the key, so say ex semaphore, take does the name of the API. And this here takes the name off. The key name of the key is our new tax I.D.. Over here. The new text we created in Cuba makes its code. You add a new tax on those who control the copy. And then I'm going to put this here and then we're going to add some delay here, such as it is a form of a timeout. So I'll say put Max DeLay and put Max DeLay means this is, um, infinite timeout. Meaning don't move on, too, until you get a key. You can put an amount of time here, such as fry them as such that if the key doesn't arrive in five, Emmis, break the door and enter. But if you put port max delay means if the key doesn't arrive. You cannot open the door. The door is still locked. But if we put something before, put an actual number here, which is not put to Max DeLay 10 M as hundred M as it means, if the key doesn't arrive within this time, you can go ahead and try to enter. Right. And you can think of the bathroom being that you got that you are the driver, the restroom being the driver. So wait, wait for infinite time until the key arrives before you can enter the restroom, which is the driver once you are done. You can return the key. We this uh this API should be you at take. I forgot to put a word here.

```
 19.    for(;;)
        {
            //Thread_1_Profiler++;
            // HAL_GPIO_TogglePin(GPIOA,GPIO_PIN_5);

            xSemaphoreTake(uart_mutexHandle,portMAX_DELAY);

            HAL_UART_Transmit(&huart2,message,24,10);

            x|  I

            osDelay(10);
        }
    /* USER CODE END Thread1Func */
    }


    /* USER CODE END Header_Thread2Func */
    void Thread2Func(void const * argument)
    {
        /* USER CODE BEGIN Thread2Func */
        /* Infinite loop */
            uint8_t message[24] = "Greetings from Thread2\r\n";

        for(;;)
```

Once you are done you can return the key by saying x semaphore. You can give back the key x semaphore. Give like this and the name of the key is you are to new text Hondo. Right. And when given the key there is no time involved. So this is it. So the same thing is going to be done for our threat to thread two would also need to take the same key. The key name is the same. And we say, wait two. The key arrives. Wait. An infinite amount of time once you are done. You can also return the key. The same key. Like this. OK. I hope you understand the analogy so we can build now and see what we have a quicker way here to build. It's built successfully. Click here to get it onto the board. It's downloadable. It's downloading. OK. It's, quote, onto the board. Click here to stop. so now we can go to war to return to see. Select. I was to report from here. This one over here, then change the board bodyweight. It's the correct rate. Now we can see the returns from the third greeting from threat to almost equal amount of threat one and three, two. In fact, they have equal amounts of access to the U. S. So this is the beauty of the new tax. And you apply the same method when dealing with an LCD screen. If we replace you with an LCD screen, let's say we wanted to send the same message onto the screen. We would need to just use the dramatics to do that.

CODING CREATING THREADS MANUALLY

So let's say you have generated your code with a Cuba mix and when you arrive here, you realize, oh, I would need another threat. Well, you can just follow up how the other threats were created. We start off by creating the arm, by creating a threat I.D. So I'm just gonna copy the threat idea here. I'm going to create threat three. So I renamed this threat Hando to Threat three. Hando Once the I.D. created, we come over here and then we use the U.S. threat death to create a threat. I'm going to create an exact replica of the threat. Wanted to copy this over here and then paste it. So what is happiness? We are always threatened. The first argument is the threat. Name. The first argument is the threat. Names who are called as threat to a threat. Three. The second argument is the threat function, which we should define later. Our code is Threat three funds. The argument of today is the priority and then the argument that we have zero debt. If we want to know more about this argument, we can actually view this and the threat that the threat would see fall, which you can find over here. I'm gonna keep this zero argument to what it is. This is the stock size. Um, I think I've forgotten what a zero stands for. Um, we can find that out. Let's see. So to find this out, I'm gonna come to the, um.

```
     4

43
49   int main(void)
50   {
51
52       HAL_Init();
53
54       SystemClock_Config();
55
56       MX_GPIO_Init();
57       MX_USART2_UART_Init();
58
59       osMutexDef(uart_mutex);
60       uart_mutexHandle = osMutexCreate(osMutex(uart_mutex));
61
62       osThreadDef(defaultTask, StartDefaultTask, osPriorityNormal, 0, 128);
63       defaultTaskHandle = osThreadCreate(osThread(defaultTask), NULL);
64
65       /* definition and creation of Thread1 */
66       osThreadDef(Thread1, Thhread1Func, osPriorityNormal, 0, 128);
67       Thread1Handle = osThreadCreate(osThread(Thread1), NULL);
68
69       /* definition and creation of Thread3 */
70       osThreadDef(Thread3, Thhread3Func, osPriorityNormal, 0, 128);
71       Thread1Handle = osThreadCreate(osThread(Thread1), NULL);
```

Console
-terminated - FreeRTOS_TasksAndMutex: Debug (STM32 Cortex-M C/C++ Application) ST-LINK (ST-LINK GDB server)
Debugger connection lost.
Shutting down...

Build Anal
FreeRTOS_TasksAndMutex.elf
/FreeRTOS_TasksAndMutex/Debug
Jun 1, 2020 3:28:35 PM
Memory Regions Memory Details

To the middle where a third party free ARTUS source and then I'll go to tasks to see. And then what we are looking for is the US threat def. This is something DeNardo controls. Let's see if we have it here. OK. It doesn't exist here and always threatens def. It doesn't exist here. OK. The reason it doesn't exist here is this should be found in the Ms. Ms is always dot h. This is not this is. No this is not a call if we are to use a function. This is the function that was wrapped around free Archos by Simms. So let's find a Simms's fault and find the meaning of that. We simply need to come up here in our main dot C file and then. Right click on CMC Spoilsports H Coutu declaration. And this will also give us the chance to see the different aspects, such as the number of priorities and other things we have. So what is the CMC Stone Age for the API? We are using are from this file over here. So you can spend some time looking at this. OK. So these are the priority levels. We have the ideal priority.

This is the lowest minus three. We always have low priority. This is minus two. Below normal. It's minus one. Normal is your priority above. Normal is plus one. We have high priority. We have real time priority. We have. Priority. These are the priority types. And they are always status types, which we've not looked at. And then, um, all we are looking for is a while. Always the red dev function. This is it. Always the red death. The first name is a pointer to the thread name. The second name is the start address of the thread function, which is basically the thread function. This is the priority. What is the zero that was confusing us is this one here. Number of instances. So you can have a single thread and have multiple instances of the same threat. So we pass in zero days because we now create infinite instances. So this argument is the number of instances. And the last one, of course, is the stock size. And if you want to learn more about the API available, you can certainly spend more time on this, followed by here. So we know what that means. Now, this is a number of instances. So zero instances.

This is the stack size. So once we've used the OS thread def. To set these parameters. We come here and then we use the always threat create and then to create a threat who is threat create and then is threat three over here. And this is going to return to the threat under which we shall store in the threat I.D. that we created. So it's gonna be stored here. Right. So change the comment here to threat three. Remember, we have threat three over here. So the steps. Step one, we declared a handle to store the threat handle. When it returns. And then we use the always threat def to define DRM, the parameters of the threat. And then we create the threat using the OS threat. Great. Once that is done, we have to go ahead and define the threat function. So I'm gonna come down here and the threat function has to take this format. It's void.

```
187          OSDelay(1);
188     }
189     /* USER CODE END 5 */
190 }
191
192
193  void ThhreadlFunc(void const    argument)
194  {
195     /* USER CODE BEGIN ThhreadlFunc */
196     /* Infinite loop */
197     uint8_t message[24] = "Greetings from Threadl\r\n";
198     for(;;)
199     {
200         //Thread_1_Profiler++;
201         // HAL_GPIO_TogglePin(GPIOA,GPIO_PIN_5);
202
203         xSemaphoreTake(uart_mutexHandle,portMAX_DELAY);
204
205         HAL_UART_Transmit(&huart2,message,24,10);
206
207         xSemaphoreGive(uart_mutexHandle);
208
209         osDelay(10);
210     }
211     /* USER CODE END ThhreadlFunc */
212 }
```

It takes constant point-I argument. So I'll copy this pasted over here. I copy the lymphoid conclusory to copy control to paste open and close. And then I'm gonna change this to threat three func. Remember we already told our OS threat def that the threat function is called Threat three fund. As you can see over here. So that is why I'm using the same name. OK. And its priority is just like the others. And in here you can just put your infinite loop. Remember threats. Main threats have to have infinite loops. The other forms of threats that are time are threats, interrupt threats. Those don't don't have infinite loops. Those have to return. And just to RAAM to make sure it is working. Let's add our profiler to it. Let's profile this threat and see. So in our profilers, I'm going to come over here at a new one thread, three profilers like this, and then I'm simply going to go and increment. So I'm going to come down here. This is our threat three function. I'm simply going to this profiler. So now let's go and see if this increment unless she did I forget to train this to Profiler three. Okay. When I posted this here, he had to be three. Okay. So let's go and see when I click to build. Click over here to build. It's built in. We've got to rush. Let's see. Let's see, let's see. Right. Three functions are good to work with. Okay, I should be up there somewhere. Who is the threat or those who see it over here? Huh? Okay, so I suspect I know the reason is because our thread function, the prototype of the function, has to be placed on the top of the fall. Remember, the function is declared below this line. So it's not accessible because of that. We've got to put a prototype of thread three. You see, we have the prototype of all our threat functions at the top here. So copy this pasted over here. Change this to number three like this and then click over here to build. It's Putin. We still have two errors. Let's see what it says? Three. Oh. Okay, so the other issue is I have a typo in this word here. It should be one H. And yeah, I'll fix that here. Three, three fingers, one each. Okay, let's build and see. Click over here to build. We have one error. Let's see. This time somewhere else has to be done here. All right. Three phone calls for gonna open this up a bit on a defined reference to threat, three funk. We still have our two H's over here. Share a border. Click over here to build. It appealed successfully, gonna get onto the board and go to the debugger by clicking here. It's opening. So I'm going to profile thread number three. I'm going to remove all of these from the old project or old experiment or copy thread three profiler, go at it over here. Remember, thread three has the same priority as the other threats or tasks. Click over here to run and you can see it is running. So our new task or threat is executing as well. Right

CODING SENDING NOTIFICATIONS BETWEEN THREADS

So let's go to a new threat, threat three, and we are going to, um, we're going to add that also to these threats for sending the four taken and sending the message. Basically, we're going to let it take, Becky. The key to the restroom and also be able to use the restroom, which is that you are out in our story. So using the same new text, we can use this as well. I'm going to copy this book over here and then paste it in our new thread, which is thread three. I'm going to comment this out. Patients over here. And, um, we're going to send a message. This message is going to be hello from threat to three. Going to come up here. And I know I'll say hello from three to three, right? And they know where to put the same amount of delay, which is tenements. So now we have hello from thread one, thread two and thread three. And then. Put this over here like this. Okay, let's put it aside and see what we have. Click over here to build. Putin. To build successfully. And then click to debug.

```
193
194 void Thread3Func(void const * argument)
195 {
196
197     uint8_t message[24] = "Greetings from Thread3\r\n";
198
199     while(1){
200         //Thread_3_Profiler++;
201         xSemaphoreTake(uart_mutexHandle,portMAX_DELAY);
202
203         HAL_UART_Transmit(&huart2,message,24,10);
204
205         xSemaphoreGive(uart_mutexHandle);
206         osDelay(10);
207
208     }
209
210 }
211
212 void ThhreadlFunc(void const * argument)
213 {
214     /* USER CODE BEGIN ThhreadlFunc */
215     /* Infinite loop */
216     uint8_t message[24] = "Greetings from Thread1\r\n";
217     for(;;)
218     {
219         //Thread_1_Profiler++;
```

Problems Tasks Console Properties
<terminated> FreeRTOS_TasksAndMutexr Debug [STM32 Cortex-M C/C++ Application| ST-LINK (ST-LINK GDB server)

Verifying ...

It's loaded, okay? We use terror time in this experiment. So I'm going to exit this quickly over here to come out of it and I'll come over here for a term, then select this three sort of baud rate to the appropriate value. This one over here. And then, click away to reset. we get in a bit of a conflict. Lizzie. And yet it's understandable why we should get this, OK? So what happens is the threats have the same priority. So if one threat has the key and the threat. Right. Loses the key. The other two threats, stop fighting for a key. So in a way, that is what creates this, um, this issue with you. So when we have just two threads, one releases the key data, one just picks it up and then uses the key. But now we have two threads waiting. And they both have the same priority. So it's the one the other one believes is the key. No one is ahead of the other. The key is dropped. And then there's a conflict for who gets the key. That is I think that is what is manifested into the second one. It's up this way. But anyway, this is not the experiment we run in here that we can synchronize the threat further to, um, to let this arm. To let all of them work peacefully. We can, um. We can do that. But that's not an experiment. We're going to see how to notify you. Between threads. And furthermore, actually, we can um. Uh, a simple issue will be to reduce that learmount between the threats.

So that all work peacefully. Uh, a proper issue is to apply another form of synchronization between the threats. Well, let's go ahead and look at the notification. I'll leave this for you as an assignment. If you've not found a way to make them more, you know what? Peacefully, then, um, leave it. And the questions and answers area. Why should it be an issue? Let's see how to create notifications. So we are going to notify thread number three from thread to using the, um, the push. But we were so when we pressed the push button, which is often what is going to be read into it that a notification should be sent to thread three to use the, um. You ought to transmit its message, which is greetings from threat three. So let's do that. So I'm going to enable the, um, the push button and thread to again, um, this is what we did. I'm gonna come over here and then remove the comment and then, um, we can. No, I'm just gonna fetch all of this. This is how a. You quote them using UTX. Cut this. And then our place here. So to, um, to send a notification, we need to use the, um, the task notify function. Come over here and say X task. Notify the first argument is the. It's the task you want to notify. And you have to pass the task on the. Remember the task on the list, like the idea of each task. We want to notify Task three. We need to do 300 tasks. Copy. Task or threat three from. Yeah. Come down here. Post this over here. The second argument is a flag that we can set, we can, um, there's a range, I think, you know, eight others up to eight PYT range of flags that we can set. This flag would be used to identify the notification. I'm going to set E X zero one and then I'm going to pass the E set bit. So there are ways of notifying you to either set pits or disable it. So here we are set in bits. So our pass is set. Yeah. So we send in the notification to thread three three three. We have to wait for the notification to arrive.

```
226
227              xSemaphoreGive(uart_mutexHandle);
228
229          osDelay(10);
230      }
231      /* USER CODE END Thread1Func */
232  }
233
234
235  /* USER CODE END Header_Thread2Func */
236  void Thread2Func(void const * argument)
237  {
238      /* USER CODE BEGIN Thread2Func */
239      /* Infinite loop */
240      uint8_t message[24] = "Greetings from Thread2\r\n";
241
242      for(;;)
243      {
244          //Thread_2_Profiler++;
245          xTaskNotify(Thread3Handle,0x01,eSetBits);
246          if(HAL_GPIO_ReadPin(GPIOC,GPIO_PIN_13)== GPIO_PIN_RESET){
247
248              xSemaphoreTake(uart_mutexHandle,portMAX_DELAY);
249
250              HAL_UART_Transmit(&huart2,message,24,10);
251
252              xSemaphoreGive(uart_mutexHandle);
```

So I'm going to go to thread three words or thread three. This is to reach over here. And here we are going to use the next task. Notify wait. Function say X task. Notify wait and then pass PD force over here. And it's your X, F, f. And then at five values. And then PD Mux delay of port must delay. So we passed this here because we don't want it to reset the flags upon entry. And this one here resets all the flags before leaving. So upon entry, do not reset the flags and here reset the flags when leaving and the notify value. Here's the value that will be received. And this is what we would use to confirm this is the notification we want. And postmarks delay means waiting indefinitely for this notification to arrive if we don't use postmarks delay. And we use that time such as 5:00 a.m., as it can wait for five a.m., as if the notification doesn't arrive. It would proceed to execute the other lines of code. But here we are saying wait indefinitely. So we have to define the notify value here. So you inferred this underscore to. That's Five-fold. So, um, this variable here would have the notification value, you would have it. So we basically would declare an empty verbal to start the notification value. And we've got to check the notification value if it's the one we're waiting for. And we can use the end, um, the logical end to do this. We can say if the notified value contains our expected value. So I'll say it over here. And say, and your ex sure won because you can have notification coming from different tasks. If this is three quarters of zero. Right. If that's the case, then we can know it's the right notification, we can, um, transmit our data. Or just cut this and put it in the. Right. So we will receive a notification because remember when we said send notification, we added this threat threat 3s, thread I.D. would that notification arrive. And we confirm if this or X were one, then this is the notification that tells us to go ahead and use the U. We can have another notification coming from another thread, and that could be through extra, too.

And we can check if it's so X to do this other action. Right. So what is this thread, too? I'm going to make sure that notification is sent when we press the button. So I'm going to cut this over here. The task notify function. I'm going to put it here. This is the action that we take when the pattern is pressed. So won't the button be pressed. We want to do two things. We want to send notification to thread three, as well as print our threat to message. But this is not really relevant here. OK. But we can keep it. And then let's Putin see what we have. Let's hope we have no errors. OK. We've got no arrow. Let's get onto the board. Click over here. It's downloaded. Download in. OK. It's downloaded. Going to escape by coming out of it. I'm going to make a terror attempt to see where we are. AK. When I select the port, this one over here, then I set the board rate to the appropriate value. This one over here, we have Cretans from threat one. As I pressed the button, we saw Cretans from threat three and threatened to let me just increase the font size so that we all see what we see properly. It's open. A select 14 here. Then I'm going to use this one. See the council. so this is it. Greetings from threat one. The Botin is not prest. So I'm going to select 14 over here and then use this font. And now it's bigger. OK. So this is the third one only sent. Remember, we only send a message from three to when the button is pressed and at the same time we send a notification as well. So the button is not pressed. No, I'm going to press the button. You can see we find greetings from Threat three and then greetings from threat to us. Well, right. Because of what we are threatening. OK. So in threat number two, just to point out. When a botanist presses, we send a notification and then we print out what threat to message. And when we send a notification threat, three receive the notification. And then it printed a message. So this weather is how to send notification between friends or even amongst threats. I advise you to, um, experiment more, try to send a notification coming from threat one as well. And then check that it is the right notification. Just give it a different notification value and then take an appropriate action.